W9-AFO-391

29.95

U.S. INFLUENCE IN LATIN AMERICA IN THE 1980s

POLITICS IN LATIN AMERICA,
A HOOVER INSTITUTION SERIES

General Editor, **Robert Wesson**

Copublished with Hoover Institution Press,
Stanford University, Stanford, California

U.S. INFLUENCE IN LATIN AMERICA IN THE 1980s

Edited by
Robert Wesson

Library of Congress Cataloging in Publication Data
Main entry under title:

U.S. influence in Latin America in the 1980s.

   (Politics in Latin America)
   Bibliography: p.
   Includes index.
   Contents: Introduction / Robert Wesson—Chile,
successful intervention? / Paul E. Sigmund—Argentina,
pride and weakness / Kenneth F. Johnson—[etc.]
      1. Latin America—Foreign relations—United States.
2. United States—Foreign relations—Latin America.
3. United States—Foreign relations—1981-
I. Wesson, Robert G.   II. Title: United States
influence in Latin America in the 1980s.   III. Title:
U.S. influence in Latin America in the 1980s.   IV. Series
F1418.U67   327.7308   81-22721
ISBN 0-03-061603-4   AACR2

*The Hoover Institution on War, Revolution and Peace,
founded at Stanford University in 1919 by the late President
Herbert Hoover is an interdisciplinary research center for
advanced study on domestic and international affairs in the
twentieth century. The views expressed in its publications
are entirely those of the authors and do not necessarily
reflect the views of the staff, officers, or Board of Overseers
of the Hoover Institution.*

Published in 1982 by Praeger Publishers
CBS Educational and Professional Publishing
a Division of CBS Inc.
521 Fifth Avenue, New York, New York 10175 U.S.A.

© 1982 by Praeger Publishers

3456789   052   98765432

Printed in the United States of America

095498

Contents

Preface

Although there has been an enormous amount of discussion of problems of international relations and foreign policy, and much is made of the growth or decline of Soviet or United States influence in various areas, little attention has been given to the closer analysis of the subject, that is, the assessment of levels of influence. While actions and events are amply chronicled, the ability of one power to sway another is mostly implicit, an assumed element of the situation.

Credit must go to Alvin Z. Rubinstein for focusing closely on the question of influence. As a specialist in Soviet foreign policy, he undertook to analyze and evaluate the results of Soviet efforts to gain influence over such powers as India and Egypt—treating the latter in his *Red Star over the Nile.* He broadened his approach to organize a series of volumes (currently being published by Praeger) on the influence of both superpowers on many representative countries. He kindly requested that I do one of these, which was published in 1981 as *The United States and Brazil: Limits of Influence.*

The present volume borrows Professor Rubinstein's approach (with his permission) to try to develop some ideas regarding the means and magnitude of U.S. influence in Latin America, something obviously in decline over the past 15 years or so but still very important. It seemed unnecessary to try to cover all 20 of the republics; 10 were selected for various reasons: Mexico and Cuba for their direct importance as neighbors; Brazil, Colombia, Argentina, and Venezuela for general economic and political importance; Chile because of the controversial nature of its relations with the United States; and Panama, Nicaragua, and El Salvador because of the very large role formerly or currently played by the United States in their political life. The writers, most of whom are authors of monographs in the Hoover Institution series on Latin American politics, concentrate on the most recent period, generally the last five or ten years, instead of analyzing in detail such well-documented episodes as the overthrow of Chile's Salvador Allende or the 1964 military coup in Brazil. In each country the factors are different, and the authors naturally differ in approach and perceptions. It may be hoped, however, that they add up to a fairly coherent picture of the influence of the United States in what was once considered its very own sphere, as the nation advances into a new decade under a new administration with new approaches to Latin America.

U.S. INFLUENCE IN LATIN AMERICA IN THE 1980s

1

Introduction

Robert Wesson

Discussion of the foreign policy of the United States usually takes on moral-ideological tones, as opposing sides contend that this country should or should not support friendly dictators, try to impose respect for human rights, combat radical movements, protect commercial interests, and so forth. The debate is usually between those who lay more weight on abstract values and those who emphasize the supposed political or material interests of the nation. Whatever the usefulness of such debate about what we should do, it lacks solidity unless it is based on an understanding of what we can do at costs we are prepared to pay. Realistic thinking about foreign policy must start from an assessment of the capacity of the nation to implement its preferences, that is, its present or potential influence.

This is not easy. Influence is a rather intuitive concept, with a strong subjective aspect. It is commonly inferred either from expectations, as one assumes that obviously superior strength means influence, or from results. The only proof of influence is behavior more to the linking of another power than would be expected in the absence of influence. Except when backed by overwhelming force and willingness to use it, influence is unreliable. A nation (like a person) supposedly much under the influence of another may rebel, even at some risk and economic cost, for political or psychological rewards, and reject its subjection. Czechoslovakia, for example, was steadily reducing its subordination to the Soviet Union and Soviet policies in the first part of 1968, and might have entirely departed the Soviet political sphere had it not been jerked back by a stronger form of influence, military force. Egypt, thanks to its location, was more successful in 1972, casting off without difficulty what had seemed to be strong Soviet influence. Cuba from 1898 to 1959 was so much under the influence of the United States that at times its sovereignty appeared to be little more than nominal. But from 1959 to 1961, Fidel Castro effectively cut loose and nullified U.S. influence on the island, replacing it with Soviet influence.

The concept of influence is closely akin to that of power, but the former is more diffuse and general, carrying less implication of force and coercion and more of persuasion. Influence rests on many of the same things as power, the national capabilities, political, economic, military, or whatever, all that makes the nation an effective actor on the world scene.[1] It is a relation of inequality, of strength against weakness, riches against poverty, technological advancement against relative backwardness. In ordinary human psychology, it is pleasant to exercise influence, irksome to be subject to it. To some extent the weaker may influence the stronger, but this occurs because the stronger needs the cooperation of the weaker partner or desires goodwill. For example, Panama, by making it seem that hostility might jeopardize the canal and by appealing to all possible international forums, led the United States to renegotiate the canal treaties and yield sovereignty over the Canal Zone. Much of the behavior of the United States toward Latin America is conditioned by the desire to maintain a positive image and to assure the generally favorable disposition of the Latin republics.

From their point of view, however, the essential reality is their weaker bargaining position and the lack of complete autonomy. Latin Americans write much less of influence, which implies something of the will, than of dependence, an objective condition. For example, Cuba before Castro was not only subject to influence in that the U.S. ambassador was an extremely important person, but it was also dependent on U.S. trade and investment, especially the sugar quota that gave Cuban sugar preferential access to the U.S. market. When the quota was canceled, Cubans rejoiced at liberation from dependence. However, in becoming independent of the United States, Cuba had to seek Soviet support. Dependence on Soviet subsidies and military backing was translated into strong Soviet influence, both in alignment with Soviet foreign policy and in implantation of Soviet political patterns and the indoctrination of the population in Soviet doctrines and values.

Influence has three major bases: military, economic, and cultural. The military is, of course, final and perhaps incontestable if ruthlessly applied. Its utility, however, is marginal. Latin Americans know that U.S. military power may place some limits on their freedom of action, but they hardly test those limits. Military measures are inhibited in part by the fear of unleashing a calamitous nuclear conflict. Short of the most extreme circumstances, troops of a superpower are not likely to be sent where they might clash with another great power. General attitudes also restrain the use of violence. For example, at the height of the petroleum crisis there was no likelihood that U.S. forces would be sent to secure supplies from the Near East, and Mexico or Venezuela could cut off shipments of petroleum with little fear of invasion. The United States has employed very little military force in inter-American relations since the 1840s, and never against South American countries. The marines have been sent into three very weak countries (Nicaragua, Haiti, and the Dominican Republic) that were in conditions of disorder, but never against concerted national resistance; casualties have been minimal. A naval threat was used in 1903 to deter Colombian reconquest of Panama, but it was only a supplement to a native insurrection. Intervention has been categorically forbidden by treaties since 1936. The use of the marines in the Dominican Republic in 1965 had to be presented as a collective measure.

Indirect military influence has been far stronger. The United States has developed close relations with most Latin American armed forces through military sales and assistance, training programs in the countries concerned, and education of officers in U.S. institutions. These entail dependence on the United States as source of equipment (implying replacements and spare parts from the same source), respect for the producers of the equipment, acceptance of U.S. ideas and doctrines, and probably friendships with Americans and positive feelings for this country.

Economic influence is much broader and more complex in its many aspects. The fact that the United States is the biggest market for and supplier of nearly all Latin American countries is of prime importance. One does not lightly offend one's best customer, and intensive trade relations bring travel, financial links, and cooperative arrangements that are not easily broken. The fact that the United States is the largest supplier of manufactured goods is not so conducive to goodwill, since nations appreciate less their having to pay than being paid; but selling also gives some leverage and implies positive relations. Americans go to the Latin countries along with their goods, and natives gain from importing and merchandising them. Some products are unobtainable elsewhere, or only at higher costs; a threat to withhold them would cause concern. Cuba would very much like access to the U.S. market not only to sell but also to buy. Trade, however, is a broad source of influence, not an implement easily usable for specific purposes. As it is carried on by a multitude of private firms interested in their own profit, the U.S. government cannot easily turn it on or off; it can only exercise a degree of marginal control through licensing of certain products, use of credits, and cumbersome tariff adjustments. Most trade controversies have, in fact, been conducted out of the political realm; it would probably be counterproductive if the United States should attempt to coerce a Latin American country by threatening to cut trade with it for political purposes. The embargo on trade with Cuba certainly facilitated Castro's communization of the island's economy. However, dependence on trade with the United States (and other market economies) tends strongly to keep Latin American countries within the basic outlines of pluralistic society.

Investments of U.S. corporations in Latin America are more controversial and complex in effects. The big foreign corporation, with its superior financial, technological, managerial, and marketing capacities, represents a power in the land. It probably has access to the highest spheres of government, and it may apply its resources in many ways, not all necessarily legitimate. On the other hand, the foreign corporation is very visible, its exploitation of national resources and labor for foreign profit is resented, and it is politically vulnerable. How much U.S. investments increase the leverage of this country is unclear. To some extent, the foreign investment is hostage to the national government, increasing its bargaining power. The corporations act on their own behalf, not for the State Department. Interests, however, often coincide. There was formerly extensive collaboration between corporations and government agencies working abroad, and there still is some. Most countries, despite political costs, wish to attract foreign capital. Dependence on foreign investment, as on foreign trade, acts as a general constraint, keeping policies within limits generally acceptable to the capitalist-dominated world economy.

The perennial need for loans and credits also reduces freedom of action. The restrictions the International Monetary Fund imposes on its largess are a very visible form of influence, although they are not directly political and are theoretically intended only to strengthen the economy of the petitioner. It is important for needy countries to keep the goodwill of the world's bankers. Yet dependency goes both ways. When countries such as Mexico and Brazil manage to indebt themselves in amounts of scores of billions of dollars, the bankers cannot afford to provoke them to default.

Cultural influence is even more diffuse and difficult to estimate than economic. From the anthropological point of view, it is very significant if youths (the generation in process of finding itself being most susceptable to foreign fashions) wear U.S. college T-shirts, listen to U.S. records, see U.S. movies, and so forth. But it does not translate directly into political effects. People seduced by U.S. modes may (like Americans at home) be strongly opposed to policies of the U.S. government. We may assume, however, that those who enjoy American shows, drink Coke and Pepsi Cola, or read American novels are less likely to be hostile to the United States than those who hate such modes. The use of jeans in Eastern Europe does not make people necessarily procapitalist democrats, but it is a breach of communist discipline. The United States, with its immense ferment of ideas and chaotic creativity, is exceptionally inventive in all realms, from science fiction to marketing; this may be its most massive impact on the world. The effects are not altogether positive. The cultural impact creates resentment, like the corporate presence, although much less so. The U.S. government, however, has made little effort to put this amorphous asset to political use, and perhaps cannot really do so within the limits of the American political system. Even more than economic influence, the cultural penetration is diffuse and has only the most general political effect.

The government has tried to exert economic and cultural influence directly through aid and informational or educational programs. These are a postwar phenomenon; earlier it had hardly occurred to strong states that they should advance their interests by making gifts (except as charity after natural disasters) or advertising themselves and their beliefs. The ability to extend or hold back sums of money large in relation to the resources of poor countries has been a lever of some importance. For example, a few hundred million dollars of loans helped persuade Bolivia to hold proper elections in 1980—but not to adhere to the results. The threat to cut off aid if a country expropriated properties of Americans without compensation (the Hickenlooper Amendment) has never been applied, however; it is practically a dead letter. Gratitude for foreign aid programs (the benefits of which may not be obvious to the masses) is short-lived, while cutting them off is regarded as positively injurious. In recent years, economic aid has ceased to be a major factor in U.S.-Latin American relations. Official cultural relations are likewise trivial in comparison with the mass of unofficial exchanges.

The political significance of influence depends, of course, on the political potential of the persons being influenced. The United States is commonly accused of standing with the upper classes against the masses in Latin America. Politically, this is highly desirable unless the possessors are likely to be dispossessed and expelled from power by revolutionaries, like the Sandinistas in Nicaragua, who blame the United States for having supported their Somocist oppressors. The coincidence of interests between the United States and the wealthy and powerful in Latin America is almost unavoidable, since they profit from U.S. trade and investment (usually) and support the status quo and values of order and stability against which the Soviet Union raises (at least theoretically) a threat of revolutionary change. Where societies are deeply divided, as Latin American societies generally are, to appeal to one side means to antagonize another. For example, the effort to promote democratic reforms under the Alliance for Progress disturbed conservatives and irritated nationalists because they were foreign imposed. Jimmy Carter's effort to castigate governments violating human rights won the applause of many liberals and intellectuals, but it irked the officers in power. The net result for U.S. influence in militarily governed countries is debatable.

Influence is exercised mostly through a minority. The Soviet Union has tried to use the proletariat, primarily the factory workers, for this purpose since 1917, without striking success. Despite contrary inclinations of some presidents, such as John Kennedy, U.S. influence in Latin America has flowed mostly through those near the top of the social pyramid, the wealthy (commercial or industrial elites much more than the traditional landholding classes), the successful politicians, and the military leadership. The co-operative elite may be very small; in pre-1979 Nicaragua it was almost limited to the Somoza family and intimates. This implies the risk that a country will turn hostile when a narrow pro-U.S. rulership collapses, as in Cuba in 1959 or Nicaragua in 1979.

That the United States is supported by elites does not imply that these groups have been prepared to act for foreign interests, but that their interests have usually paralleled those of the United States, while the United States has almost always felt most comfortable in dealing with those in power. It is not easy to find instances where Latin American elites acted contrary to their own interests and desires in compliance with the wishes of the United States. If they are frequently denounced as puppets of imperialism, it reflects the fact that it is politically more advantageous to attack them as betrayers of the homeland than simply as holders of privilege whose interests coincide with those of the United States.

The United States thus has very large assets in its dealings with Latin America though its power rests in the background, in economic strength, cultural pervasion, the appeal of its ideals, and the general congruence of its interests with those of most members of the elites. These things, plus some customs of deference and often of admiration, add up to a potential for substantial influence, not causing nations to follow blindly U.S. policies but to incline them toward choices favored by this country. To what extent this potential is realized depends on the last major ingredient of influence: political will and skills. Influence is dubious unless there is a will to use it and acumen in doing so, while a strong will, together with craftiness in disarming opposition, may magnify it. Leadership carries far; Yugoslavia was for many years a prime leader of the so-called nonaligned nations, despite feebleness of military and economic resources, by virtue of the independent drive and skill of Tito.

The influence of the United States on Latin America has usually been much less than its potential because there has not been any strong drive to achieve anything in the area, much less to dominate in the way that overwhelming strength makes possible. Both the temper of the United States and its political structure have stood in the way of systematic empire building, European style, permitting only a loose sort of hegemony. The attention of Washington has mostly gone elsewhere. Where the United States has felt its security at issue, it has moved with some dispatch and vigor; otherwise, its actions have usually been inept, commonly entrusted to amateur diplomats. United States influence in Latin America declined during the Nixon and Ford administrations because of neglect. It declined further during the Carter administration, not only because of the domestic troubles of the United States and the continued shrinkage of its world stature, but also because Carter policies were seen as contradictory and thus not to be taken seriously. An administration with more tact and consistent purpose in dealing with Latin America might well restore something of the losses—in part, they are lasting—without larger resources or expenditures.

THE SPHERE OF INFLUENCE

Latin America has been and in some degree still is a region in which the power of the United States has been predominant, a sort of mild and informal empire without annexation or legal control and without the type of military presence that has underpinned the Soviet sphere in Eastern Europe. Much of the predominance of the United States has consisted simply in the political exclusion of competing powers. This was expressed by the Monroe Doctrine.

Stated in 1823, the Monroe Doctrine was practically the cornerstone of U.S. foreign policy from the latter part of the nineteenth century until the 1930s.[2] In its original statement, however, this famous doctrine was considerably less than a fence around the hemisphere to make it a preserve of the United States. The operative language was merely that this country "would consider any attempt on their [European powers'] part to extend their system to any portions of this hemisphere, as dangerous to our peace and safety," leaving open what might be done about such danger. Under the circumstances of 1823, this was not much; the United States lacked the means to ward off a determined effort by a major European power to intervene in Latin America. That this region did not become an object of successful European colonization in the decades after 1823 was due to the British navy, Britain's unwillingness to seek new territories in the Americas at the cost of antagonizing the United States, and the weakness of Spain, the power that was most interested and that made some efforts to recover its colonies long after being militarily defeated in the 1820s.

Through the nineteenth century, British investments in and trade with Latin America were much larger than those of the United States, while culturally the region looked to France, secondarily to Britain. The influence of the United States was strong only as a political model. The young republics of Spanish America (and Brazil toward the end of the century) admired the material success of the United States and made many efforts to emulate its institutions and to copy its constitution. Only in the 1880s and 1890s did the United States begin seriously to overshadow the remainder of the hemisphere.

In the first zestful decades of the young republic, there was a feeling that its system should expand more or less indefinitely, not only to spread to the

Pacific but probably to include Canada, perhaps to include more or less of Latin America. However, Canada proved not easily attainable, energies were occupied in taking and filling the western lands, and the suggestion that the United States incorporate all of Mexico in 1846 was rejected in favor of annexing the sparsely inhabited territories in the latitude of the original states. Subsequently the slavery controversy consumed American energies, and the country turned inward during the Civil War and the period of reconstruction. An opportunity to acquire the Virgin Islands was declined, as was the petition of Santo Domingo to be annexed to the United States.

Toward the end of the 1880s, however, the country began increasingly to look outward in an expansionist mood. Contiguous expansion had long ended and the internal frontier had been wiped out. The nation was rapidly building up heavy industry and there was a growing awareness of the desirability of foreign markets. In the thinking of the day, markets were to be assured by political control; the major European powers were giving an example by slicing up most of Africa and the independent parts of Asia (except China and Japan). Germany and even Japan were building navies, and Admiral Mahan was eloquently preaching the strategic meaning of seapower. The United States began expanding its much neglected fleet and looking for bases in Hawaii, across the Pacific, in the Caribbean, and in South America. It was a time of confidence in the Manifest Destiny of the singularly blessed United States, reinforced by vague neo-Darwinist ideas of the racial-cultural superiority of Anglo-Saxon civilization and the blessings it should confer on the less fortunate races.

This confidence, which lasted until the Great Depression of the 1930s, led to the assumption of a sort of protectorate over the weaker lands of this hemisphere. In demanding that Britain submit a boundary dispute with Venezuela to arbitration in 1895, Secretary of State Richard Olney expressed this lofty presumption: "Today the United States is practically sovereign on this continent, and its fiat is law upon the subjects to which it confines its interposition."[3] This was something of an exercise in truculence, unjustified by any real threat to the independence of Venezuela, but U.S. intervention in the complex Venezuelan controversy was a major step toward interventionism in Latin America.

A much larger step was the Spanish-American War. Despite the search for crasser motives, it is probably fair to say that the chief reason for going to war was the feeling, whipped up by irresponsible journalism, that it was the responsibility of the United States to liberate the suffering Cubans. The war was forced on a reluctant McKinley by popular and congressional impatience.[4] The victory was satisfyingly easy and quick, and as a result the United States came into possession of a piece of Latin America, Puerto Rico, and a protectorate (through the Platt Amendment authorizing intervention at the discretion of the United States) over a larger piece, Cuba. This was not annexed because Congress had grandly passed a self-denying resolution. Such was the zeal for spreading civilization that the distant and populous Philippines were taken under the American wing despite the vigorous resistance of the people to be civilized.

The war with Spain opened an era of intermittent interventionism in Latin America that lasted until after World War I. An important step was the acquisition of the Panama Canal Zone in 1904. Panama had been a province of Colombia, although accessible only by sea. Colombia turned down a proferred treaty for U.S. construction of a canal; the Panamanians were prepared to rebel, and President Theodore Roosevelt intervened to the extent that he later boasted, "I took Panama." By the treaty ceding the zone and related rights to the United States, Panama became, in the common estimation, a colonial dependency. Commitment to the interoceanic canal meant commitment to control of the strategic approaches and to holding the Caribbean as something of an American lake.

Around this time, however, the situation in the Caribbean was complicated by a threat of European intervention. The Dominican Republic owed sums to Britain, France, and other nations much beyond its ability to pay. The international law of the day was generally held to sanction the use of force to collect debts and secure the rights of investors in less civilized lands. But if force were to be applied in this hemisphere, the United States was resolved to be the power to apply it. In 1904 Roosevelt accepted the implication of the Monroe Doctrine that since outsiders were denied the right to exercise police powers in this hemisphere, the United States should do so.

In accordance with this "Roosevelt Corollary," the United States in 1904 undertook the administration of Dominican customs and debts—as desired by the Dominicans. A few years later, however, it was necessary to deploy troops to keep order, and finally the United States came to a full-scale occupation in 1916. Much more than other interventions, this represented an imposition of arbitrary power, as U.S. naval officers took over the government.[5] Despite growing hostility, the marines remained until 1934, leaving behind an effective police force commanded by Leonidas Trujillo, who ruled the country as his private property for 30 years.

Meanwhile, in 1912 marines had gone into Nicaragua in a chaotic situation. They remained—although usually only a few hundred strong—until 1933, with a break in 1925. Haiti was under a U.S. customs receivership from 1904 to 1941, and was occupied from 1915 to 1930. Woodrow Wilson, who was in principle a firm noninterventionist and a thorough democrat, undertook in 1913 to overthrow Mexican President Victoriano Huerta, who had seized power by the murder of his predecessor, Francisco Madero. To this end Wilson occupied the port of Vera Cruz, but he aroused the general hostility of the Mexicans and had to pull back. He also sent General Pershing chasing Pancho Villa across the deserts of northern

Mexico after Villa's raids over the border. Less violently, Wilson advocated intervention for high ideals by the nonrecognition of unconstitutional regimes.

The prime years of intervention were thus from 1904 to 1914. It was also the time of what was called "Dollar Diplomacy." This was not so much the application of diplomacy to the pursuit of dollars as the use of economic power for political influence. The State Department urged businessmen and bankers to invest abroad.[6] Dictators in small countries welcomed investments and were willing to play up to the United States in return. Intervention was primarily to secure stability, and the countries intervened—Haiti, Dominican Republic, and Nicaragua—were among those holding the least U.S. investments. Only in Nicaragua were business interests a major factor. Given stability, business should take care of itself.

There was little resistance to intervention. The Dominicans, wearied of their exceptionally turbulent politics, several times during the nineteenth century asked other powers to take responsibility for the island, and for a few years returned to the status of a Spanish colony. United States intervention in Cuba from 1906 to 1908 was sought by President Tomás Estrada Palma. There was little or no protest against these interventions by other Latin American nations. It is to be emphasized that the U.S. hegemony asserted in this period applied in practice to Central America and the Caribbean basin. These set the tone and were the subject of pronouncements, but U.S. influence fell off sharply to the south and was slight in the Southern Cone. Only later did the South Americans begin to fear that they might undergo the fate of the islands and small republics subject to the sway of Washington.

There was reason for such fears because U.S. potential for influence in Latin America expanded enormously during World War I and shortly after. The war removed Germany from the Latin American scene, where the rising Reich before 1914 had been making much progress, especially in the southern quarter of South America. It relegated France to little more than a cultural presence; and it gravely weakened Britain, which had held the greatest economic stake in Latin America. While the European economies had suffered great destruction or at least exhaustion, the United States had boomed. After the war this country produced well over half the world's goods. The U.S. economic position was correspondingly strengthened in Latin America as elsewhere. In 1913 the United States accounted for 16.7 percent of the foreign trade of South America; by 1927 the figure was 27 percent. In 1913 the United States had 18.4 percent of private foreign investment in Latin America, while Britain had 47.4 percent. From 1913 to 1929, U.S. investment in Latin America tripled, while that of European countries was static, the U.S. share being thereby raised to about 45 percent.[7]

The position of the United States was strengthened in numerous other ways. The German military missions, sought because of the efficient

Prussian wars of the nineteenth century, departed as Latin America was aligned more or less with the Allies and Germany was discredited by defeat. They were replaced by missions from France or the United States. Latin American officers began the trek to U.S. training schools, which became a major source of influence. Cultural penetration multiplied. The new art of the cinema, in which the United States was the leading producer from the beginning, exposed Latin Americans, down to the gauchos of the pampas, to something of the United States. In 1916 and 1919 the Associated Press and United Press began service to Latin America, elbowing aside the European agencies that had been furnishing news, often with an anti-U.S. slant.[8]

Despite massive strengthening of the basis for increased U.S. hegemony in this hemisphere—as everywhere—military interventions were halted, pressure grew to withdraw marines where they were stationed, and the United States was led or pushed to renounce intervention entirely. This was partly because the United States felt more secure; no longer did it seem necessary to use U.S. forces to preclude Europeans taking advantage of disturbed conditions. But it was primarily because of the changing atmosphere and values abroad in the world. Nationalism and democracy were the order of the day, the values in the name of which World War I was fought and the peace treaties were dictated. Racial superiority had lost appeal, and nations were held to be more equal. No longer were peoples expected to welcome foreign troops to help sort out their politics, and no longer would the world, including public opinion in the United States, look on so benignly.

A harbinger of the new age was the Mexican revolution, which began in 1910 and sputtered on for nearly ten years. Beginning as a purely anti-dictatorial movement, it became egalitarian and antiforeign in reaction to the deference of Porfirio Díaz to foreign interests. Asserting the primacy of social needs, it claimed mineral rights for the nation and attacked foreign, chiefly U.S., holdings. It was the first serious challenge to U.S. domination in the northern part of Latin America; never since has Mexico been so amenable to the wishes of its big neighbor as it was before 1910. In the Dominican Republic, Haiti, and Nicaragua, opposition to the presence of the marines swelled, either because they outstayed their welcome or because of the changing temper of the times. In Haiti and Nicaragua there was armed rebellion.

Emphasis was also shifting toward multilateral consultations with Latin America, meetings in which the Latins were better able to defend their interests. The inter-American system began as far back as 1889, when a conference was assembled in Washington to promote, it was hoped, a customs union. It succeeded only in establishing a bureau for the distribution of commercial information,[9] but in the 1920s pan-Americanism prospered and multilateral forums multiplied. One of the main items of their agenda was to demand the general acceptance of the principle of nonintervention, which the U.S. government was gradually pushed to acknowledge despite the reluctance of Republican administrations from 1921 to 1933.

A major move in this direction was the treaty of 1922 in which the United States paid Colombia amends and in effect apologized for having facilitated the independence of Panama (only the fury of Theodore Roosevelt prevented an explicit apology). Secretaries of state became more hesitant in defending the right to intervene. The upsurge of disorder in the world after the calm of the latter 1920s, and the desire of the United States to check aggression anywhere, strengthened noninterventionism in this hemisphere. In 1931 Secretary of State Henry Stimson, chastising the Japanese for the invasion of Manchuria, was embarrassed by the presence of marines in Nicaragua for the purpose of keeping order, the same purpose that the Japanese alleged.[10]

A new course in policy toward Latin America, as in domestic policy, came with the populist administration of Franklin Roosevelt. He changed the basis of U.S. influence in Latin America by withdrawing the military threat and promising that the United States would be a simple "good neighbor" among the brother republics of the hemisphere. The last marines were pulled out of Haiti and the Dominican Republic. By use of nonrecognition and a naval display during 1933 and 1934, Roosevelt forced the resignation of the popular Cuban President Ramón Grau San Martín whom Roosevelt suspected of communist sympathies. But he did not invoke the Platt Amendment, and in 1934 this substitute for the annexation of Cuba was abrogated. The Montevideo Pan-American Conference subscribed to the doctrine that, "No state has a right to intervene in the internal or external affairs of another." In 1936 the United States Senate unanimously ratified an unequivocal statement of nonintervention adopted by the Buenos Aires Pan-American Conference.

In 1938 U.S. adherence to this principle was tested by the first big attack on foreign business in Latin America: the expropriation of U.S., British, and Dutch oil properties by Mexico's dynamic Lázaro Cárdenas. The owners and other adherents of the sanctity of private property agitated strongly for the use of force. Roosevelt held back, however, and ultimately accepted a rather modest settlement. One reason for restraint was the concern growing in the latter 1930s over German influence spreading in Latin America, and fear that violence would cause a dangerous anti-U.S. reaction and incline the Latins to look to the challenging power for support.

World War II was, practically speaking, a second chapter of the contest begun a generation earlier; it had similar effects on the position of the United States and its standing over Latin America. Again, Europe was weakened while the United States was strengthened. In the first postwar years this country again accounted for well over half the world's product. With the atomic bomb it was more than ever militarily dominant, at least in potential.

United States investment in Latin America had declined somewhat because of the long depression from 1929 to 1940, but between 1940 and 1950 it increased by 64 percent while most European holdings were liquidated. The U.S. share thereby rose from 45 percent to 67 percent.[11] The U.S. share of Latin American foreign trade, slightly under one-third in 1938, was nearly half in 1948 and 1958.[12]

Cooperation in World War II both demonstrated and increased the strength of U.S. influence in Latin America. In World War I only Brazil plus Central American and Caribbean countries had become cobelligerents with the United States, while Mexico, Colombia, Venezuela, Chile, Argentina, and Paraguay did not even break relations with the Central powers. In World War II some states declared war immediately after Pearl Harbor. A conference at Rio de Janeiro in January 1942 recommended breaking relations with the Axis powers, and almost all the participants did so rather soon, except that Chile delayed and Argentina held out until near the end of the war. Brazil sent a force to the European battlefield, and various others collaborated actively; the United States had bases in Brazil, Mexico, Ecuador, Panama, and Cuba. The Argentine government was taken by pro-Axis army officers in 1944, but even that holdout declared war as the Nazi state was crumbling.

The war meant a big rise in U.S. standing (which could well be called hegemony) throughout Latin America, because the United States-United Nations' cause was respectable and popular. Moreover, practical aspects of cooperation brought the United States and Latin republics closer together. The United States became the only important source of manufactured imports, while the bulk of exports went north, increased by a huge demand for many strategic materials. Military collaboration placed a pro-U.S. imprint on the Brazilian armed forces that was strong for 20 years after the war and has not been entirely erased to this day. The Latin republics, with the sole exception of Argentina, became accustomed to political and diplomatic cooperation with the United States.

During and shortly after the war, the inter-America system, which almost amounted at this time to the system of U.S. influence, rose to its height. The ending of the war naturally slackened the bonds of alliance, but in the cold war that soon took hold the United States was able to muster general adherence. Latin American governments were no more disposed toward communism than was the United States. In 1947 the United States secured unanimous adoption of the Rio Treaty of Mutual Assistance. This was the first of the cold war pacts, predecessor of NATO. It provided for cooperation against an armed attack on any signatory, in effect an anti-Soviet commitment. In 1948 at Bogotá (against a backdrop of enormous leftist rioting sparked by the murder of Eliecer Gaitán), the Organization of American States (OAS) was established as a sort of regional United Nations Organization, with theoretical equality but de facto U.S. leadership. The OAS was endowed with peacekeeping powers, by two-thirds vote, and it was assumed that the threat to the peace was from international communism.

Latin American adherence to the cold war policies of the United States was mostly passive, however. Not long after Bogotá, the North Koreans launched their offensive to reunify the country, and the United States quickly took up the challenge. Although numerous European countries joined the United States by sending at least token forces to fight under the U.N. flag, only Colombia of Latin American nations did so, and this was because the strongly conservative Colombian government was engaged in something like civil war.

In 1954 Guatemala provided a sharper test of influence by consultation. Washington became concerned at the growth of the communist party in Guatemala after the 1944 overthrow of the Ubico dictatorship. The first constitutional president, Juan José Arévalo, was acceptable; but the second, Jacobo Árbenz, seemed to be leading the country toward revolution. He took leading communists into his entourage, permitted communist domination of labor and peasant organization, and let communists manage land expropriations, including most of the immense holdings of the United Fruit Company. Further, the government arranged a shipload of arms from the Soviet bloc, a great audacity for those days. At an OAS meeting in Caracas, Secretary of State John F. Dulles was able to secure the necessary majority for a resolution condemning communist penetration in principle. Mexico and Argentina (plus Guatemala) refused to subscribe[13] and the OAS gave no effective support. However, undemocratic governments of Nicaragua and Honduras did. With their assistance, the CIA was able to arm a mini-invasion of Guatemala that, together with the advertised disapproval of the United States and grave internal difficulties, sufficed to persuade the Guatemalan military to retire Árbenz and accept the pro-U.S. General Carlos Castillo Armas.

This outcome illustrated a weakness of the U.S. position in Latin America during the cold war: dictators were apt to be more cooperative than more popularly based governments, and they were appreciated accordingly. An exception occurred in 1953 when the Eisenhower administration accepted the radical but non-communist Bolivian revolution and granted it generous economic aid, thereby deflecting it from extremism in a successful exercise of economic influence. But the usual reflex was to distrust populist movements, which were probably hostile to foreign investment, and to lean on strongmen as bulwarks against dangerous tendencies. Thus the United States was prepared to entertain, decorate, and grant loans to such sturdy characters as Trujillo (Dominican Republic), Somoza (Nicaragua), Rojas Pinilla (Colombia), Pérez Jiménez (Venezuela), Batista (Cuba), and Stroessner (Paraguay), who generally returned the favor by outlawing communism (and other opposition movements), supporting the United States internationally, and usually furnishing favorable conditions for foreign (especially U.S.) corporations.

This tendency to treat as friends those who showed themselves friendly was ultimately to make the position of the United States in Latin America less solid. It was self-reinforcing; the impression grew that the superpower favored dictatorships; hence popular movements were more inclined to be hostile to it; hence the United States became more distrustful of any movement tending to radicalism as potentially communist of anti-American. As the identification of the United States with wealth, power, and privilege took hold, the journalists, intellectuals, and reformers, all of whom in 1945 had been wholly pro-U.S., turned distrustful and hostile. To be critical of the United States and foreign corporations was an easy way to popularity for many politicians. The two world wars had taught that peoples should be free and independent; this idea was increasingly turned against European colonial powers in Africa and Asia, and against the hegemonic power in Latin America. How far this alienation had proceeded was apparent in 1958, when governments quite favorable to the United States were unable to prevent masses of their peoples from jeering, throwing rocks, and spitting at Vice-President Richard Nixon.

One reason for this turn was that administrations after World War II had seen no great urgency in Latin American relations. Relations seemed in quite satisfactory shape for over a decade, with the exception of Guatemala, which had proved manageable. There were far more urgent calls for attention from devastated Europe, Greece, China, Korea, and other areas. The Latins, however, felt neglected as their dreams of postwar prosperity faded. After the Nixon episode, the administration looked to increased aid, especially loans through the Inter-American Development Bank, to pump up economies and restore U.S. influence. Little was done, however, because the dominant philosophy remained that the private sector would produce for development if only governments gave it a fair chance.

While Nixon's party was being roughed up, worse troubles were being prepared for the United States in the highlands of eastern Cuba. By March 1958 the United States had repented of its support for the crude, corrupt, and ruthless Batista, and cut off arms supplies for him. This indicated that the Cubans were free to overthrow him, and they proceeded to do so in the last part of that year. Cuba had reached considerable prosperity, with one of the highest GNP per capita of Latin America; but its prosperity was unequal, unstable,and humiliatingly dependent. On attaining power, Fidel Castro found it suitable to use anti-Americanism as a means of rallying support. With great boldness for the ruler of an island in the closest U.S. zone of influence, he defied the United States, confiscated the property of American citizens, and proclaimed his state the "Liberated Territory of the Americas."

Through a series of moves and countermoves and reprisals to reprisals, he led Cuba into the Soviet bloc, even to some extent made it a Soviet military post and naval base.

By way of punishment, the United States, operating under the assumptions of an earlier age, cut off diplomatic relations, trade, and travel, thereby ironically depriving itself of its chief means of influence and increasing Cuban dependence on the global antagonist. An ill-planned effort of Cuban exiles, with logistic support of the CIA, to invade the island ignominiously failed and consolidated the Castro government. With armed action now being ruled out, the United States seemed devoid of ideas to alter the unpleasant situation.

Attention turned to preventing the infection from spreading. Presidents Kennedy and Johnson enlarged the Monroe Doctrine by stating that no more communist states would be tolerated in the hemisphere. Cuba was excluded from the OAS (by a bare two-thirds majority), and nearly all the republics (Mexico being the outstanding exception) were brought to cut off all dealings with Castro. On the more positive side, President Kennedy launched the Alliance for Progress, a grandiose scheme whereby, with large public and private investments, Latin America should achieve rapid economic growth, which was to be accompanied by democratic reforms—unacceptable to most Latin American governments—to make prosperity meaningful for the many. The unrealistic Alliance achieved very little, and it rapidly faded away after the assassination of its author in 1963. It was the last great effort of the United States to act as hemispheric leader.

In 1965 the Johnson administration was alarmed at what was taken to be a potentially procommunist turn in one of the innumerable conflicts of Dominican politics and rushed in a force of marines. They hardly engaged in combat, but they served to give victory to the conservative military officers. In deference to prevalent feeling, the administration sought to cover itself by securing the support of the OAS—which approved by a bare majority— and converting it into a nominally OAS operation under the nominal command of a Brazilian general, who had a modest Brazilian contingent at his disposal. The subsequent effort to establish a permanent OAS force, which would in practice have been dominated by the United States for future missions of repression of disorders received little Latin American backing.

Even in Panama, which had been a semicolony by virtue of the U.S. control of the canal and adjacent territory, the superpower found itself pressed. Riots in 1964 over the flying of the Panamanian flag in the Canal Zone set in motion negotiations eventually leading to a new treaty, finally ratified in 1978, for the liquidation of U.S. sovereignty over the Zone and the gradual transfer of the canal to Panamanian control. The best event of the 1960s from the U.S. viewpoint was the overthrow of the leftist and increasingly unfriendly government of João Goulart in Brazil, and its replacement by a military rulership very friendly to the United States and disposed to cooperate in opposition to communism.

Since the latter 1960s, U.S. influence in various countries has risen and fallen. In Peru in 1968, for example, a military group took power with a commitment to nationalize U.S. petroleum properties, and it took a markedly leftist, although noncommunist, stance. In and after 1975, however, Peru turned toward more moderate and pro-American policies. In Chile, the election of Allende in 1970 represented a considerable defeat—hailed by leftists worldwide—for the United States. His overthrow by the military, with considerable but perhaps not indispensable assistance from the United States, might indicate that, if Washington uses its resources sagely, it is difficult for a government to take a strongly contrary line. Allende, however, had many troubles besides the hostility of the United States, especially the disunity of his coalition and the fact that he could never bring the armed forces under his control.

Overall, the influence of the United States in Latin America has tended to wane ever since it reached an exceptional high in the wake of World War II. This is an expectable result of the recovery of the war-devastated economies and the success of most of Europe and Japan in keeping up higher growth rates than the United States. The result in Latin America is summarized by the drop of the U.S. share of the region's foreign trade from nearly half in 1957 to 37.7 percent in 1967 and 29 percent in 1977.[14] The industrialization and economic growth of Latin American countries has also contributed to growing feelings of independence; amounts that the United States could allot as foreign aid loomed large in the 1950s, but were hardly significant in the latter 1970s for the major republics.

The grinding down of the cold war has also decreased U.S. influence. As long as upper and middle classes were convinced that communism was a real danger to them, they were ready to side with the United States. If that threat comes to seem unreal, the power they perceive limiting their freedom of action is the old hemispheric hegemon.

The Vietnam war too, was a major cause of decreased U.S. influence after about 1967, as the anticommunist military effort began to seem a failure. The prestige of the United States sank with its inability to bend a small poor country, North Vietnam; sympathies increasingly went to the guerillas fighting against bombers and napalm. The United States was tormented by dissent and growing disorders. As the Nixon administration reluctantly withdrew and the Ford administration could only watch as the North Vietnamese rolled to final victory, the United States seemed to have lost the will to act abroad that is an essential component of national influence.

What has happened in ten countries of Latin America is detailed in the chapters that follow. It is clear, however, that the United States has lost a large part of what was once a very strong position in Latin America; the ability of this country to sway its neighbors, never so complete as often imagined, has been much reduced. The formerly dominant U.S. holdings in basic industries, such as mining and petroleum extraction, have virtually all been nationalized. The multinationals are still welcome nearly everywhere except in Cuba, but they are subject to a multitude of restraints. The OAS, which long seemed a triumph of U.S. policy and a useful means of its diplomacy, became more like a forum for making demands on this country.

The feebleness of U.S. powers was demonstrated by general noncompliance with the Carter administration's call for a boycott of the 1980 Moscow Olympic Games in reprisal for the invasion of Afghanistan. Only the dictatorial or military-governed countries of Argentina, Bolivia, Chile, El Salvador, Guatemala, Haiti, Honduras, and Paraguay heeded Carter's call,[15] assuredly for their own anticommunist reasons. The grain embargo to punish the Soviets for their aggression only encouraged the principal agricultural exporters, Brazil and Argentina, to increase their sales. The fact that pro-Castro radicals could take power in the small Caribbean island of Grenada in 1979 and remain defiant and unscathed showed the superpower to be a rather shackled giant. American ambassadors in Latin America countries exaggerate when they claim to have no influence at all, but they are not entirely unrealistic. Yet the material assets of the United States are still very large and may potentially be used if there should be a political will to do so.

NOTES

1. A brief discussion of the nature of influence is given in Robert Wesson, *The United States and Brazil: Limits of Influence* (New York: Praeger, 1981), pp. 1–9.

2. Gordon Connell-Smith, *The United States and Latin America* (London: Halsted Press, 1974), p. 5.

3. Richard J. Walton, *The United States and Latin America* (New York: Seabury Press, 1972), pp. 51–52.

4. Samuel F. Bemis, *The Latin American Policy of the United States* (New York: Harcourt, Brace, and Co., 1943), p. 136.

5. Walton, *United States and Latin America*, pp. 91–92.

6. Bemis, *Latin American Policy*, p. 166.

7. United Nations, Economic Commission for Latin America, *External Financing in Latin America* (New York: United Nations, 1965), pp. 18, 19, 33.

8. John T. Reid, *Spanish American Images of the United States, 1790–1960* (Gainesville: University of Florida Press, 1977), pp. 147–48.

9. Connell-Smith, *U.S. & Latin America*, p. 110.

10. Connell-Smith, *U.S. & Latin America*, p. 152.

11. United Nations, *External Financing*, p. 33.

12. United Nations and International Bank for Reconstruction and Development, *Direction of International Trade* IX (New York: United Nations, 1958), p. 12.

13. Connell-Smith, *U.S. & Latin America*, pp. 213–14.

14. United Nations, *Direction of International Trade* (New York: UN, IMF, and IBRD joint pub., 1958), p. 12; International Monetary Fund, *Direction of Trade Annual, 1963–1967* (Washington, D.C.: IMF, 1967); IMF, *Direction of Trade Yearbook 1980* (Washington, D.C.: IMF, 1980), p. 46.

15. *New York Times*, July 14, 1980, p. 12.

2

Chile:
Successful Intervention?

Paul E. Sigmund

Although Santiago is farther from New York than is Moscow, Chile has exerted a strong fascination for Americans in recent decades. Ideological groups from the extreme left to the extreme right have interpreted its recent stormy history as a confirmation of their own views of political, economic, and international relations. Although Santiago only has a population comparable to that of Philadephia, and the whole country less than that of New York State, it has been the object of a particular interest and attention by U.S. policymakers and political commentators ever since the radicalization of the Cuban revolution awakened Americans to the fact that Latin America existed. United States interest and attention have had an impact on the course of recent Chilean history, which has been better publicized and more thoroughly evaluated than U.S. relations with any other Latin American country—even Mexico. This chapter will attempt yet another evaluation— without, it is hoped, the partisan bias that has characterized many such analyses in the past—in order to determine the character and effects of U.S. influence on Chile over the last 20 years.

This discussion of U.S. influence will inevitably focus principally on official policies, both because they are easier to identify and because they have had a clearer impact. Yet it will also consider the influence of nongovernmental groups based in the United States, particularly banks, multinational corporations, trade unions, and educational institutions, since it is clear that at certain moments they have had an important effect on Chilean politics, economics, and society. No attempt will be made to consider the degree to which the U.S. relationship to Chile can be described as "imperialistic," or the Chilean relation to the United States as one of "dependency," despite the considerable literature from the advocates of these positions. In any case, "influence" is a more accurate description of the relations between sovereign nations than the rigid categories of domination or subordination that are the etymological roots of imperialism (Latin, *imperare*—to command) and dependency (Latin, *dependere*—to hang from).[1] The etymological core meaning of influence is a flow entering from outside (*influere*), and the flows involved can be of many kinds: diplomatic, military, economic, cultural, and ideological. The flows may be in either direction, but in the case of Chile and the United States the relationship is clearly asymmetrical.

PRE-1960 INFLUENCE

While Chile was settled principally by Spaniards, a significant element of which was of Basque origin, after independence other ethnic groups made their influence felt, especially the English and Germans. There was extensive contact between Chile and California at the time of the gold rush in the middle of the nineteenth century and up to the opening of the Panama Canal, but no important American colony established itself in Chile. The United States recognized Chile in 1823, but during the nineteenth century Chile was more oriented toward Europe. American entrepreneurs, notably William Wheelwright in steamships and Wheelwright and Henry Meigs in railroads, helped to develop the country, but U.S. investment was not significant until the twentieth century when the Guggenheim interests developed large copper mines at El Teniente and Chuquicamata, the latter being sold to the Anaconda Company in 1923.[2]

With the initiation of the pan-American movement at the Washington Conference in 1889, the United States began to take a more active role in inter-American affairs. In the twentieth century, as investments in copper, nitrate, and iron increased, U.S. influence in Chile rose dramatically as the expansion of trade led it to replace Britain as Chile's number one trading partner. By the 1920s 90 percent of Chilean copper was U.S.- owned, and one-third of Chile's exports and imports was with the United States.

Chile contributed to the Western war effort during World War II by agreeing to keep the price of copper stable, but it did not formally participate in the conflict. In 1947 it joined the United States and other Latin American countries in the Rio Treaty of Mutual Assistance, which provided for collective defense against external attack. At Bogotá in 1948, along with the other Latin American republics, Chile participated in the establishment of the Organization of American States, which was an important channel of U.S. influence until the 1970s. After the initiation of the Korean War, strong

Chilean resistance developed to the unilateral action of the U.S. government in once again setting a fixed price for copper for the duration of the conflict. In May 1951 a Chilean delegation to Washington secured an increase in the price and the right to sell 20 percent of its output on the London market where prices fluctuate everyday. An attempt to establish a Chilean government monopoly on the sale of copper in 1952 failed because it coincided with the drop in copper prices at the end of the Korean War, but the copper question continued to be an important issue between the United States and Chile.

An additional channel of U.S. influence was established in the 1950s as the U.S. Military Assistance Program began to send advisers to Chile, and the Chilean military participated in training programs in the United States and in the Panama Canal Zone. President Truman's Point Four Program had already initiated a small number of technical assistance projects in Chile. In 1955 a team of U.S. economic advisers, the Klein-Saks Mission, carried out the first of many efforts to reduce Chile's rampant inflation. The principal impact of the United States on Chile in the 1950s was through the considerable expansion of U.S. investment (mainly, but not only, in copper). The Eisenhower administration was reluctant to embark upon the large-scale program of economic assistance that was urged upon it by Chilean and other Latin American economists and political leaders.[3]

In summary, previous to the 1960s the influence of U.S. investors on the Chilean economy, especially in copper, was considerable. However, the diplomatic presence of the United States was largely restricted to fostering Chile's integration into the emerging inter-American security system, along with the occasional exercise of good offices in smoothing over difficulties between Chile and U.S. copper companies.

THE CUBAN REVOLUTION AND THE ALLIANCE FOR PROGRESS

After the Cuban Revolution, the United States began to take a more active interest in Latin America. In August 1960 the OAS established the Interamerican Development Bank (IDB) to provide public assistance to Latin American programs of economic and social development. In August 1961 the United States approved the Alliance for Progress to provide $20 billion in public and private assistance to promote reforms in taxation, land tenure, education, housing, medical care, and other social programs—all designed to respond to the Cuban challenge by demonstrating that reform could be carried out under the auspices of political democracy. The U.S. military, already engaged in training and joint maneuvers with its Latin American counterparts, offered new courses in antiguerrilla combat and "civic action" designed to win popular support. At the same time, the cultural programs of the United States Information Agency emphasized the common democratic values of the hemisphere and opposition to communism.

Washington looked for a showcase of democracy in Latin America, and one of the places where it found one was Chile—which except for interruptions in 1891 and from 1925 to 1932 had been governed by civilian constitutional regimes since 1833. Despite its conservative orientation, the government of President Jorge Alessandri was ready to cooperate in the program of the Alliance. At the outset of the Alliance for Progress, Chile benefited from a U.S. aid program for earthquake relief, and the first Peace Corps advisers arrived in mid-1961. Responding to the Alliance program, Alessandri secured the adoption of an agrarian reform law in 1962 which was succeeded by a much stronger measure in 1967. Less visible evidence of expanded U.S. influence was the CIA funding (exposed late in the decade) of noncommunist student, labor, peasant, and community development groups in Chile, which were supporting democratic alternatives to the programs of the Marxist movements. A Catholic president in the White House with a Spanish-speaking wife added to the impact and attraction of the United States to Chileans at the time.

Perhaps the high point of U.S. influence in Chile was the period immediately before and after the landslide victory of the Christian Democratic candidate, Eduardo Frei, over Salvador Allende in the September 1964 presidential elections. It was later revealed that the U.S. embassy had played an important role in the preelection maneuvering that led to Frei's victory and that the CIA had spent a total of $2.6 million in support of Frei's campaign. With the arrival in December 1964 of U.S. ambassador Ralph Dungan, one of the late President Kennedy's closest advisers and a man who became a personal friend of many members of the Frei administration, U.S. influence reached its peak. It was exerted in public support of the Frei reform programs, especially his efforts to pass a stronger agrarian reform law and to acquire part ownership ("Chileanization") of the U.S.-owned copper mines. In the mid-1960s Santiago was filled with U.S. advisers in the areas of military assistance, education, agriculture, science, law, community development, trade unionism, and the organization of peasants and slumdwellers. In addition to official aid programs, U.S. foundations were active in many areas, including a program of fellowships for graduate study in economics (principally at the University of Chicago) that was to have significant consequences for official economic policy a decade later following the 1973 coup.

There were a number of reasons why U.S. influence declined in the latter half of Frei's six-year administration. CIA covert funding of many Chilean organizations was exposed.[4] The Christian Democrats who had been doing well both electorally and in their economic programs began to run into difficulty beginning in 1967. The inflation rate that had been dropping began to increase as government spending exceeded tax receipts. The Christian Democratic reform programs became increasingly controversial and expensive. This alienated the right-wing parties that had supported Frei earlier out of fear of an Allende victory, and they began to promote the candidacy of ex-president Jorge Alessandri for the 1970 elections. The left wing of the Christian Democrats took an increasingly anticapitalist and anti-American line, while the deepening U.S. involvement in Vietnam undermined American prestige. In late 1967 Edward Korry, Dungan's successor as ambassador, adopted a "low-profile" policy for the U.S. presence in Chile, which was extended to the hemisphere as a whole by President Nixon when he came to power in January 1969. The U.S. Congress began to limit military credits and sales to Latin America, and the military in Chile increased its purchases of arms from Europe. In 1969 the Frei government forced the Anaconda Company to sell it majority ownership of the mines that had not been included in the earlier Chileanization effort, and it imposed an excess profits tax on all U.S.-owned copper companies. In the same year the centrist Radical Party moved to the left, joining the newly formed Popular Unity electoral alliance with the Marxist parties, which after lengthy negotiations nominated Allende again for the 1970 presidential race.

Chilean opinion became more divided, and elements on the right, the center, and the left were increasingly critical of the United States. Despite CIA expenditure of $200,000 in covert funds in the 1969 congressional elections to help them, the Christian Democrats continued to lose ground electorally. The possibility loomed that in a three-way election in 1970 (as opposed to what was basically a two-way fight in 1964) the left, which controlled about one-third of the Chilean vote, could emerge triumphant.

THE 1970 ELECTIONS

Much more information is available about U.S.-Chilean relations during and immediately following the September 1970 presidential elections than about any other period. It has been the subject of extensive investigations by three committees of the U.S. Congress, many books and articles by Chileans and Americans, and personal testimonies by participants that continue to be published. What they reveal is a deep and continuous U.S. involvement in 1970, both by various elements of the U.S. government and by American companies, which was directed at preventing the installation of Salvador Allende as president of Chile. United States involvement included support for covert CIA funding of anti-Allende propaganda, substantial campaign contributions by American companies to right-wing candidate Alessandri, as well as unsuccessful efforts by Nixon to use the CIA to promote a military coup in September and October 1970 in order to prevent Allende from coming to power. Yet the very fact that all of the U.S. efforts came to naught demonstrates the limits of U.S. influence at this point, and the strength and autonomy of Chilean political and military leadership.

The U.S. involvement in Chile during the 1960s and at the time of the 1970 presidential election was substantial but not decisive. Despite the claim in the Senate Select Committee report that CIA involvement converted what would have been a Frei plurality into a Frei majority in 1964, it seems likely that once the right wing had decided to throw its support to Frei in a desperate attempt to stop Allende from achieving the victory he had come close to gaining in 1958, Frei was assured a majority, since in repeated elections from 1958 to 1973 the Chilean electorate had divided its votes three ways—among the right, the center, and the left. In the election and party maneuvers of the late 1960s, CIA and embassy manipulations probably led to several splits in the Socialist and Radical parties, but neither of those parties was important in the Chilean political scene. Despite Henry Kissinger's assertion to the contrary in his memoirs, the U.S. government's decision not to support Alessandri directly, but only to engage in an anti-Allende "spoiling" campaign in 1970, was not significant in influencing the outcome, since American companies gave Alessandri very sizable sums. Only if the United States could have persuaded the Christian Democrats to name a candidate who could succeed in persuading the right to withdraw the Alessandri candidacy, or if the Christian Democrats had withdrawn in favor of Alessandri, thus making it a two-way race, would the election results have been different. However, this would have required total U.S. control of Chilean politics in the late 1960s rather than the pattern of declining influence that has been traced.[5]

The White House-CIA involvement in support of military intervention in the period after the popular election also did not alter the final results. It did, however, communicate to some military leaders that the United States would not be adverse to a coup against Allende when, for their own reasons, they decided to do so three years later. It also directly contradicted basic American democratic principles since it involved reversing the results of a free election—even if it was defended as an effort to prevent the establishment of a Marxist dictatorship. The link between the CIA activities and the death of Chilean Army Commander-in-Chief René Schneider, at the hands of rightists who were attempting to kidnap him in order to prevent a congressional vote for Allende, has been extensively studied by a Senate committee. The committee concluded that there was no direct U.S. involvement with the kidnapping attempt; however, one writer believed that the extensive CIA support of the anti-Allende right at this time indicates that "If the CIA did not actually shoot General Schneider, it is probably fair to say that he would not have been shot without the CIA."[6]

U.S. INFLUENCE DURING THE ALLENDE YEARS

Again because of the extensive controversy after the 1973 coup, a great deal is known about U.S. actions in Chile in the Allende years (November 1970 to September 1973). While the official policy as announced by President Nixon in January 1971 was to have "the kind of relationship with the Chilean government that it is prepared to have with us," there seems to have been an informal program of economic pressure on Allende, principally by discouraging lending to Chile by U.S. banks and international financial institutions. It is true that the United States voted for a loan by the Interamerican Development Bank in January 1971, but this was the last loan by IDB or the World Bank to the Allende government, although IDB used indisbursed earthquake relief funds to aid Chile after the Valparaiso earthquake in mid-1971, and the World Bank had a smaller agricultural loan ready for approval at the time of the 1973 coup. Whether because of U.S. government pressure or simply because Chile did not look like a very good credit risk, U.S. bank loans and credit lines dropped off, and the Export-Import Bank moved Chile to a lower category of credit worthiness.

United States aid, except for humanitarian purposes (including Food for Peace powdered milk that was used to fulfill an Allende campaign promise), declined to a trickle, although there was no diminution of military assistance and training programs. Allende described the U.S. pressures as an "invisible blockade." This is not an accurate description of a program that did not cut off trade or normal commerical activity and made no effort to prevent the Allende government from securing spectacular increases in lending from banks and governments in the rest of Latin America and Western Europe, which more than made up for the decline in U.S. assistance.[7]

The U.S.-owned copper companies were nationalized with little or no compensation in mid-1971, and many other U.S. companies were taken over by forced purchase or through legal loopholes ("intervention" because of a government-incited labor dispute, or "requisition" because of problems in the production of "articles of basic necessity"). Those actions resulted in heavy pressure for U.S. government action by the affected companies, and led to a strong statement against nationalization without "prompt, adequate, and effective compensation" by Nixon in January 1972. The compensation question was also brought up by the United States during the Chilean multilateral negotiations to secure the refinancing of its debt in 1972.

In the area of covert action, a total of $6 million was spent between 1970 and 1973 to support the opposition to the Allende government. Beginning in early 1971, the CIA channeled money to the opposition parties and after September 1971 to opposition newspapers and radio stations, including $1.5 million to *El Mercurio*, the prestigious conservative newspaper that was the Allende government's most influencial critic. In September and October

1972 the CIA also began to help opposition business and labor associations, and some funds they received seem to have been used for two nationwide general strikes against the Allende government in October-November 1972 and July-September 1973, which had much to do with Allende's overthrow. The CIA also financed a small anti-Allende news pamphlet directed at the armed services, and in one instance passed false information and documents to a Chilean military man outside of Chile. It was also in touch with various coup plotters among the military, although in May 1973 when it became clear that a coup was likely in the next several months, the CIA station in Chile was ordered to avoid any action that might be interpreted as supporting or encouraging a coup.[8]

When the coup finally took place, it was the result not of U.S. intervention but of runaway inflation (a 323 percent annual rate in July 1973 by official statistics, with unofficial estimates running much higher), political polarization between a president elected with 36 percent of the vote and the opposition-controlled Congress and courts, and the threat posed to the military monopoly of the instruments of coercion by the growth of armed extremist groups on the right and left. (The rightist group Patria y Libertad had received $38,500 from the CIA in 1970 and 1971, but Senate investigators found no evidence of such support after it resorted to terrorism in 1973.) Despite charges that the 1973 coup was directed from a U.S. weather plane in Argentina (Chile's long-time enemy) or by the U.S. military in Panama, and that the presidential palace was bombed by American pilots (in British planes!), no evidence of U.S. involvement in the coup has been produced.[9]

The Senate Select Committee report, *Covert Action in Chile*, concludes that during this period the United States moved from support of what it "considered to be democratic and progressive forces in Chile . . . to advocating and encouraging the overthrow of a democratically elected government." Except for the Nixon-CIA efforts to promote a military coup in September and October 1970, this seems to be something of an overstatement. The Senate report itself indicates that the ambassadors and the State Department opposed both intervening in the electoral process in 1970 and engaging in economic warfare with the Allende government thereafter. Because he thought it would provoke a coup, Ambassador Nathaniel Davis successfully opposed funding the strikers—although, as noted above, some money seems to have been given to them by other recipients of CIA support, despite an express prohibition of such action.[10] In this writer's interviews with embassy personnel two months before the coup, it appeared on repeated occasions that the current embassy strategy was to support the democratic opposition in the hopes of a massive repudiation of Allende at the polls in 1976. The CIA steered clear of direct coup involvement, although it is possible that in their earlier contacts with military opponents of Allende they may have encouraged such thinking. The *Covert Action* report mentions the "disinformation" that it circulated in 1971, and arrest lists that the CIA prepared but never turned over to the military. There is no evaluation in the report of the influence of the U.S. Military Assistance Group, except for evidence uncovered in the investigation of the Schneider assassination that one attaché had encouraged some of the October 1970 plotters.

What would have been the course of Chilean history between 1970 and 1973 had the U.S. influence not been exerted in the way it was? Much less would have been published or broadcast by opponents of the regime, *El Mercurio* might have gone bankrupt because of economic pressure from the government, and the two general strikes probably would not have spread as quickly nor lasted as long as they did. But the coup would probably have occurred in any case, given the politically motivated and disastrous course of the Allende economic policy of massive deficit financing, the polarization of politics, and the spread of arms on the extreme left and right. At least one observer concludes that without CIA covert support the coup would have occurred *sooner*, since there would have been less hope by the opposition that it could survive through the democratic process.[11] At the very least, there is no evidence that the United States had any direct role in provoking the coup or overthrowing the Allende regime. However, its influence was clearly not exerted in support of Allende—and in September and October 1970, it was not even exerted in support of the democratic process.

THE UNITED STATES AND THE PINOCHET GOVERNMENT

After the coup of September 11, 1973, the covert action program was sharply reduced, but CIA support for propaganda programs in progress was continued. One book in English that had already been in preparation, Robert Moss's *Chile's Marxist Experiment*, was rapidly completed, translated into Spanish, and widely distributed with CIA financing. The junta issued a white book a month after the coup that was prepared in part by CIA collaborators, and the CIA was authorized in October to cover the travel cost of anti-Allende labor leaders to Europe and the United States, as well as to continue support of an opposition radio station. However, within a few months one of the opposition newspapers that seems to have been principally supported by CIA funds was closed for financial reasons, and the *Covert Action* report indicates that the last covert expenditure took place in June 1974, when $50,000 was authorized to cover commitments made before the coup to the Christian Democratic Party.

The most important immediate result of U.S. influence in Chile, however, was the availability of a skilled group of economists and technocrats who had been trained in the United States over the preceding 15 years and who had a clear program for the economic reorientation of the bankrupt Chilean economy. With Pinochet's support, the so-called Chicago boys began to reduce tariff protection, eliminate subsidies and price controls, sell off most of the 500 enterprises that had been taken over by the Allende government, reform the tax system, and introduce massive reductions in public expenditure—notably by reducing the number of government employees. (Any post-Allende government would have been required to introduce many of these changes—although not necessarily in as ruthless a fashion—since the state-owned enterprises were running at a deficit that equaled half the national budget, while 53 percent of the budget itself was deficit financed.) At first the program was implemented gradually, but in early 1975 after the price of copper, Chile's principal export, dropped and the cost of oil jumped as a result of OPEC price increases, the government economists initiated a brutal "shock treatment" to bring down inflation and reduce government expenditure.

The removal of price controls and subsidies meant that the official inflation rate for 1973 jumped to 700 percent, but in succeeding years (particularly after the 1975 shock treatment) it was drastically reduced, leveling off at about 30 percent at the end of the decade and dropping further in 1981. However, the social cost in unemployment—which rose to over 20 percent—industrial bankruptcies, and reduced living standards was high. The rigid ideological approach of the Chicago boys—most trained by Arnold Harberger rather than Milton Friedman—was blamed.

Critics of U.S. policy toward Allende also noted that shortly after the coup, the Commodity Credit Corporation granted the regime two credits for wheat purchases that had been delayed in the last days of the Allende regime. In 1974 when the Export-Import Bank reopened its credit lines, AID asked for $25 million in new U.S. assistance. The United States then reached an agreement on debt rescheduling that it had not been able to reach with Allende, and therefore, was accused of ideological discrimination in granting and withholding aid, and even of deliberately provoking the overthrow of Allende and propping up a dictatorial regime. When private banks rushed to grant loans to the new regime (arguing that its conservative economic policy made it eminently creditworthy) and the Pinochet government worked out compensation arrangements with U.S. copper companies, the right-wing thrust of U.S. influence seemed to be confirmed.

The criticisms were intensified by the extreme brutality—indeed savagery—of the Pinochet regime's treatment of the opposition. Political parties and trade unions were suppressed, the Marxist-controlled radio stations and newspapers were shut down, the universities were placed under the control of military men, and thousands of Allende sympathizers were "detained," tortured, and killed. (Two Americans were among those killed under mysterious circumstances in the postcoup period.) Senator Edward Kennedy took a leading role in denouncing the repression, citing the wheat credits as "the latest symbol of our willingness to embrace a dictatorial regime which came to power in a bloody coup and which continues to conduct summary executions, to burn books, to imprison persons for political reasons, and to deny the right to emigrate." Kennedy used his chairmanship of the Refugee Subcommittee of the Senate Judiciary Committee to publicize the violation of human rights in Chile. The Latin American Subcommittee of the House Foreign Affairs Committee conducted five sets of hearings on human rights and the U.S. role in Chile in the fall of 1973. On the other side the House Internal Security Subcommittee offered an opportunity to defenders of the junta to introduce evidence concerning the imminence of civil war or a communist coup in Chile, which had been averted by the action of the Chilean military. A year after the coup the *New York Times* revealed the secret testimony of William Colby, the head of the CIA, concerning U.S. covert assistance to the opponents of Allende. The revelations led to the initiation of a Senate investigation of the CIA; the detailed report of that investigation has been a major source for this chapter.[12]

The continuing reports of atrocities in Chile, and the strong reaction against the Pinochet regime by U.S. church, labor, and human rights groups was an important factor in the development, several years before the advent of the Carter administration, of a U.S. human rights policy that had a special application to Chile. In October 1973 Senator Kennedy introduced an amendment to the Foreign Assistance Act to cut off all aid to Chile, except humanitarian assistance, until Chile improved its human rights record. The amendment was not adopted, but the act as adopted in December directed the president to "call on" Chile to respect human rights. In September 1974 Secretary of State Kissinger was reported to have rebuked Ambassador David Popper for raising the human rights issue with the Chileans. Kissinger urged Popper "to cut out the political science lectures," but by the end of the year the evidence on Chilean repression was so overwhelming and the American reaction to it so strong that the Congress voted to cut the president's request for economic assistance to Chile and to eliminate all U.S. military aid "unless the president reports to Congress that Chile is making fundamental improvements in the observance of human rights." Congress also voted to prohibit CIA clandestine operations for other than intelligence-gathering purposes unless the president certifies that "each such operation is important to the national security of the United States and reports, in a timely fashion, a description and scope of such operations to the appropriate committees of the Congress."

By 1975 relations between Washington and the Pinochet government had further deteriorated as a result of Chile's refusal to admit an OAS Human Rights Committee as previously agreed upon with the United States. At the end of the year the U.S. delegation to the United Nations voted in favor of a resolution condemning repression in Chile. In October the House adopted the Harkin amendment to cut off aid to all countries that engaged "in a consistent pattern of gross violations of internationally recognized human rights." It also created an Office of Humanitarian Affairs in the State Department, which in the next administration became the Bureau of Human Rights and Humanitarian Affairs. No request was made by the Ford administration for military aid to Chile, and in early 1976 Congress voted to extend the ban on military aid to include *all* Chilean military purchases in the United States after June 30, 1976, and to condition economic aid on an improvement in Chile's human rights record. In June 1976 even Kissinger spoke out on the human rights issue in a speech at on OAS meeting in Santiago. Here he supported the OAS Human Rights Commission and underscored the necessity of the observation of certain "fundamental standards of human conduct."

How did the Pinochet government react to the U.S. pressures? At first it denied that human rights violations were taking place at all; then it accused its critics (including Kennedy) of being part of a worldwide communist campaign against Chile. In 1975 and 1976 Chile issued decree-laws containing guarantees for the detainees, but they were known to be violated by the National Department of Intelligence (DINA), which had become a virtual state within a state with 4,000 employees and an estimated 16,000 informers. In the mid-1970s Chile began to release some political prisoners on condition that they leave the country. Arbitrary arrests and disappearances continued, although at a reduced rate, and several outspoken critics of the regime were summarily deported. The regime could resist the U.S. pressures because "pipeline" aid, under contracts signed before the military aid cutoff, continued until at least 1979, and needed military supplies could be secured elsewhere—from Brazil, France, and Israel, who were happy to sell Chile arms on easy credit terms. Chile's economic problems could be resolved by loans from American, European, and Japanese banks that were awash with petrodollars as a result of the OPEC price hikes. (Despite Chile's open policy to foreign investment, few U.S. companies made new investments in Chile after the coup, and most of those were in the mining sector.) Thus the influence of U.S. official policy was undercut by the actions of the private sector. Despite calls from congressional liberals for legislation to control private bank loans to Chile, there was no disposition to take such drastic action.

The Chile question was not a major issue during the 1976 presidential campaign in the United States, but "American interference in the internal affairs of Chile" was criticized in the Democratic platform. Jimmy Carter attacked the Republicans in a television debate in October for overthrowing an elected governement in Chile and helping to establish a military dictatorship. Just before Carter's election the Pinochet government announced that it would no longer participate in the U.S. aid program ($27.5 million had been voted by Congress in economic assistance, a sharp cut from the $100 million requested by the Ford administration) because of the congressional cuts and Chile's improved economy. Immediately following his election, Pinochet announced that 300 political prisoners would be released and allowed to leave the country.

The Pinochet announcement was made in anticipation of what was accurately perceived to be a likely increase in the U.S. emphasis on the human rights issue under the Carter administration. The human rights policy was supported by Zbigniew Brzezinski, Carter's national security advisor, both in order to contrast the new administration's approach with the Kissinger *realpolitik*, and out of a belief that U.S. prestige and power in the world would be enhanced by a stronger public commitment to freedom. The Human Rights Bureau was reorganized and headed by an activist, Assistant Secretary of State Patricia Derian. An Interagency Group on Human Rights and Foreign Economic Assistance—the so-called Christopher Committee— determined that Chile was one of a number of countries to be denied aid on human rights grounds. After Congress voted to require a report from the Department of State each year on the human rights records of recipients of U.S. aid, Chile once again rejected all U.S. assistance.

On the surface the U.S. pressure on Chile concerning human rights did not seem to have much of an impact on Chilean policy, but in 1977 two important changes took place—both related to U.S. policy. First, in July 1977 Pinochet announced a tentative timetable for return to civilian rule, with a constitutional plebiscite by the end of the decade and elections in 1985. More important, a month later the dreaded DINA was replaced by a National Intelligence Center (CNI) with more limited powers and a different leadership. Critics predicted that the reorganization would make no difference; but in retrospect it appears to be directly related to a sharp reduction in repression, the virtual ending of disappearances, and the appearance in mid-1977 for the first time of criticism by the Chilean press of the actions of the security services.

Those changes were affected, it is now clear, by the U.S. investigation of the assassination of Allende's ambassador, Orlando Letelier, in Washington in September 1976. One of the most serious violations of human rights by Pinochet's security forces had been a campaign of assassinations of exiled opponents of the regime. In 1974 ex-General Carlos Prats, a leader of the constitutionalist military at the end of the Allende period, was killed in Buenos Aires; Bernardo Leighton, a Christian leader with good contacts with the left, barely escaped with his life when his car was blown up in Rome in

October 1975; unsuccessful efforts were also made to kill several leftist leaders in Mexico; and in September 1976 Cuban rightists working with Michael Townley, an American DINA agent who had lived in Chile most of his life, blew up the car of Orlando Letelier, Allende's ambassador to the United States and one of the most skillful of the anti-Pinochet lobbyists in Washington. (An American coworker, Ronnie Moffitt, also died in the explosion.) The ensuing investigation moved slowly, but by June 1977 the FBI had identified the Cuban assassins and demonstrated their direct connection with the DINA. The American investigating attorney then confronted the Chilean ambassador with the evidence. A month later the DINA agent who had been in contact with the Cubans was identified by picture and pseudonym, and the DINA was reorganized. In November as the trail came closer, Manuel Contreras, the former head of DINA, announced his resignation as head of CNI. The following March when Townley was identified as an American citizen and the mastermind of the assassination, Contreras announced his resignation from the army. In April, after Ambassador George Landau had reportedly threatened to release information linking the Chilean government to the Letelier assassination, Chile turned Townley over to the U.S. authorities.[13]

The revelations about the DINA activities and the political opening in Chile were beginning to threaten Pinochet's hold on power, which he had consolidated during the years of repression. However, he had alredy demonstrated that he was a far more skillful politician than he had been given credit for at the time he took power in 1973. The reorganization of the DINA and the removal of Contreras insulated Pinochet from the possibility of a Chilean "Watergate." He followed this up with a suddenly announced plebiscite on his rule at the beginning of January 1978 in which he won over 75 percent of the vote.[14] This was followed by the removal from the governing junta in July 1978 of his only likely military rival, Air Force General Gustavo Leigh, and the resignation of most of the top generals in the Chilean Air Force. Having yielded to U.S. pressures on Townley, Pinochet then drew the line at Washington's request to extradite Contreras and two other DINA officers implicated in the Letelier case, although he did turn the request over to the Chilean courts and ordered the confinement of the three officers to Santiago's military hospital pending a court decision. Over a year later, long after a U.S. court had sentenced Townley and the three Cubans to prison terms for the assassination, the Chilean Supreme Court rejected the extradition request on the grounds that it was based on the tainted evidence of Townley as part of a plea-bargaining arrangement, and the three military men were released. In early 1981 a Chilean military court absolved them from all responsibility.

The Carter administration retaliated for the Chilean refusal to extradite by cutting its military and diplomatic representation, forbidding loan guarantees to Chile from the Overseas Private Investment Corporation and loans from the Export-Import Bank, and excluding Chile from the "Unitas" joint naval maneuvers. Since Chile was already not receiving U.S. economic or military aid and it had ready access to loans from private banks, the sanctions were purely symbolic; they had no effect in Chile except to demonstrate once again that the Carter administration disapproved of the Pinochet regime. This disapproval was demonstrated once again in September 1980 at the time of a plebiscite on a new Chilean constitution that granted Pinochet an eight-year term as president beginning in March 1981, with the possibility of another eight years through an additional plebiscite. When Pinochet received a two-thirds vote of approval in the plebiscite, the State Department declared that it regretted "the lack of meaningful choice" in the plebiscite and expressed the opinion that neither the plebiscite nor the constitution's transitional provisions marked an advance toward democracy.

Throughout the Pinochet period the U.S. embassy in Santiago and the government in Washington, as well as leading members of Congress such as Senator Kennedy, kept in touch with the leading members of the opposition, especially Christian Democrats such as former president Eduardo Frei. Leader Grants given by the U.S. embassy went to noncommunist labor leaders and centrist politicians, rather than to supporters of the government. The U.S. military continued to maintain good relations with their Chilean counterparts, and U.S. businessmn and bankers were generally highly favorable to the economic policies of the regime. American labor leaders, on the other hand, were highly critical of Pinochet's labor policy. In late 1978 the AFL-CIO threatened a boycott of Chilean goods unless Chilean workers were allowed to organize and to strike for higher wages. Just before the boycott deadline, a long-promised labor code was issued that allowed union organization and, within strict limits, strikes—although only on the level of the individual plant. As a result, the threatened boycott was called off; U.S. influence seems to have accelerated the liberalization of labor relations.

At the end of 1978, relations between Chile and Argentina deteriorated sharply over their long-standing border conflict concerning the Beagle Channel in the extreme south. The conflict was referred to the Vatican for arbitration, partly, it was said in Santiago, as a result of behind-the-scenes activity by the United States.

The Chicago boys remained in control of economic and social policy, and in 1978 began to introduce what they described as "the Seven Modernizations." These involved restructuring of government social and administrative programs on the basis of efficiency, competition, and the private market. For example, private health plans were encouraged, and the social security system was completely reorganized to promote the creation of private retirement funds among which the individual worker or employee could choose to invest his compulsory social security deduction. Private universities were initiated and students were supported with loans rather than grants on the basis of nationwide competitive examinations designed by the Educational Testing Service in Princeton. Primary and secondary schools were turned over to local school boards, and even the long-standing professional corporate groups (*colegios*) were no longer officially recognized by the government as representatives of their professions. The theory and practice for these changes was in the hands of young economists with American Ph.D.s (cynically referred to by the opposition as "the pretty boys behind the bayonets"). They flew American professors such as Friedrich Hayek, Arnold Harberger, and James Buchanan to Santiago to express their approval of the new programs. (William Buckley wrote a column endorsing the social security reforms and recommending them to the incoming Reagan administration.)

With the Reagan victory, the Pinochet administration anticipated a decided improvement in U.S.-Chilean relations. While Roger Fontaine, one of Reagan's closest advisers on Latin America, had declared on a visit to Santiago before the election that "U.S. concern for human rights did not begin with the Carter administration and it will not end with it," there is no doubt that the expressed preference of the Reagan team for "quiet diplomacy" in the area of human rights and the distinction made by Secretary of State Haig between authoritarian and totalitarian regimes were approaches that appealed to the Pinochet government. In 1981 when Reagan removed the Export-Import Bank ban, announced that Chile would participate in the next Unitas maneuvers, and that the United States would no longer vote against loans to Chile by international financial institutions, it seemed that relations would improve between the two governments. However, Chileans still complained that Argentina got more favored treatment. Argentine General Roberto Viola was invited to Washington at the time he took office in March 1981, and Reagan attempted to remove the congressional ban on military sales to Argentina while leaving the Chilean prohibition still in force. Chileans did not understand that, at least until the publication in April 1981 of Jacobo Timerman's book on his imprisonment and torture in Argentina, there was much stronger domestic U.S. opposition to lifting sanctions on Chile despite the fact that its human rights record had improved since 1977. (There were no disappearances although there were still occasional explusions and internal exile, as well as many detentions for questioning; in 1980 one Chilean student died as a result of mistreatment by a rightist paramilitary group.)

As he took office under the new constitution on March 11, 1981, President Pinochet referred to the ideological rapprochement between the two regimes:

Seven years ago, we found ourselves alone in the world in our firm anti-Communist position in opposition to Soviet imperialism, and our firm decision in favor of a socio-economic free enterprise system, contrary to the socializing statism that prevailed in the Western World . . . Today we form a part of a pronounced worldwide tendency—and I tell you, ladies and gentlemen, it is not Chile that has changed its position.[15]

While there is no doubt that the United States had neither the same kind of extensive influence in Pinochet's Chile that it possessed during the Frei administration, nor the deep covert involvement of the Allende period, it still remained the most important foreign actor on the Chilean political scene. The human rights issue loomed very large in the mid-1970s, but after the Letelier affair had produced a sharp reduction in the degree and kind of repression (although not its elimination) and the Carter administration began to run into domestic problems with its human rights policy, the tension subsided. In some cases Pinochet ably exploited Chilean nationalism against the foreign pressures to increase public support (which was easier to do when there was no effective opposition press), and in other cases he gave just enough ground to diminish the force of the criticism. In 1980 the Chilean regime took on the trappings of constitutionalism—however manipulated and artificial—and adopted a timetable for return to civilian rule—however distant in the future—just at the beginning of a new administration in Washington that was much more in tune with its thinking on both economics and international relations.

While Japanese economic influence in Chile visibly increased under Pinochet, his international isolation made it difficult for Chile to look elsewhere than to the United States. Frei's Christian Democrats had attempted (without much success) to involve the Western Europeans with Chile to a greater degree, while Allende had done the same with the Soviet Union and Cuba—again without much in the way of results except to frighten the middle class and the military. Since it had border problems with all its neighbors, Chile could only look to Brazil for support in South America; but Brazilian politics were entering a period of opening (*abertura*) in 1974 just as Chile's politics were closing down, while the Brazilian economic model involved much state control and ownership than were favored by Chile's policymakers. Thus for good or for ill, Chile remained in the U.S. sphere of influence, but it felt much more comfortable there in 1981 than it had in the mid-1970s.

CONCLUSION

Over the past several decades, U.S. influence has been exerted on Chile to secure varying objectives. From the end of World War II until the early

1960s, it was principally concerned with protecting U.S. investments, securing copper at as low a price as possible, and maintaining Chilean support for the inter-American system of collective security. In this it was largely successful, although the copper question caused some problems in the 1950s. Then with the initiation of the Alliance for Progress in 1961, U.S. influence was exerted in favor of social reform under democratic auspices— especially as articulated by the leadership of the Christian Democratic Party. Here it was successful at the outset, but as the Christian Democrats ran into domestic difficulties, U.S. enthusiasm and support for them waned. In the early 1970s the United States tried to prevent Allende from becoming president, and then supported the opposition forces during his presidency. It failed in the first objective, but was successful in the second, although the result was a bloodbath after the coup that contributed to the pressure in the United States for a new emphasis on human rights as one of the central objectives of its foreign policy. Chile moderated its repressive policies after 1977, but this had more to do with the after-effects of the investigation of the Chilean-organized assassination of Orlando Letelier than with U.S. aid cutoffs and adverse U.N. votes. With the reduction of repression and the adoption of a new constitution—and the advent of a more conservative administration in Washington—U.S. official influence is likely to be less clearly targeted on inducing changes in Chilean behavior than at any time in the past 20 years.

Throughout the period under discussion, but especially in recent years, the general cultural influence of the United States on Chile was powerful and pervasive. *Time* magazine and American television programs, products, and films all had a deep effect on the values and habits of an expanding Chilean middle class that thought of itself as part of an international consumer society, the model for which was "made in USA"—and specifically in Chicago.

Because of the original and far-reaching nature of the latest changes in Chile's social and economic structure, there are those who argue that in the 1980s the influence will flow in the other direction: from the Chilean experiment in free enterprise economics and decentralized and competitive social programs, to an American policy that has become disillusioned with state regulation and the growth of the centralized welfare state. But that influence cannot be effective unless it is accompanied by the return of political democracy, and this still seems far in the future for Chile.

NOTES

1. The classic expression of the theory of imperialism is Lenin's *Imperialism, the Highest State of Capitalism,* which was written in 1916 and borrowed some of its central concepts from the English liberal J.A. Hobson. The best evaluation of the theory is Benjamin J. Cohen, *The*

Question of Imperialism (New York: Basic Books, 1973). The most widely known of the large number of books and articles on dependence are Osvaldo Sunkel, "Big Business and *Dependencia*, a Latin American View," *Foreign Affairs,* April 1972, and Fernando Cardoso and Enzo Faletto, *Dependency and Development in Latin America* (Berkeley, Cal.: University of California Press, 1979 [revised version of 1969 Spanish text]). The best criticism is David Ray, "The Dependency Model of Latin American Development: Three Basic Fallacies," *Journal of Inter-American Studies,* February 1973.

2. On U.S.-Chilean relations, see Frederick B. Pike, *Chile and the United States, 1880–1962* (South Bend, Ind.: University of Notre Dame Press, 1963). On the Guggenheims, see John H. Davis, *Guggenheim: An American Epic (*New York: Morrow, 1979).

3. On U.S. relations with Chile in this period see Claude Bowers, *Chile from Embassy Windows, 1939–1953* (New York: Simon and Schuster, 1958). On the Klein-Saks mission, see Albert O. Hirschman, *Journeys towards Progress* (New York: Twentieth Century Fund, 1963), pp. 161–223.

4. For details, see Eduardo Labarca, *Chile Invadido* (Santiago: Editorial Austral, 1968).

5. For Kissinger's view, see *The White House Years* (Boston: Little, Brown, 1979), Ch. 17. For the U.S. role in the 1970 elections and during the period between the September 4 popular election and the congressional runoff 50 days later, see Paul E. Sigmund, *The Overthrow of Allende and the Politics of Chile, 1964–1976* (Pittsburgh: University of Pittsburgh Press, 1977), Ch, 6, and the following government sources: U.S. Congress, Senate, Committee on Foreign Relations, Subcommittee on Multinational Corporations, *Multinational Corporations and United States Foreign Policy—Hearings on the International Telephone and Telegraph Company and Chile, 1970–71,* March 2-April 2, 1973, 2 volumes (Washington, D.C.: U.S. Government Printing Office, 1973); U.S. Congress, Senate, Select Committee on Intelligence Activities, *Covert Action in Chile, 1963–73,* Staff Report (Washington, D.C.: U.S. Government Printing Office, 1975); U.S. Congress, Senate, Select Committee on Intelligence Activities, *Alleged Assassination Plots Involving Foreign Leaders,* Interim Report (Washington, D.C.: U.S. Government Printing Office, 1976), pp. 225ff. The history of the U.S. role is still being debated. See, for instance, *New York Times,* February 9, 1981, for evidence that U.S. Ambassador Korry had no knowledge of the Nixon-CIA effort to promote a military coup, and that the cable cited in the ITT hearings as giving "a green light" to all efforts to stop Allende short of landing the marines was sent not to Korry but to the CIA station in Santiago. For a left perspective on these events, see James Petras and Morris Morley, *The United States and Chile: Imperialism and the Overthrow of the Allende Government* (New York: Monthly Review Press, 1975), Ch. 2. For a liberal internationalist criticism, see Robert C. Johansen, *The National Interest and the Human Interest* (Princeton, N.J.: Princeton University Press, 1980), Ch. 4. On the ITT role, see Anthony Sampson, *The Sovereign State of ITT,* rev. ed. (Greenwich, Conn.: Fawcett, 1974), Ch. 11.

6. Thomas Powers, *The Man Who Kept the Secrets: Richard Helms and the CIA* (New York: Knopf, 1979), p. 237. See also Select Committee on Intelligence Activities, *Alleged Assassination Plots,* pp. 245–47.

7. See Paul E. Sigmund, "The Invisible Blockade and the Overthrow of Allende," *Foreign Affairs,* January 1974; the debate between Sigmund and Elizabeth Farnsworth, "Chile: What Was the U.S. Role?" *Foreign Policy,* Fall 1974; and Richard Fagen, "The United States and Chile," *Foreign Affairs,* January 1975.

8. *Covert Action in Chile,* pp. 26–39. See also David Atlee Phillips, *The Night Watch: 25 Years of Peculiar Service* (New York: Atheneum, 1977), Ch. 9.

9. See respectively, Gary MacEoin, *No Peaceful Way* (New York: Sheed and Ward, 1974), p. 169; Thomas Hauser, *The Execution of Charles Horman* (New York: Harcourt Brace Jovanovich, 1978), p. 65; and Gabriel Garcia Marquez, "The Death of Salvador Allende," *Harper's,* March 1974.

10. Contrary to a September 1974 *New York Times* report, the strikers did not receive "a

majority" of the CIA funds expended in Chile during the Allende period.

11. Frederick M. Nunn, "El Chile antiguo y el nuevo; la politica de transición, 1973–79." *Cuadernos del Instituto de Ciencia Politica,* (Santiago) no. 28 (1979), p. 16.

12. See the series of articles by Seymour Hersh in the *New York Times,* September 8–20, 1974 and by Laurence Stern in the *Washington Post,* September 8–17, 1974. For the Kennedy statement, see U.S. Congress, Senate, Judiciary Committee, Refugee Subcommittee, *Refugee and Humanitarian Problems in Chile,* Hearing, September 28, 1973 (Washington, D.C.: U.S. Government Printing Office, 1973), p. 54 (Statement, October 5, 1973). The House Latin American Subcommittee has published its hearings on Chile along with a useful collection of articles in U.S. Congress, House, Foreign Affairs Committee, Subcommittee on Interamerican Affairs, *United States and Chile during the Allende Years, 1970–1973,* (Washington, D.C.: U.S. Government Printing Office, 1975). The Internal Security Committee hearings are published as U.S. Congress, House, Internal Security Committee, *The Theory and Practice of Communism, Part 6, (Marxism Imposed on Chile-Allende Regime)* (Washington, D.C.: U.S. Government Printing Office, 1974).

13. For details on the Letelier case, see John Dinges and Saul Landau, *Assassination on Embassy Row* (New York: Pantheon, 1980).

14. The plebiscite followed a U.N. General Assembly vote cosponsored by the United States and the Soviet Union that condemned Chile for violating human rights. The Chileans were asked to vote yes or no to the statement, "In the light of the international aggression unloosed against the government of our patria, I support President Pinochet in his defense of the dignity of Chile and I reaffirm the legitimacy of the government of the Republic to lead sovereignly the process of institutionalization of the country."

15. *El Mercurio* (International Edition), March 5–12, 1981, p. 8.

3

Argentina: Pride and Weakness

Kenneth F. Johnson

THE INTERNATIONAL SETTING

Since the end of World War II, U.S. influence in Argentina has varied according to the commitments of those wielding power in Buenos Aires. The first government of Juan Domingo Perón (1946 to 1955) openly sympathized with the erstwhile leaders of Nazi Germany who went to a welcoming Argentina to recoup. During most of the war the United States had not kept an ambassador in Buenos Aires; the first one sent since 1943 was Spruille Braden, a man with little admiration for Perón, who moved into the U.S. embassy in 1945. In this year, pressure from the Allied powers forced Argentina's military government to end its proscription against political parties and to open up the political system to competitive pluralism. That included Juan Perón, who as an army colonel and minister of labor had put together the proletarian grass roots of a movement eventually to be known as *justicialismo.*

In October 1945 a group of officers imprisoned Perón, seeking to curb his growing power. On October 17 his proletarian followers, the shirtless ones or *descamisados,* desended on the main square of Buenos Aires, the Plaza de Mayo, and demanded his release. Perón's captors gave in, and the colonel proclaimed his presidential candidacy for the approaching elections. These dramatic events generated even more of a following for the eager and ruthless Perón. The significance of October 17, 1945 is critical, for it meant the first genuine politicization of the working classes in Argentina. It also meant the installation of an ideology that, while anticommunist, was also anti-United States. Peronism, *justicialismo,* was proclaimed as a third position in the rapidly growing East-West cold war.

Juan Perón's election as president in 1946 ushered in a low point in U.S.-Argentine relations. Perón campaigned on his labor reform record and received some unexpected help from his nemesis, former U.S. ambassador Braden. After he had returned to Washington as assistant secretary of state for Latin American affairs, Braden published through the State Department a Blue Book that detailed Perón's ties with Nazis and his admiration for Italian fascism. Perón had belonged to a group called the United Officers Block (GOU), which publicly subscribed to the Axis cause during World War II. Perón had also been in Italy during Mussolini's regime and was known to have admired what he saw there. The opportunistic Perón turned the U.S.-sponsored Blue Book to his own advantage. He held it up as blatant U.S. intervention in Argentina's internal political arena. The voters of Argentina were then offered the alternative of "Braden or Perón," as the slogan went. The theme of the United States as villain would continue in Argentina up to the early 1980s.

Perón was forced out of the presidency by a violent military coup in 1955. He remained exiled for 18 years, mostly in Spain, while surrogates purveyed his influence in Argentina. A new generation of Argentine political activists who had not known the excesses of his regime came to revere the exiled leader. The myth of status and largesse for the proletariat via Peronism was kept actively alive. During the years of Perón's exile a succession of soldiers and civilians tried unsuccessfully to govern Argentina. In 1971 the nation was in the grip of an economic crisis and faced a hardening guerrilla insurgency of major proportions. The generals then in power had had enough. They agreed to allow Perón's return in the face of rising popular demands. This mistake was compounded by the fact that the public, when faced with the rarity of a popular election, made Perón and his third wife Isabel president and vice-president. When Perón died in 1974 he left economic disaster and widespread political violence as a legacy to his wife, who became the hemisphere's first woman president. Isabel, unqualified to govern, was overthrown in March 1976 by the military, which has since sought to restore order at home and Argentina's credit and credibility abroad. The present chapter is mainly concerned with United States relations with military governments since 1976. Were a civilian government in power, be it a Radical, Conservative, Christian Democratic, or Peronist government, the thrust of this chapter would be quite different.

There is one diplomatic tradition that most recent governments, including Perón's, came to share: the notion of Argentina as representing a Third Position between capitalism and communism, between the United States and the Soviet Union. Perón made more of this than have most other governments; his posture toward the United States was openly hostile, while other civilian and military regimes have been cooperative, albeit independent. It is fair to say that Argentina today seeks to be no one's puppet, desires to maintain amicable relations with most nations, and hopes it can maintain an independent diplomatic profile. President Arturo Frondizi (1958 to 1962) sought to promote Argentina's industrial growth so as to free his country from dependence upon the whims of the world marketplace for agricultural products. Frondizi favored hemispheric solidarity and opposed the expulsion of Cuba from the OAS, yet at the same time he tried to improve relations with the United States. Frondizi was too willing to collaborate with the Peronists for military tastes, however, and he was ultimately removed by a coup. Frondizi's contract with multinational companies had been intended to build Argentina's economy. But following a caretaker government and new elections in 1963, the government of Arturo Illia reversed what Frondizi had done and cancelled many of the multinational contracts, in particular those dealing with petroleum. Illia, again, wanted to assert Argentina's independence in the Third Position tradition. He also tried to curtail the adventurism of his generals, but in 1966 one of them led a coup against him.

The government of General Juan Carlos Onganía (1966 to 1970) was significant for Argentine domestic politics because of the repression he unleashed and the insurgent reaction that ensued. That insurgency plagues Argentina to this day and has foreign ramifications. Onganía's government was highly personalist and his foreign policy stamp was anticommunist, hostile toward Third World leftist revolutionaries, antagonistic toward Fidel Castro, and cold toward the Soviet Union. Under Onganía the multinationals were welcomed once again and close relations prevailed with the U.S. government. Many observers felt that Onganía conservative economic policies might get Argentina back on its feet.

During the Onganía regime the peso was devalued from 250 to 300 to the dollar. By the end of his government in 1970 it had dropped somewhat more, but the bottom never fell out as occurred during the mid-1970s and thereafter. In 1972 the government of General Alejandro Lanusse decreed a change in the currency in which a "strong peso" was created by simply removing two digits from each bill (a note for 1,000 pesos became 10 pesos). But this did not disguise the inflation and currency devaluation that was to follow. Whereas during Onganía's government it would cost 300 pesos on the average to buy one dollar, by the time of General Videla's government in 1980, 300,000 of these same pesos went for a dollar. This monetary instability had, and continues to have, a dire effect on Argentina's fortunes; the ability of United States creditors to extend credit and refinance loans to Argentina plays an important part in the overall U.S. impact on that country.

Following the ouster of Onganía in 1970 Argentina was governed by two generals, including Alejandro Lanusse, who early in 1971 turned out to be a surprise in both domestic and international politics. His approach was ideological pluralism, which meant setting up working reationships with the Peronists and courting socialists abroad. Lanusse sought closer ties with the leftist Allende government in Chile and worked to offset the growing power of Brazil in the Southern Cone region. Lanusse facilitated the elections that ultimtely returned Juan Perón to the presidency and opened a disastrous epoch in Argentine politics.

INTERNATIONAL IMPLICATIONS

Argentine governments since the overthrow of Perón in 1955 have oscillated between classic liberals and statist nationalists. The former have had some economic success; the latter have generated more popular support and national enthusiasm. Neither has been able to come to grips comprehensively with Argentina's malaise, be it domestic or international.[1]

Apart from the idiosyncrasies of any given regime, one can point to a few general international goals that prevail in Argentina as a prelude to considering U.S. relations with the two most recent military governments. Argentina seeks a favorable balance of trade (as does any nation), but it also seeks to solve the problem of flight of capital, which is tied to political instability and results in a perpetually undermined currency. Governments that pay their domestic bills by running off unsupported currency on the presses only exacerbate the international dimensions of the currency instability. In the words of a Radical leader, Argentina must strive to become a country where people go to live and save, rather than to loot and flee.[2] Argentina needs to become a country whose peso is respected worldwide.

It is also a major Argentine goal to control the use of the foreign technology that it is forced to import. This is an especially tough and continuing issue between Argentina and the United States, whose firms part with their patents and controls with great reluctance. If a U.S. firm can prohibit an Argentine subsidiary from selling its manufactures in a given market, that may deprive Argentina of foreign exchange. The last Perón government forced Argentine subsidiaries of U.S. automakers to sell cars to Cuba or be nationalized. The State Department yielded and Castro got his cars.

In a number of economic and technological areas, the influence of the United States on Argentina is potentially great but at present ineffective. Argentina and the United States could join with Canada and Australia in a grain cartel to balance the OPEC oil cartel. This could include a boycott on grain sales to the Soviet Union as a diplomatic lever. In recent years this has not worked despite United States efforts. Also, Argentina seeks to become an independent nuclear power despite the efforts of Washington to discourage such developments. Like its northern neighbor Brazil, Argentina has had assistance in developing a nuclear capability, much of it coming from West Germany and Canada.

Washington would prefer to keep nuclear power in South America limited to thermoelectric and other peaceful purposes. An Argentine-Brazilian nuclear arms race could rapidly grow into a hemispheric nightmare. Such weapons might be used to settle water and border disputes between those countries should diplomacy fail. Other Argentine goals with potential for conflict with U.S. interests are national prestige and, of course, national security. The present military regime has avoided the anticommunist excesses of its predeccessors, especially the Onganía government. The Videla government even appointed socialist leader Américo Ghioldi as its ambassador to Portugal, and allowed both socialist and communist publications to circulate informally providing they kept a very low profile. The Argentines are not so anti-Marxist as some in Washington might like them to be.

Currently Argentina has a serious territorial dispute with Chile in the far south. Those two nations have rattled swords so many times that no one expects real war to break out, but it is possible. United States interests in the economies of both nations would be hurt by a war between them; however, since Washington is a major supplier of arms to both nations, U.S. pressure could prevent any such conflict. Another potential problem area for Argentina is illegal worker migration from its neighbors, a theme that has been treated elsewhere in greater detail.[3] Border problems over illegal aliens could damage economic cooperation in the Río de la Plata basin.

Argentina has its own limited arms industry. It sold weapons to the Somoza dictatorship in Nicaragua during 1979 at a time when the United States had frozen such sales. Argentine arms sales could become a future problem for the United States, especially if Argentine collaboration with Libya should involve nuclear arms transfers. This dramatizes another area of contradiction for Argentina: its often professed Third Position drive to be a leader of the Third World while at once desiring major power (First World) status.

Argentine indebtedness to the United States should not be overlooked. Since World War II the total of economic assistance (loans and grants) to Argentina from the United States has been $199.1 million. Of this, $131.4 million had been paid back as of 1979, leaving a balance of $67.7 million. Argentina has been one of the hemisphere's greatest beneficiaries of U.S. military aid. For the same period cited above, Argentina received $263.6 million in military goods and services, of which $118.7 million has been paid back, leaving a balance of $144.9 million.[4] The amount is not so great (considering the millions the United States poured into Brazil during World War II), but the fact of the assistance and the indebtedness always reminds Argentines that they needed and accepted Yankee help.

Cultural and economic penetration of Argentina by United States interests is considerable, but seldom do its political implications become a matter for public debate. During the second Perón era the far left made great cause against U.S. economic "imperialism" in Argentina. American-based interests control (not necessarily own) some of Argentina's major industries, including the automotive, pharmaceutical, and electrical industries. Granting U.S. firms contracts to develop Argentina's oil wealth has frequently been a controversial issue. The Onganía government welcomed the U.S. firms whose contracts its predecessor government, the constitutional regime of Arturo Illia, had canceled. The Peronists generally favor local control of petroleum, and some military sectors agree. The current government of General Viola has made the U.S. firms feel welcome once again.

Even though cultural and economic penetration is quite visible in Argentina, the Argentines are fiercely proud of their national tradition and seek to give the impression that "made in Argentina" means that a product is theirs, despite whose capital was brought in to underwrite the venture. They may use American words and cultural expressions to name products, styles, and phenomena (like soccer teams), but it is understood that these are Argentine choices that were not dictated from the exterior. The Argentines also have a unique speech pattern, which lends itself to the impression of arrogance, and they are quick to stress their Europeanness when cultural heritage is mentioned. They are, in a word, open to outside influence, even American influence, so long as its terms are optional and not imposed. Americans seeking to influence Argentines or their government will do well to guide the process by which options are chosen in a subtle and delicate way. Imposed choices are likely to be doomed, especially those that violate the clan structure that pervades Argentine political life. The Argentines are tightly knit families, and it has been observed that they do not mix well, particularly with pushy foreigners.[5]

THE ISSUE OF HUMAN RIGHTS

The Argentine government, and the people generally, take very seriously what Washington does and says. Criticism by the Carter administration of human rights abuses in Argentina led that government to reduce its military presence in Buenos Aires during the World Cup games of 1978. In that same year a group of American congressmen visited Argentina on a fact-finding mission. Their concern for two key themes, human rights and the economic promise of Argentina as a place to invest, was not missed in Buenos Aires. Congressman William Moorhead told the Buenos Aires press corps that there was probably "less anti-semitism in Argentina than the North American press alleges."[6] Congressman Dante Fascell was quoted as opposing the foreign aid ban against Argentina legislated by the U.S. Congress in 1977.[7]

Argentine leaders felt that they and other leaders of Latin American nations were capable of forging their own political life, without being prodded toward democracy by President Carter. They cited the cases, then recent, of Ecuador and Peru, where democratic openings were being made under military auspices. They alluded to the plebiscites planned in Chile and Uruguay in a similar vein. The Argentine government had affirmed publicly its commitment to returning to pluralistic democracy when the country was prepared for it. Brazil, where visible restorations in political liberties were under way, was another example of liberal military stewardship that Argentines could point to. Whether U.S. pressures by the Carter State Department spurred these steps toward democratization can never be known in a hard and fast way. But criticism of Argentina for its lack of democracy was unwelcome, as was the Carter administration's constant dwelling on human rights.

Terence A. Todman, President Carter's Assistant Secretary of State for Inter-American Affairs, made several tours of Latin America. He set forth during February 1978 a set of "commandments" for U.S. diplomatic actors and programs in Latin America. His pronouncement was a reproach to critics who had challenged the Carter administration with having gone soft on right-wing regimes in the hemisphere. Todman insisted on getting the facts straight, not expecting reform overnight, putting each phenomenon in its real-life context, not assuming the incumbent stewards of power are always liars, and avoiding ethnocentrism. He held that denying aid to the poor is not the best way to castigate their government, that public ridicule of another government is counterproductive, and that nations must work incessantly through the OAS and its Inter-American Commission on Human Rights to alleviate suffering throughout the hemisphere.[8] Todman was a seasoned diplomat with experience in both Africa and Latin America. In responding publicly to his North American critics, he was sure to draw a response from Latin America. From Argentina his remarks drew these commentaries:

Augusto Comte Macdonnel (Christian Democrat): "Todman reaffirmed his defense of human rights and support for his position grows daily. Argentina must join this effort."

Bernardo Grinspun (Radical): "The well-balanced position of Todman should be followed in Argentina with the support of all the people in ending the repression and bringing the guilty parties to justice. Along with this should go respect for social and economic rights to a secure life and income plus freedom from the tyranny of subversion."

Enrique Osella Muñoz (Justicialista): "Todman backs up what he and I discussed in various conversations all within the spirit of the United Nations' charter. The steps he cites are part of a prolonged process that must be incorporated into our historical reality."[9]

Officially the Argentine government said nothing, but the above could not have been published without at least the tacit approval of the military junta. The Carter administration had made its human rights stand more palatable for the time being. Todman had left the impression that he saw improvement in Argentina's human rights situation.

A softening of the Carter administration's position on human rights in Argentina was evidenced by changes in the lending policy of the Export-Import Bank in Washington. Early in 1979 the Eximbank resumed granting dollar loans to Argentine firms without setting any political conditions. Previously the Carter administration had suspended such loans as a reprisal against Argentine human rights violations. Members of the U.S. Congress who were identified with the human rights cause (for example, Senator Culver and Representative Harkin, both of Iowa) had carried Carter's campaign into the legislature amid considerable controversy that the United States was abandoning its "friends" in the interest of intervening in the private domestic affairs of other nations.

The resumption of economic cooperation and loans in 1979 did not mean a lifting of the ban on weapons sales to Argentina. This remained in place until early 1981, when the Reagan administration expressed willingness to resume sales of some $100,000 in arms to Argentina. Senator Thomas Eagleton condemned that development, saying that "fundamentally, there is little difference between the violent tactics of terrorist groups and the systematic brutality of some governments," referring clearly to Argentina, South Africa, the Philippines, and other authoritarian governments.[10] In contrast to Eagleton's sentiment, the Reagan administration announced that it would plan joint naval exercises with both Argentina and Chile. The controversy over U.S. collaboration with, and support for, Argentina would be a continuing one.

Parenthetically, one should note the considerable support that had gone to the Argentine government (post-Peronism in 1976) in the form of loans from U.S. private banks. Controversy over this emerged in 1980 when Carter named A. W. Clausen, a Republican and retiring president of the Bank of America, as successor to Robert McNamara, then retiring from the presidency of the World Bank. Clausen's appointment was seen in some Third World countries as a defeat for them and their effort to fill the spot with a non-American. Worse, from the viewpoint of some Third World nations, Clausen's bank had "financed the Argentine government six months after the Videla coup with a loan of 40 million dollars."[11] Clausen thus was identified with having financed a number of the most repressive governments in the hemisphere, including Chile and Brazil. Carter's nomination of this conservative Republican only five days before the presidential election was seen by some as a last-ditch, cynical effort by Carter to save himself. This attitude, perhaps, is why the Carter human rights campaign had so little impact.

Carter himself was highly inconsistent in applying his doctrine to foreign governments and in naming persons to sensitive positions vis-à-vis human rights.

The same sanctions applied against Argentina had been used to help bring down the dictatorship of Anastasio Somoza in Nicaragua in 1979, and here Carter can claim credit for having pursued his human rights commitment rationally and consistently. Yet the following year Carter yielded to pressures at home and halfway propped up the sagging junta in El Salvador, then cut aid when reports of atrocities surfaced, and later restored some of the aid. Carter's human rights policy in Latin America was widely seen as inconsistent and ineffective, despite what he may have accomplished in Nicaragua. Nicaragua was not Argentina. Continuing to deny Argentina loans from the United States would not have toppled the military junta in 1979 any more than would refusal by the Reagan administration to sell arms to Argentina in 1981. As components of United States influence, such actions would only have hastened the economic disorder that broke loose once again soon after the change of Argentine governments in March 1981.

NONMILITARY U.S. ASSISTANCE AS INFLUENCE POTENTIAL

In 1980 the U.S. Eximbank offered some $700 million in loans for the Argentines to purchase turbines and generating equipment for the Yacyretá hydroelectric plant in the northeast. Additional funds were made available for a range of capital equipment. The United States hoped to counteract the Soviet Union, which was also bidding on the project and whose turbines were aready being used on the Salto Grande hydroelectric scheme. It is important to underscore the significance of the hydroelectric issue in Argentina, as that country's hydro resources are such as to give it the potential for major industrial power within the next decade. Harnessing those resources is a major goal shared by all recent Argentine governments. The issue has been especially pressing since Brazil, in collaboration with Paraguay, has taken control of the headwaters of the Paraná River. If the United States can assist Argentina in its own coveted industrial development, then U.S. potential influence in that country can be enormous.

Argentina is seriously concerned about the growing economic and political power of Brazil. Argentina has superiority over Brazil in nuclear development, in petroleum, and in certain agricultural pursuits (grains and livestock in particular). Brazil has superiority in industrial capacity, in human resources, in geographic size, and in international political influence. The threat of Brazilian imperialism from the north is believed very real in Argentina. Anything the United States does to help Argentina keep up with

Brazil (without alienating Brazil at the same time) means influence potential for Washington.

The hydroelectric issue between Argentina and Brazil is geopolitical. Since 1978 the Brazilian-Paraguayan dam project known as Itaipú (and other smaller dams) has retained river waters of the Paraná, Uruguay, and Río de la Plata to the detriment of Argentina in the south. Argentina proposes to construct a dam called Corpus just south of Itaipú that would capture hydroelectric power and preserve some of the river's navigation potential. In 1970 all nations in the Río de la Plata basin agreed that none would monopolize the river to the detriment of the others. Subsequently Brazil dissented, claiming exclusive rights to headwaters within its territory regardless of the consequences downstream, and began building the Itaipú Dam with Paraguay. Argentina then entered into another project of this type, also with Paraguay, that would be completed in 1985 and would be known as Yacyretá. This is the project for which the U.S. Eximbank loaned funds in 1980 and entered into competition with the Soviet Union for provision of turbines. Complicating the picture further is the Salto Grande project that started partial operation in 1980 and in which Soviet-made turbines are being used. This venture was between Argentina and Uruguay, but involved all the nations of the Río de la Plata basin and a number of European countries and firms. At stake in this complicated set of developments is the basis for a major regional industrial power having worldwide scope and political impact if all the parties can get together. If they cannot, the industrial development opportunity will be postponed or lost. United States influence in bringing the area's development to fruition will, therefore, be important.

The fact that the Carter administration and the Videla government worked out an economic rapprochement has been attributed to the labors of their respective ambassadors. American Ambassador Raúl Castro went to Washington with evidence that the Argentine government was making a reasonable effort both to stop the terrorism without further sacrifice of lives and to solve the mystery of disappeared persons, even to the point of publishing a list of persons officially detained under the National Executive Power.[12] Castro sought to convince Washington that many acts of violence occurring in Argentina were done by persons who, although perhaps associated with the police or security forces, were not acting under official blessing, and that Videla and the military junta were not to be held morally responsible for subunits that they were trying, albeit unsuccessfully, to control.

Argentina's envoy to Washington, Ambassador Jorge Aja Espil, also worked to "unfreeze," as the Argentines say, relations between the Carter White House and the Videla Casa Rosada. Not only was Aja Espil charged with smoothing out matters concerning human rights allegations and international credit, but his task also included handling Washington's desire for

Argentina to sign the Nonproliferation Treaty for Nuclear Arms. Argentina seemed the most advanced of Latin American countries in nuclear arms development, with Brazil a close second. The military junta guarded this capability jealously; the American initiative, if pressed too far, could make diplomacy difficult. After the United States embargoed arms sales, the Argentine government saw nuclear development as even more urgent. Canada and West Germany were already collaborating with Argentina in the development of nuclear energy, and economic pressures from the United States intended to limit these developments served only to stimulate them further.

RECENT U.S.-ARGENTINE ISSUES
OF CONTENTION

At the beginning of the 1980s, the principal issues of contention in U.S.-Argentine relations were nuclear proliferation, international credit and assistance, grain sales to the Soviet Union, and human rights. The position of the Reagan administration was to play down human rights and underscore the eradication of terrorism in the hemisphere. On the other hand, continued grain sales to the USSR and growing economic closeness between Buenos Aires and Moscow were of concern to Washington. The United States could not object to the grain sales, however, as President Reagan announced in 1981 that his government would resume grain sales to the Soviets. It appeared that Washington's most promising area of influence vis-à-vis Argentina's governing establishment was in the area of economic assistance, particularly in the matter of hydroelectric development.

Argentina is quite capable of acting independently of the United States where its perceived vital interests are at stake. Argentina boycotted the 1980 summer Olympic Games in Moscow, heeding U.S. pressures following the Soviet invasion of Afghanistan. But at the same time Argentina stepped up its grain sales to the USSR, replacing much of what the United States withheld and enabling the Soviets to channel some of their grain internationally to aid Nicaragua and Cuba. In fact, in 1979 Argentina had a surplus balance of trade in its favor with the USSR amounting to more than $300 million, a credit the chronically weak peso could not stand to lose.[13]

During 1980 President Carter had sent General Andrew Goodpaster on a goodwill mission to Argentina that was generally successful. By this time the State Department had virtually accepted the defeat of its human rights effort in Argentina as originally conceived. But following the Goodpaster visit, relations between Washington and Buenos Aires cooled again on the occasion of the July 1980 military coup in Bolivia, which ended that country's brief flirtation with democracy. The new regime of General García Meza expressed open admiration for the military junta in Buenos Aires, and President Videla was widely quoted in the Latin American press as having supported the Bolivian coup so as to maintain friendly regimes on its borders. It was simply a matter of good geopolitics for the Argentines, then embroiled in a bitter territorial dispute with Chile (which had been referred to mediation by the Vatican), to want a friendly regime in Bolivia in case of war. Bolivia had a long-standing animosity toward Chile over the loss of Bolivia's Pacific coast during the late nineteenth century, but the incumbent caretaker regime then in power in La Paz could not be counted on to support Argentina militarily against Chile should that eventuality occur. The Bolivian generals could be counted on, so Argentina supported their coup. There are many hemispheric precedents for such intervention, but for Argentina this was a major departure away from the tradition of nonintervention. However, this further strained Argentina's relations with the United States, given the State Department's commitment at that time to fostering the nonviolent development of political democracy in Latin America. Noteworthy also was Argentina's need for Bolivian natural gas, which seemed less likely to be interrupted under a military government.

Therefore, in a perhaps unusual move for an Argentine head of state, President Jorge Rafael Videla admitted publicly that his government had supported the July 1980 coup in Bolivia. It had previously appeared likely that a socialist would ascend to the presidency of Bolivia.[14] Videla said that Bolivia had two options: one was the "correct" or legal path of permitting the democratic process to take its course; the other option, which Videla specifically termed "incorrect," was the military coup. He then said that he sympathized with the legally "incorrect" option given the risks involved in allowing democracy to proceed and risk of having created "in South America that which Cuba has become to Central America."[15] He stated also that "we did not support the OAS motion to condemn the new government of Bolivia simply because we did not want to end up with Cuba at our backs."[16] Finally, and with great candor, Videla said that his government had made both weapons and military advisors available as backup forces to guarantee the success of the Bolivian coup. He termed this military cooperation an ongoing relationship between Argentina and Bolivia, and admitted that his action was a departure from Argentina's traditional position of nonintervention. The menace of communism in the Southern Cone and the need for an ally should war come with Chile over the southern territorial disputes were so weighty that Argentina felt forced to abandon its diplomatic tradition in this instance.[17] So once again, Washington's ability to influence Buenos Aires had been nil.

THE QUEST FOR DEMOCRACY VIS-À-VIS
THE REAGAN DOCTRINE

There was no secret of the Argentine government's delight when Ronald Reagan defeated Jimmy Carter in the November 1980 presidential election. The rhetoric from Reagan's political camp suggested he would have approved of Argentina's intervention in Bolivia given the "linkage" significance of a communist advance in South America. At the same time, even before taking office, Reagan was meeting unofficially in 1981 with Mexico's President Jośe López Portillo, who urged the president-elect not to intervene in the affairs of Central American nations. But notwithstanding Reagan's desire to court López Portillo, the two men were far apart on the matter of intervention, just as Carter had been at odds with President Videla over Argentina's involvement in Bolivia. Thus it is well to inquire into the Reagan Doctrine in Latin America (insofar as it can be identified during the first presidential year) and its relevance to Argentina.

The Reagan Doctrine, not yet fully clarified, would appear to consist of a number of tenets that have been attributed both to the president and to his ambassador to the United Nations, Jeane Kirkpatrick. One of these is that long-time friends of the United States, albeit dictators, should be defended to the degree that they impede the growth of communism in the hemisphere. A corollary is that some torture and repression by the autocrat is an unavoidable evil that must be tolerated if the pro-American status quo is to be preserved. Further, it is asserted that association with leftist rebels is sufficient cause for the United States to ostracize political groups and actors within a given country's political spectrum.

Other parts of the doctrine are the belief that revolutionary-socialist regimes are irreversibly destined to become communist-totalitarian ones, and that conservative regimes are more malleable; thus there are better prospects for democratic conversion when a society has reached a state of preparedness such as to make democracy work.[18] Implicit also in the Reagan Doctrine for Latin America is the notion that major social overhead capital investments, like the hydroelectric projects for Argentina discussed earlier, will have the "halo effect" of spreading socioeconomic well-being as a basis for the growth of democratic practices. But peace, economic growth, and stability, not democracy as such, seem to be the prime goals of the Reagan Doctrine. That high investment in capital-intensive industrialization may also generate high levels of unemployment, and hence sociopolitical unrest, is a risk that will be examined toward the end of this chapter. Suffice it to conclude that the Reagan Doctrine favors generous military assistance to Latin American friends within the linkage theoretic context, and it is assumed that the recipients can best decide how such assistance may be used. Reagan thus places the evaluation of Latin American actors and events in a context of

Moscow-to-Washington linkage and competition; by contrast, Carter tried to stress the human rights context of what was done, and to whom, as the principal criterion for deciding U.S. assistance policy. Carter was not always consistent in applying his policy; it remains to be seen how Reagan will fare in this respect.

It is appropriate to ponder what renewed aid under the emerging Reagan Doctrine might mean for Argentina, and whether this will contribute to the Viola government's commitment to political democracy. Considering Argentina's chaotic record of democratic civilian governments that ended disastrously, it is not at all certain that political democracy in the Anglo-American context is appropriate for Argentina. What seems clear is that Argentina's incumbent leaders (including President Viola) and the leaders of political outgroups do want democracy. Viola has promised to return the country to democracy at the earliest possible time.

Argentina's two most recent presidents, Videla and Viola, genuinely wanted democracy to work. It is a melancholy truth that Argentina's most recent civilian governments were horrendously corrupt and chaotic, making military intervention imperative if the country were to be spared civil war and total economic collapse. This is not to excuse the carnage involved in reestablishing order, but the civilians and their consitutional government during recent years have proved themselves so incompetent to govern that extended military rule becomes a practical and fair option for Argentina. Nevertheless, as noted above, Argentina's current rulers and opposition politicians all say they want political democracy within a constitutional framework, and they have promised to bring it to fruition.

CONCLUSIONS AND ANALYSIS

Argentina, as a politically unstable nation of great hemispheric importance, is more susceptible to U.S. influence in the economic sphere than in the diplomatic, cultural, or strictly military sphere. Any U.S. influence must not collide with Argentine pride if it is to be successful. One might think this a platitude, yet so sensitive are the Argentines in the matter of how one treats them formally that it is imperative to stress the issue. Telling them in public how to manage their human rights is unlikely to work. It is therefore not surprising that President Viola would develop better relations with President Reagan than existed under President Carter. Whether such relations will benefit the people of Argentina is a question that cannot be answered here.

However, Washington will have to come to terms with the human rights charges against the government it now supports in Buenos Aires. The testimony from the exiled Anglo-Argentine Robert Cox, and from the exiled

Jewish-Argentine Jacobo Timerman, leads one to conclude that there is official terrorism in Argentina. Making matters worse are the stories told by these men of Argentine policemen wearing Nazi swastikas while carrying out their grim tasks in torture chambers.[19] There are other severe dilemmas in this, including the silent complicity of the Jews themselves:

> Most distressful for Timerman, however, is the realization that even the Jewish community in Buenos Aires has fallen into this same "silent complicity" despite overwhelming evidence that anti-Semitism is alive and well.[20]

Testimony of this sort has motivated the efforts of Senators Percy, Pell, Zorinsky, and others to prevent resumption of military aid to Argentina without human rights guarantees. Some reports of General Viola's March 1981 visit to Washington indicated his willingness to publish lists of "disappeared" persons and give human rights guarantees. Others said the general had repudiated such statements.[21]

The human rights issue will not go away, and Washington is under considerable domestic and international pressure not to support the Argentine regime unless the human rights question is solved. How the Reagan Doctrine is adapted to fit this challenge will be crucial for U.S. influence in Argentina during the next few years. Even if Congress vetoes the attempt to give Argentina military aid, there is always economic assistance, as I documented above. Moreover, if Washington shuts off aid there is always the New York banking community. As the Latin American saying goes, "if Washington cuts us off New York will finance us. Who needs Washington anyway?"[22]

Argentina seems able to accept U.S. influence when it is convenient to do so. Washington cannot legislate away Argentine pride, nor its monetary instability, nor its human rights abuses, nor its nuclear adventures,[23] nor its sale of wheat to the USSR. In its drive to become a major world power, Argentina is likely to remain impervious to U.S. influences except as convenience dictates. One major exception may be the area of international indebtedness and international monetary exchange. Argentina's natural resources will enable it to survive world depression and probably, for a time, internal revolution. Cutting of U.S. assistance will not topple a given regime as in Nicaragua; but cutting off *all* forms of assistance and loans from anywhere in the United States, plus U.S. influence against Argentina in the multinational arenas, probably could. Given the apparent emerging priorities of the Reagan Doctrine, and barring some natural disaster or major international war, it is not likely that any such U.S. influence will materialize before 1985. At that point the American national political process will come into play. Much will depend on whether Argentina's government is still in military hands and, if not, which part of the domestic political spectrum is the controlling power of state.

Here, then, are two analytic views of the influence dilemma of U.S. foreign policy toward Argentina. The Argentine generals in 1976 took on their "historic project" of suppressing and exterminating the existing violent subversion at almost any price. But, *essentially*, this was a process whose goal was economic stability. Argentina had had a recent history of acting contrary to U.S. wishes. Washington was concerned that too great an emphasis on human rights might jeopardize other U.S. interests there, especially economic and diplomatic ones. The United States also hoped to persuade Argentina to limit its nuclear development programs to peaceful endeavors. The United States employed sanctions like cuts in aid and suspension of military sales, along with the promise of graduated rewards if the worst of the human rights abuses were to be ended. Since the Carter administration viewed President Videla as a moderate, care had to be taken so as not to undermine the general with too tough an implementation of the human rights policy. Thus U.S. Ambassador Raul Castro urged Washington not to disrupt diplomatic relations just because the host government was taking a hardline approach to liquidating the guerrilla subversion. It is claimed that Castro reported the "bad news" from Buenos Aires only reluctantly, thus giving Washington the impression that more progress in the human rights field had taken place than was really true.[24] Argentina was able to secure arms and financing from non-U.S. sources, principally European, thus weakening the effect of the U.S.-imposed arms and aid sanctions.

Washington had little choice other than to deal with the military government. The Peronists were discredited, demoralized, and divided. The Radicals and Christian Democrats were weak and unpredictable. The Marxists lacked a solid base and existed only because the military tolerated them. Assistant Secretary of State Todman's visit to Buenos Aires in 1977 generated confusion because he gave the impression in Argentina that human rights were being respected, but the subsequent aid and arms sanctions by the United States seemed to contradict that diplomatic effort. In 1980 the State Department issued a high-level paper criticizing human rights violations, but then proceeded to send new emissaries to Buenos Aires to smooth relations. Not surprisingly, the Argentines were confused and suspicious of U.S. diplomacy.

In the next few years the tone of bilateral relations with Argentina will depend on U.S. ability to relate to the military government without giving the impression that human rights have been abandoned completely as a goal of diplomacy. Any such goals sought by the United States must be pursued within a process of astute maneuvering that is sensitive to the subtle nuances of Argentine pride. A sense of human rights as a moral value was communicated successfully by the Carter administration, and this should not be lost sight of in American diplomacy.

A second and somewhat distinct view is that the thrust of Argentine politics since the coup of March 1976 has been essentially political and a struggle against the agents of international terrorism, which unavoidably resulted in inadvertent human rights violations. The reward emerging from this process was the subsidiary goal of economic stability and the restoration of stable governing institutions that would lead eventually to a democratic government, but with a strong military participation. The Reagan administration removed barriers to arms sales to Argentina and announced it would not oppose multilateral loans to Argentina, Chile, Paraguay, and Uruguay via international lending agencies.[25] This was a near-total reversal of the Carter policies. Repeal of the Kennedy-Humphrey amendment of 1977 (restricting military assistance and arms sales to governments violating human rights) by the Congress at the request of the Reagan administration is therefore justified on a number of grounds. These include evidence that human rights violations have been significantly reduced in Argentina since 1977, especially during 1979 to 1981.[26] Disappearances of persons have also drastically declined. Moreover, the restoration of human rights in Argentina had little to do with U.S. sanctions and owes more to the success of the Argentine security forces in liquidating subversive elements. Also, the subversives themselves were guilty of human rights violations that turned much of the Argentine public against them (as occurred in neighboring Uruguay during the antisubversive campaign of 1970 to 1972). The Kennedy-Humphrey sanctions did not prevent Argentina from purchasing all the arms it needed in Europe and elsewhere, at a loss to the U.S. economy. It is also argued that the Carter administration's tough human rights stand may have actually encouraged Argentina not to join the grain embargo. The Kennedy-Humphrey sanction may also have been counterproductive since it did not allow the executive branch sufficient flexibility to conduct the nation's foreign affairs.

This line of analysis argues that elimination of the above-mentioned sanctions will not be taken in Argentina as U.S. abandonment of human rights, especially in view of General Viola's public commitment to that cause. To the contrary, dropping the sanctions will be taken "as a signal that a policy of self-damaging and counter-productive hostility towards Argentina has come to an end, and that a new era based on constructive dialogue and cooperation has begun, in which the interests of both countries will be better served."[27]

Whichever interpretation one chooses, there is a central element that must be considered in estimating potential U.S. influence in Argentina: the political constant of wasteful corruption. It is seen in the overstaffed and wasteful state-run enterprises and in the propensity of governments to pay their domestic bills by running off unsupported currency. Both features drain the public treasury and visit chaos on society and the economy. Neither military nor civilian governments in Argentina have been willing to attack this continuing problem; it seems the trouble existed at least back to the first Perón era. The consequences of waste and corruption, socioeconomic disorder, and internecine political violence affect Argentina's political stability and alter whatever quest for democracy may exist. Between 1975 and 1980 the scholarly image of Argentina's democratic status dropped notably.[28] United States influence probably cannot foment democracy where the climate is unfavorable. On the broad plane,then, the U.S. influence in Argentina seems limited to key areas of economic policy and military affairs.

NOTES

1. Edward S. Milenky, *Argentina's Foreign Policies* (Boulder, Colo.: Westview Press, 1978), p. 16. See also the two-volume work by Robert A. Potash, *The Army and Politics in Argentina* (Stanford, Calif.: Stanford University Press, 1969 and 1980).

2. Interview with Alfredo Concepción, August 8, 1975, Buenos Aires.

3. See Kenneth F. Johnson and Miles W. Williams, *Illegal Aliens in the Western Hemisphere* (New York: Praeger, 1981), passim.

4. U.S. Agency for International Development, *U.S. Overseas Loans and Grants: July 1, 1945–September 30, 1979* (Washington, D.C.: USAID, 1980), p. 36.

5. See interview with Robert Cox in *World Review Press*, January 1979, p. 20.

6. *La Opinión Revista*, Año 11, No. 87, 12-18 January 1978, p. 12.

7. Ibid.

8. *La Opinión Revista*, Año 11, No. 87, 23 February-1 March 1978, p. 13.

9. Ibid., p. 14.

10. As quoted in the *St. Louis Post-Dispatch*, March 25, 1981.

11. As reported in *Uno Más Uno* (México), 14 November 1980.

12. *La Opinión Revista*, Año 111, No. 100, February 1979, p. 13.

13. "Quarterly Economic Review of Argentina," *The Economist* (London, 3rd. Quarter, 1980), p. 7.

14. Bolivian elections were held in June 1980. Since no candidate for the presidency was triumphant with a majority, the decision was left to the parliament. It appeared that the plurality holder and former president Hernan Siles Suazo might be chosen. The Argentine government preferred to intervene rather than face a socialist in the presidential chair of neighboring Bolivia.

15. *Diario Las Américas* (Miami), 7 August 1980.

16. Ibid.

17. Ibid.

18. The case of Nicaragua in 1979 does not support this contention. See Tom J. Farer, "Reagan's Latin America," *New York Review of Books*, March 19, 1981, pp. 10–16.

19. Interviews reported by columnist Anthony Lewis in the *St. Louis Post-Dispatch*, June 16, 1981 and March 24, 1981 plus Jacobo Timerman's interview broadcast on national PBS, "Bill Moyer's Journal," May 1981.

20. Henry A. Christopher, "A Jew Tells of Nazi Torture in Argentina," *St. Louis Globe-Democrat*, June 14, 1981. Terrorism against Jews in Argentina is documented extensively by Robert Weisbrot, *The Jews of Argentina: From the Inquisition to Perón* (Philadelphia: Jewish Publication Society of America, 1979).

21. WOLA, *Update Latin America*, Washington D.C.: Washington Office on Latin America, May/June 1981, Vol. VI, No. 3.

22. *Uno Más Uno* (México), 14 November 1980.

23. See John R. Redick, *Military Potential of Latin American Nuclear Energy Programs* (Beverly Hills, Calif.: Sage Publications, 1972).

24. Richard E. Feinberg, "U.S. Human Rights Policy: Latin America," *International Policy Report*, October 1980, Vol. VI, No. 1, pp. 11–12.

25. *Diario las Américas* (Miami), 10 July 1981.

26. Statement of the Hon. James D. Theberge before the Subcommittees on Inter-American Affairs and Human Rights and International Organizations of the Committee on Foreign Affairs, House of Representatives, Washington, D.C., April 1, 1981, mimeographed, p. 2.

27. Ibid., p. 4.

28. See Kenneth F. Johnson, "The 1980 Image-Index of Latin American Political Democracy," *Latin American Research Review*, forthcoming, 1982; by the same author, "Scholarly Images of Latin American Political Democracy in 1975," *Latin American Research Review*, Vol. XI, No. 2, Summer 1976, pp 129–40; also "Measuring the Scholarly Image of Latin American Democracy: 1945–1970," in Wilke and Ruddle, eds., *Methodology in Quantitative Latin American Studies* (Los Angeles: UCLA Latin American Center, 1976); with Miles W. Williams, *Democracy, Power, and Intervention in Latin American Political Life* (Tempe-Arizona State University, Center for Latin American Studies, 1978), p. 29. For a good substantive coverage of United States relations with the Southern Cone, giving a broad historical perspective, see also Arthur P. Whitaker, *The United States and the Southern Cone* (Cambridge, Mass.: Harvard University Press), 1976.

4

Brazil: Independence Asserted

Robert Wesson

Since 1964 relations between the United States and Brazil have evolved rather steadily, straightforwardly, and perhaps more predictably than with any other major Latin American country. The chief trend, after the armed forces extinguished the leftist and somewhat inimical government of João Goulart, has been away from very close alignment to Brazil's recent emphatically independent stance.

For most of the history of the two countries, their relations were simple, friendly, and untroubled. Their vital interests have never clashed sharply, and Brazil has usually been the best friend of the United States in Latin America. There have been two obvious reasons for this. One is size. Brazil has long regarded itself as something of a counterpart of the United States in the southern continent, and this perception has been shared by the United States. As a very large country, Brazil has felt more secure than smaller Latin American countries and has been largely immune to their nervousness over questions of U.S. intervention in Latin America. Through the nineteenth century, Brazil was the only Latin American country to applaud warmly the Monroe Doctrine. The second reason is that Portuguese Brazil has always—although to a much decreased degree in recent years—felt itself more or less at odds with Spanish America. Brazil has been willing to support U.S. policy in the expectation of being supported by the United States in its relations with its neighbors, especially Argentina.

U.S.-Brazilian friendship has been brought into question mostly by ideological differences, and problems have arisen largely from internal Brazilian politics. Until 1885, the existence of slavery in Brazil cast a shadow, and the fact that Brazil was a monarchy somewhat dampened the cordiality of relations. Brazil, however, became a republic in 1889; the constitution it adopted paid the American one the flattery of imitation in form, although its working in practice was very different. The special relationship of the two countries was raised to a high level in the first decade of this century, as Brazil's foreign minister, the Baron of Rio Branco, sought U.S. backing in boundary settlements with Brazil's neighbors and its rivalry with Argentina, the chief critic of the United States in this hemisphere. He also wanted to bring in the United States to offset British influence, as the British economic penetration was then felt to be quite as burdensome as U.S. penetration would be more than a half century later. At that time, although the United States was a good friend and informal ally of Brazil, it had little economic presence in that country despite being the largest buyer of coffee.

In World War I Brazil was the only Latin American country to join the United States in war with Germany. The war had the effect of greatly weakening the position of European powers in Brazil, especially Britain and Germany, and of strengthening that of the United States. Relations between these two countries continued tranquil and became even more cordial under Franklin Roosevelt's Good Neighbor Policy. However, Brazil was caught up in the ideological turbulence of the years when fascism was touted as the wave of the future. In 1937 the Brazilian president, Getúlio Vargas, tore up the constitution, abolished political parties, dismissed the congress, and set up what he called a "New State." This looked rather like a fascist state, with censorship and exaltation of the ruler, although there was no mass party and no particular ideology and repression was mild. Vargas was, in any case, seen as a near-fascist, and Brazil appeared to be a major potential ally for Hitler's Germany and fascism in the Americas.

For a short time, the danger seemed acute. Vargas appealed to nationalistic feelings directed primarily against the United States (it was already common to decry the powers of international, U.S.-dominated interests). Vargas did not hide his admiration for such successful leaders as Hitler and Mussolini, and he exalted fascistic virtues while scorning the decadence of democracy.[1] There was a thriving fascist party, the green-shirted Integralistas; and the Nazi Fatherland counted on the influential Germanic minority in the south of the country. The Nazis launched a trade offensive and had considerable success because of their willingness to take quantities of Brazilian goods unsalable on the depressed world market, paying in blocked currency. German exports to Brazil in 1938 slightly exceeded those of the United States. Even more important was Germany's willingness to supply cheap arms to the hungry Brazilian forces. In consequency, a sector of the officers' corps became pro-German.[2]

Vargas, however, was a realist who at all times wished to keep open channels to Washington. Between dallying with the Nazis, he outlawed the Nazi movement among German-Brazilians and welcomed U.S. investments. In 1940 when the Germans after the conquest of France failed to storm

Britain, Vargas came down on the side of the United States. After Pearl Harbor, Brazil broke relations with the Axis powers and began military collaboration with the United States, which was willing to supply arms in return for facilities to prevent a possible Axis bridgehead in the Northeast bulge.

In August 1942 Brazil, after numerous sinkings of its ships declared war and became the only real ally of the United States in Latin America. Brazil furnished air and naval bases, cooperated with its navy in the security of the South Atlantic, and sent a small army (22,000 men) to fight in Italy.

The war greatly and enduringly strengthened U.S. influence in Brazil. The other major industrial powers were removed from the scene; only in the 1960s and 1970s were Japan, Germany, and other European countries able fully to take their places in the Brazilian economy. On the other hand, the Brazilian and U.S. economies became meshed. The industrialization of Brazil that Vargas promoted went forward largely under U.S. auspices; this included the state-owned, U.S.-financed Brazilian steel industry. Many Americans came to Brazil and stayed, and American businesses felt encouraged to invest there. Equally important was military collaboration. The Brazilian Expeditionary Force was supplied and trained by the U.S. army, with which it worked closely. Pro-Germanism in the Brazilian army and navy was wiped out, and the armed forces became more pro-American than those of any other major Latin American country. Soldiers of the two nations got along very well, and the officers of the force generally became lifelong friends of the United States.

The special friendship of Brazil with the United States was thus taken for granted in 1945. There was a contradiction, however, between admiration for the U.S. economic and political model and acceptance of the government of Vargas. The soldiers who had fought with the United States against dictatorship in Europe in effect demanded a democracy at home, and Vargas was forced to resign when he appeared to equivocate about free elections— this was a general season of toppling dictatorships in Latin America. Brazil in 1945 and 1946 inaugurated a new U.S.-style republic in an atmosphere of optimism and the greatest cordiality toward the hemispheric superpower.

The tendency to equate Brazil's interests with those of the United States continued through the presidency of Eurico Dutra (1945 to 1950). After about five years, however, the bonds of friendship began to slacken. Brazilians felt neglected as the United States turned its attention to the reconstruction of Europe and the containment of communism on the edges of the Soviet sphere, especially in Greece, the Near East, and Korea. There was little aid left over for Brazil, which seemed in no danger of subversion. The United States even seemed, forgetting its wartime ally, to treat Argentina with equal favor. The Brazilian economy at the same time slowed as the big war-accumulated balances were consumed, and discontent was inevitably directed against the overshadowing power.

A more basic factor of change, however, was the American-inspired political system, with leadership elected by a greatly expanded electorate. Dutra was firmly conservative; but Vargas, who returned to the presidency by popular election in 1951, was a populist, as were all subsequent elected presidents. But to be a populist, that is, to appeal to the urban mass vote, meant to be something of a political and economic nationalist and to turn more or less against the politically and economically dominant foreign power. Rising economic tensions and hardships resulting from inflation and unemployment along with cityward migration caused class tensions and a tendency to lay the blame on capitalists, especially foreign capitalists, and on the United States as the bulwark of the prevalent order of inequality and injustice.

This turn became evident although not yet dominant in Vargas's administration (1951 to 1954). Several measures were passed to restrict foreign capital. To the cheers of the communists and a nationalistic sector of the military, a national monopoly of petroleum production, Petrobras, was established, specifically to exclude U.S. oil companies. The Communist Party, which had been outlawed in 1947, was tolerated. In 1954 Vargas gave those who disliked his populism grounds for the military to overthrow him, as his administration was caught up in scandals of corruption and an attempted assassination. Rather than resign, Vargas shot himself, leaving behind a melodramatic note attributing the need for his sacrifice to sinister domestic and foreign forces.The masses, which had been very pro-American a decade earlier, went on a spree of smashing windows of U.S. affiliates; it became accepted among leftists that the CIA or U.S. interests engineered the downfall of the man who cared only for the people.

The next elected president, Juscelino Kubitschek (1956 to 1961), was of the Vargas camp. Since he relied on loans from the United States and foreign investment to push industrialization, he followed quite moderate policies. However, he complained of neglect by the United States, began exploring possibilities of trade with communist countries, and toward the end of his administration broke with the International Monetary Fund over its conditions for a loan, to the applause of the nationalists.

His successor, Jânio Quadros, was of the anti-Vargas camp, but he played up to the increasingly leftist-nationalist masses. Although his economic policies were rather conservative and pleasing to Washington, he turned the course of foreign policy sharply leftward and toward neutralism. He made friendly gestures toward Castro's Cuba and Communist China, then abhorred by the United States, and wanted Brazil to lead the Third World rather than follow the United States. After only seven months he resigned, blaming foreign reactionaries; it has been assumed that the United States caused his downfall, like that of Vargas.

The vice-president, João Goulart, was known for his strongly leftist views. The pro-U.S. leaders of the armed forces tried to exclude him from the succession. In the first part of his administration (1961 to 1964), however, he acted quite moderately. He even went to U.S. Ambassador Lincoln Gordon for advice on important problems and reversed Quadros's turn to neutralism.[3] But the United States and Brazil diverged as Goulart was disappointed in the financial support offered, and the State Department became concerned over the leftism of his followers. Washington tended to make loans conditional on Goulart's stabilizing the economy (which required unpopular austerity measures) and checking the growing influence of communists and near-communists in the administration and labor unions. This he did not care to do, as it meant turning against his supporters. In 1963 he turned sharply left, embracing neutralist if not pro-Cuban, anti-U.S. positions in foreign affairs, and appealing to anticapitalist, antiforeign, and anti-U.S. sentiments of the organized leftists.

This caused great apprehension in Washington. It seemed that the biggest country of Latin America, in deepening economic crisis, was careening toward revolutionary anarchy and possibly communist or at least radical dictatorship. It was a remarkable change in a few years from extremely friendly relations to emotional hostility, turning the United States from a model to a target, without any important change in the material situation. The reversal came not because of international conflict but because of domestic policy.

The course that the United States found alarming was reversed by the pro-American officers of the armed forces, primarily those who had shared in the battles of World War II. The coup of March 31, 1964 that sent Goulart into exile was desired and quietly encouraged by the United States, although "There is no evidence that the United States instigated, planned, directed or participated in the execution of the 1964 coup."[4] It has been common doctrine among all Brazilians, not only of the left, that it did just that, intervening for selfish political and economic reasons against Goulart's effort to give the workers and peasants a little economic justice and to make Brazil independent on the world stage.

The United States seemed to confirm this by welcoming the coup eagerly, and it moved rapidly to assist the new government. It also profitted greatly in terms of influence. The Johnson administration would have preferred to see the military return power quickly to a civilian administration and expressed concern about the relatively mild measure of repression taken at this time. But there could be no objection to the choice of Marshal Humberto Castelo Branco as president (1964 to 1967). He was decidedly pro-American, which may have been a factor in selecting him. Castelo Branco turned Brazil back to alliance with the United States in the struggle against communism around the world and especially in Latin America. Brazil became the most pro-American of Latin American countries, even cooperating in the 1965 intervention in the Dominican Republic (with 1,200 marines and a nominal commander for the entire interventionist force) and supporting the idea, generally unpopular in Brazil and Latin America, of an inter-American peacekeeping force. The United States, for its part, dispatched the economic aid denied the Goulart administration, and there were many programs of technical assistance. Castelo Branco decried economic nationalism, welcomed foreign investment, and improved conditions for it while stabilizing the economy and checking inflation.

Brazil did not entirely subject its foreign policy to the wishes of the United States; for example, it did not break diplomatic relations with communist countries (except Castro's Cuba, which it has steadfastly opposed), but moved toward increased commercial relations with them. Brazil declined to send even a token force to Vietnam despite pleas from Washington. The welcome for foreign capital was never unconditional, and it was sought to direct foreign investment to Brazilian needs. The Castelo Branco government believed it was simply acting to maximize growth. Yet seldom has a major power been so favorable to the purposes of the United States as Brazil was during the Castelo Branco administration.

Since then, the amenability of Brazil to U.S. policies or influence has consistently ebbed. The antileftist or anticommunist impulse of 1964 gradually diminished. As Brazilians forgot the Goulart period, nationalism reemerged; they began to see more conflicts of interest with the United States. According to a U.S. embassy cable of January 24, 1967, "The Castelo Branco government's all out support for United States policies has served to increase anti-Americanism rather than to lessen it."[5] Even conservatives turned their rhetoric against multinational corporations, the CIA, and the amenability of Brazil to U.S. purposes.

Leadership changed: Castelo Branco was replaced by Marshal Artur da Costa e Silva (1967 to 1968), who had no particular ties with or fondness for the United States and brought in a new set of advisers. The influential U.S. ambassador, Lincoln Gordon, who had close links to Brazil, was succeeded by a man who had none and never developed a good relationship with Costa e Silva and his government. Concurrently, the Vietnam war was making the United States both less impressive as a power and morally less acceptable as a model. Both the military and the intellectuals were repelled. With the Nixon administration, beginning in 1969, the United States undertook purposely to reduce influence abroad, or at least the appearance of influence, by the "low profile" and the "Nixon doctrine" of leaving it up to the peoples concerned to defend themselves against subversion. The United States was now prepared to furnish material assistance, but not to take the lead.

The two powers also diverged ideologically. The coup of 1964 had been proclaimed as a measure to protect democracy. It was generally assumed that military rule would be temporary and probably brief. Castelo Branco was indeed legalistic and as democratically minded as any of the military leadership. But the dictatorship was step-by-step hardened as his administration was pushed by the "hard line" faction to check any threat to military authority. In 1968 Costa e Silva was compelled to assume almost unlimited dictatorial powers, and Brazil was subjected to censorship and repression as never before in its history. The United States protested only mildly, but the earlier cordiality was dispelled. The next president, Garrastazu Médici, continued autocratic severity. Although the Nixon administration was not troubled by human rights violations, there was much public and congressional criticism.

Another reason for the increased independence of Brazil was economic growth. About the time that military rule was being hardened, foreign capital, encouraged by economic stabilization, began pouring in abundantly. Brazil embarked on a period of exceptionally rapid economic growth, averaging over 10 percent yearly until 1974 (and continuing more modestly thereafter despite the oil price rise and renewed inflation). Economic aid from the United States was no longer needed and was phased out as Brazil acquired confidence in its own capacity and increasingly viewed itself as a future (almost a present) great power.

It was, then, wholly to be expected that Brazil would shift priorities in foreign affairs. Costa e Silva immediately dropped support for the peace-keeping force desired by the United States. He took no interest in the moribund Alliance for Progress and complained of U.S. import tariffs. He accented Latin American relations, and Brazil began to speak more as a member of the the nonaligned nations, less as anticommunist ally of the United States. Brazil resisted U.S. pressure to sign the Nuclear Nonproliferation Treaty. The Costa e Silva government remained basically friendly to the United States and cooperated with American business interests, but it more pragmatically pursued strictly Brazilian interests.

Presidents Médici (1969 to 1974) and Ernesto Geisel (1974 to 1979) followed essentially the same course of calculated self-interest. Seeing Brazil as a rising power, they rejected in principle the dominance of the United States and the Soviet Union, as expressed, for example, in the nuclear club. They cultivated economic and political relations with their Hispanic neighbors. They expanded trade preferentially with countries other than the United States, including the Soviet Union and Eastern Europe. They were quick to recognize the communist-backed government of Angola and to develop trade with it. They took the Arab side in the Palestinian question. They expanded Brazilian territorial waters to the detriment of U.S. shrimp fishers. Far from reacting to these pinpricks, the Nixon administration, following the general logic of its approach to world affairs, upgraded Brazil and esteemed it as the leading anticommunist regional power and axis of what was left of the hemispheric system. Formally, U.S.-Brazilian relations came to an acme in February 1976 when Secretary of State Kissinger and

Foreign Minister Azeredo da Silveira signed a "memorandum of under-standing," promising that the two powers would consult on all matters of mutual concern and hold semiannual meetings at the ministerial level.[6] For the Brazilians, however, this amounted mostly to a recognition of their international status, with no particular commitment to the United States. They already had similar agreements with several European powers.

EFFORTS TO USE INFLUENCE

The Nixon and Ford administrations got along very well with Brazil by simply accepting Brazilian foreign and domestic policies without criticism. Jimmy Carter, however, proposed to remoralize U.S. foreign policy, particularly in two realms: advocacy of human rights and the prevention of the further spread of nuclear weapons or the potential for making them. Both of these policies were directed at many countries, but Brazil was an inevitable target. Carter in effect tested U.S. influence on Brazil and thereby pushed U.S.-Brazilian relations to the lowest point since 1964.

At the very beginning of his administration in 1977, Carter made Brazil a test case for his antiproliferation drive. He attempted specifically to annul the mammoth contract Brazil had made with West Germany in 1975 for the construction of as many as eight nuclear power plants plus auxiliary assistance in the mining and processing of uranium. The Carter administration particularly opposed the planned facilities for the enrichment of natural uranium and the reprocessing of spent reactor fuel, both of which might be used to produce nuclear explosives.

Atomic energy was a long-standing Brazilian aspiration, partly because it was regarded as a badge of modernization and great power status; there were moves from the mid-1950s to secure nuclear capabilities from one or another country. In 1967 the government of Castelo Branco contracted with Westinghouse for a plant at Angra dos Reis, near Rio, to be completed by 1977. In the following years, however, Brazil began seeking to lessen dependence on the United States by looking elsewhere for technology. In 1974 the question suddenly became acute because of the several-fold increase in the price of imported petroleum, on which Brazil relies very heavily; nuclear energy seemed essential for energy independence and future industrial growth. Equally important, the United States had refused to permit Westinghouse to construct enrichment and reprocessing plants in Brazil, a move that was regarded as designed to keep Brazil permanently dependent on enriched uranium from the United States. Brazil's frustration was completed as the U.S. Atomic Energy Commission renounced its guarantee of delivery of reactor fuel to Brazil (and other countries), thus making the United States an undependable supplier.

The Brazilian government reacted in June 1975 by agreeing to buy from

Germany a complete nuclear power industry, with an implied potential for the ultimate manufacture of nuclear bombs despite the international safeguards written into the agreement. There was alarm in the U.S. Congress and the press at the danger of nuclear arms in Brazilian hands, and indignation that the Germans should make big business thanks to American self-denial. The Ford administration, however, reacted only enough to meet criticisms in Congress. The ambassador in Bonn, who was briefed during negotiations, raised some objections; but after conventional safeguards against nonpacific use of the fuel were included, no further protest was made. Nothing was said to the Brazilians.

Carter, who had made the matter an issue in his electoral campaign, immediately after taking office began pressing the Germans to void the contract, using all diplomatic means available, even threatening withdrawal of U.S. forces from West Berlin.[7] The administration went first to the Germans, presumably in the belief that it had more leverage over them than over the Brazilians. But the Germans were not persuaded, and Secretary of State Cyrus Vance turned to Brazil. He argued the case several times with the Brazilian ambassador, and Deputy Secretary Warren Christopher went to Brasília early in March to present the case. But the Brazilians flatly rejected the proposal that enrichment be done in the United States or under international control. In November 1977 Vance again took up the matter while on a swing through Latin America, with no better results.

The administration was not in a position to do much more than argue, and when the arguments failed it gave up. Before Carter's visit to Brazil in March 1978, the question had been largely laid to rest with no concessions from the Brazilians. In Brasilia Carter renewed his plea diplomatically but did not let it spoil the festivities. Thereafter the administration turned its attention to more pressing matters.

The American action demonstrated the poverty of diplomatic resources, as it was not found possible to do anything forceful despite rather strong feelings on the issue. The results for U.S.-Brazilian relations were entirely negative. The Brazilians had cause for complaint in the violation of the Kissinger-da Silveira memorandum by taking up the matter with the Germans without consulting Brazil. But this document was already faded; more seriously, the Carter approach seemed a belated and unjustifiable challenge to Brazil's effort to secure energy independence. Oppositionists rallied behind the government to support the nuclear accord as a matter of national honor.[8]

For Brazil, nuclear energy was symbolic of modernization. It was unacceptable to Brazil to be told that it should not have it in full measure, from the mining of its abundant ores and the processing of uranium (isotopic enrichment) through the fuel cycle with separation of fissionable materials from rods for reuse. Brazil resented that its assurances and contractual guarantees of peaceful use should not be accepted. There was some talk of the necessity eventually to have nuclear bombs, or at least the potential for producing them; but the official position was that Brazilian purposes were wholly pacific. Brazilians viewed Washington's anxiety as primarily commercial, to keep them dependent on U.S.-processed fuel.

Only after U.S. opposition was dropped could many people in Brazil raise their voices against the program. The antinuclear lobby could not exert much direct influence on the semidictatorial government and the nuclear bureaucracy, but it could not be neglected, especially as the government moved toward democratization or "opening" (*abertura*) under President João Baptista Figueiredo (1979-   ). The antinuclear case was strengthened by the inevitable delays and cost overruns. The Westinghouse-built plant was not ready to begin operations until early 1982, five years behind schedule, and it appeared that only one of the eight plants agreed to with the Germans would be operational by 1990.[9] The program was inordinately costly at a time when Brazilian resources were stretched thin, more being spent on it than on all other energy programs in 1981. Yet it was hard to touch politically because it was still associated with the dream of "Brazil, the Great Power."[10] If the campaign against the Brazilian-German deal had been successful, it might have been disastrous for U.S.-Brazilian relations.

About the same time when the new administration was pressing the nuclear question, the issue of human rights also came to the fore. Some thought that the purpose of raising the matter of human rights must be to exert pressure in the nuclear question, where there was a visible American material interest. In regard to nuclear nonproliferation Brazil was a major target; in connection with violation of human rights, however, Brazil was a relatively minor offender.

Like the nuclear issue, the question of human rights was raised rather tardily. Through the Médici administration, which ended in March 1974, there were thousands of arbitary arrests and hundreds of cases of torture or murder of oppositionists. But the Nixon administration refrained from troubling itself or the Brazilian regime about it, although there were protests enough in Congress and the press. Violations decreased from the beginning of the Geisel administration, especially after a showdown with security officials late in 1975; they were rather few by the time the Carter administration undertook its human rights crusade in 1977. This was aimed primarily at the Soviet Union and Eastern Europe, but justice required that it be made general, and Brazil was inevitably included along with much worse violators, such as Argentina and Guatemala.

The action most offensive to Brazil, however, was a report on human rights observances by recipients of U.S. military assistance, which was mandated by law. The report, delivered to Congress in March 1977, dealt rather gently with Brazil, noted improvement under Geisel, and cited corrective actions as well as the charges.[11] It might have been little noticed if the State Department had not thrust it to the attention of the Brazilian government by sending a copy to the Foreign Office. This was intended as a courtesy, but it was interpreted as "intolerable interference." Within hours, the Brazilians denounced their military aid agreement with the United States, which had been in effect since 1952, because observance of human rights was treated as a precondition for military assistance. The gesture was inexpensive, however, as Brazil had made much progress toward building its own arms industry, and very little aid was coming from the United States. The Brazilian government was probably desirous of terminating the agreement in any case.

Some hotheaded officers were said to have talked of breaking diplomatic relations.[12] The government, however, kept the issue cool and did not use it to stir nationalistic passions. Geisel claimed to need no prodding on the question, as he was as devoted to human rights as anyone. The foreign minister defended the Brazilian record and suggested that the United States pay more attention to social and economic rights and help Brazil to develop economically so that it would be better able to advance human rights generally. Some members of the Carter administration criticized the Brazilian record; Rosalynn Carter took it up tactfully when visiting Brazil in June 1977. President Carter, in Brazil in 1977, tried to avoid either backing away from his ideals or offending his official hosts. He met several opposition leaders and spoke of the desirability of international scrutiny, but he avoided any hint of interventionism and tried to unruffle feelings. The issue, like the nuclear question, receded.

This rather mild intervention against human rights violations in Brazil— there was never a question of any material penalties, such as were applied to Argentina—was more successful or at least less unsuccessful than the antinuclear campaign. Many Brazilians, not only of the military, resented the presumption of the United States to judge actions in Brazil, and anti-Americanism became de rigueur in the army.[13] Others, however, were happy to have the moral support of the United States for human decency in their country and welcomed whatever pressure it may have exerted on official policy. Overall, the policy probably improved the image of the United States with the Brazilian people, as it certainly did among liberals and intellectuals.

There has been no admission, of course, that U.S. words swayed the government at all; if it moved toward amnesty and eventual release (by 1980) of all political prisoners, this was the avowed intention of Figueiredo from the outset. In the opinion of at least some well-informed observers, however, the Carter human rights policy helped many Brazilians, and if the government was irritated this was evidence of the need and correctness of the policy.[14]

The Brazilian leadership did not quickly forget after the Carter administration dropped the nuclear and human rights issues in 1978. To the contrary, the episode seems to have killed the old habit of deference to the United States. Relations continued correct but cool. Neither Geisel nor Figueiredo returned the Carters' visit to Brazil, although both were invited and Figueiredo accepted in principle in 1979, and both presidents traveled to numerous other countries. In October 1980 when Secretary of State Muskie proposed a visit to Brazil, it was somwhat loftily pointed out that he had not been invited; the Brazilians were irked by the technically incorrect statement of a State Department spokesman that Brazil was the only country with a nonelected government on his itinerary.[15] When Carter looked around for support in Latin America on the issue of Soviet troops in Cuba, Brazil took no notice. It likewise declined to heed the grain embargo and Olympic boycott to punish Soviet aggression in Afghanistan. Instead it negotiated increased sales and sent an enlarged Olympic team. It is typical that Brazil requires visas for the entry of U.S. citizens (because the United States requires visas for Brazilians), while allowing citizens of dozens of countries of Europe and Latin America to enter on their passports.

INDEPENDENT BRAZIL

In 1981, despite more ideological affinity with the Reagan administration, Brazil remained studiously, almost ostentatiously aloof. Figueiredo, having tripped around South America and Europe, has yet to take up his invitation to come to Washington. When Vernon Walters, military attaché at the time of the 1964 coup and an officer who once had excellent relations with the Brazilian military, was on a tour of Latin American capitals in 1981 to explain and plead for administration policy in El Salvador, the Brazilians offered only their ears and expressed disapproval of intervention in general.[16] Subsequently Brazil renewed diplomatic relations with the leftist government of Nicaragua and declined to join the Southern Cone countries in opposing communism in Central America.

While cool toward the United States, Brazil cultivates relations, especially commercial, with Latin American countries, Africa, and even the Soviet Union and Eastern Europe. Rapprochment with Argentina has eased if not erased the old rivalry, which was a major reason to look to the United States. Presidents of Brazil and Chile have visited reciprocally, and trade between their countries grows rapidly. Brazil has also reached out to Venezuela, Mexico, and other countries that share the Brazilian interest in diversification of relations. Brazil has made a strong effort in Africa, emphasizing the African share of the Brazilian heritage; it has particularly staked out an interest in Angola, quite contrary to U.S. policy, and viewed with alarm U.S. proposals to assist anticommunist guerrillas there.[17] Brazil is quite active in multilateral forums and in the councils of the less-developed nations, frequently taking positions uncomfortable for the United States.

The anticommunism of the government does not extend to business. Brazil is a leading agricultural exporter—mostly of soybeans—to the Soviet Union, and there are various projects for Soviet technical assistance in alcohol production, hydropower, and other areas; there are even plans for a joint Brazilian-Soviet hydroelectric project in Peru.[18] A high-level delegation headed by Planning Minister Antônio Delfim Neto went to Moscow in July

1981 to negotiate a large increase of trade. Figueiredo accepted in principle invitations to visit the Soviet Union and also Romania.

Brazilian foreign policy is primarily economic, intended to help trade and hasten the day when Brazil advances to status in the world commensurate with the natural greatness that is the prime article of Brazilian faith. It remains important for Brazil to keep on good terms with the United States, which is still the largest single seller to and buyer from Brazil, although its share of both Brazilian imports and exports has receded from 33 percent in 1967–68 to 20 percent in 1978–79. The share of U.S. firms in foreign investment in Brazil has likewise shrunk from 48 percent in 1967 to 24 percent in 1980, but it is still the largest national sector. Most diplomatic dealings between the two countries have had to do with economic matters, including the following: a double-taxation agreement, the promotion of U.S. exports to Brazil, Brazilian restrictions on imports of U.S. aircraft, a cocoa producers' agreement, implementation of the international coffee agreement, the law of the sea, and the North-South dialogue.[19] There are perennial problems over U.S. countervailing duties on Brazilian manufacturers. These have usually been low, but they have caused a good deal of irritation because they seem designed to deter Brazil's industrialization, that is, its march to greatness. Brazilians do not appreciate the logic of tariffs on fuel alcohol they try to export to the United States. There has also been friction over such matters as seizures of U.S. shrimpers. The United States is perhaps most concerned with Brazil's handling of its foreign debt, which was in the range of $70 billion in 1981. Brazil has long since moved out of the economic aid program, hardly because it could not use more resources but because its needs, in the billions of dollars, dwarf the entire program for the hemisphere.

Brazil is a large and diverse country, pursuing many interests, and it has multiple foreign policies as a Third World nation, a Latin American and a near-African power, and as a successful "new industrial country" and aspirant to a seat at the top. It is generally pragmatic and nonideological, seeks no quarrels, and cooperates so far as Brazilian interests are served. For example, through all frictions the United States and Brazil have kept up annual naval maneuvers, the last being held in October 1980.[20]

Under these circumstances, the ability of the United States to influence Brazilian policy is not great, and in particular matters of interest, such as commercial questions, Brazil may have a bargaining advantage because its government is more integrated. No congress is looking over the shoulder of the president and insisting on respect for this or that particular interest. Moreover, the issues are usually of relatively greater importance for Brazil than for the United States, which is the more desirous of avoiding public controversy.

It may be also that progress toward democratization and increased responsiveness to public opinion will widen the divergence of Brazil and the United States. Populism from 1960 to 1964 meant nationalism, which meant policies unfriendly to the United States and its interests; it is unlikely that the milder *abertura* of Figueiredo can fail to have something of the same effect. Although the presence of the United States is much less overwhelming than 20 years ago, it is still the primary target of nationalistic resentment. There has already been some tendency to pull back the welcome mat for foreign investors; symptomatic is the less forthcoming approach of the government to Daniel Ludwig's gigantic Jari plantation, which led him to give up the dream of Amazon development. The Brazilian government clearly feels it is desirable to maintain a certain distance from the United States. To do otherwise would mean unnecessarily to invite criticism from nationalists and leftists.

In sum, it appears that Brazil, which is strongly engaged in Western-dominated commerce and finance and shares American ideals, can be counted upon basically to support the values and broad purposes of the United States in world affairs and will probably continue to stand on the side of this country in security issues. But in lesser and economic matters, Brazil's will is very much its own.

NOTES

1. John W. Dulles, *Vargas of Brazil: A Political Biography* (Austin: University of Texas Press, 1976), p. 210.

2. See Stanley E. Hilton, *Brazil and the Great Powers, 1930–1939* (Austin: University of Texas Press, 1975).

3. Jan K. Black, *United States Penetration of Brazil* (Philadelphia: University of Pennsylvania Press, 1979), p. 40.

4. Phyllis R. Parker, *Brazil and the Quiet Intervention* (Austin: University of Texas Press, 1979), pp. 102–3.

5. John W. F. Dulles, *Castelo Branco: The Making of a Brazilian President* (College Station: Texas A & M University Press, 1978), p. 442.

6. *New York Times,* February 21, 1976, p. 1.

7. *Visão,* November 14, 1977, p. 19.

8. *Isto É,* March 16, 1977, pp. 5, 23.

9. *FBIS, Latin America,* May 26, 1981.

10. *Isto É,* April 15, 1981, p. 20.

11. Committee on Foreign Relations, United States Senate, Subcommittee on Foreign Assistance, *Human Rights Reports Prepared by the Department of State* (Washington, D.C.: GPO, 1977), pp. 111–12.

12. *Visão,* November 14, 1977, p. 20

13. Jan K. Black, "The Military and Political Decompression in Brazil," *Armed Forces and Society* 6 (Summer 1980): 625–39.

14. As in the testimony of Thomas E. Skidmore, Committee on Foreign Relations, U.S. Senate Subcommittee on Western Hemisphere Affairs, *Hearings,* October 4–6, 1978 (Washington, D.C.: GPO, 1978), pp. 19–24.

15. *FBIS, Latin America,* October 29, 1980.

16. *Isto É,* March 4, 1981, pp. 32–33.

17. *Veja,* March 18, 1981, pp. 30–31.

18. *FBIS, Latin America,* May 26, 1981.

19. Claus W. Ruser, "U.S.-Brazilian Dialog for the Future," *Department of State Bulletin 79,* September 1979, pp. 4–5.

20. *FBIS, Latin America,* October 29, 1980.

5

Venezuela: Politics of Oil

David E. Blank

Venezuela's proven oil reserves and the fact that that nation is one of the few functioning pluralist democracies in the Third and Fourth Worlds will present unique challenges and opportunities to U.S. policymakers in the 1980s.[1] In regards to oil, the United States apparently needed the experience of the Iranian revolution and the Persian Gulf war to truly appreciate the role Venezuela has played over the past half-century as a friendly, reliable, and secure hemispheric supplier of oil. The history of previous U.S. "policy incompetence" in its failing to "recognize the security value of Venezuelan oil" has been well documented elsewhere by Franklin Tugwell.[2]

A November 1980 report printed for the U.S. Senate Committee on Energy and Natural Resources, *The Geopolitics of Oil*, underlines this fact by forecasting a rather bleak future for the United States if its dependence on Persian Gulf oil is not lessened. Continued inflation, stagnated economy, and a decade or two of being "vulnerable to supply interruptions and political manipulation" comprise the heart of this forecast. In addition, national security will be severely jeopardized by a potential split in the alliance of Western industrial democracies caused by a likely "struggle for oil" and possible Soviet energy enticements.[3] The already turbulent nations of the energy-poor Fourth World would face the catastrophe of a deep depression. The Senate report concluded by suggesting that the Western industrial democracies need to diversify their energy sources outside of the Middle East, and that "Mexico and Venezuela are foremost among the countries most likely to offer the United States and our allies important opportunities for reducing our economic dependence on Middle East oil."[4]

The fact that Venezuela is also a democracy makes the continuation of a positive U.S. influence with that nation of even greater importance to the United States than is an oil linkage. The United States played an active role as a "midwife" in the initial establishment of Venezuela's contemporary democracy in the early 1960s. Venezuela was both the showcase of U.S. policy toward Latin America in the 1960s and the principal target of Fidel Castro's attempt to export his revolutionary model. Its survival as a representative democracy over the past generation and its emergence as an important voice in the councils of nonaligned Third and Fourth World nations such as the Andean Pact, the nonaligned Group of 77, and OPEC has, if anything, added to the importance of a positive U.S. influence on Venezuela.

The fundamental U.S. interests in Venezuela in the 1980s will focus on preserving that nation as a secure, long-term source of a considerable part of U.S. oil imports, strengthening the parallel international objectives both have expressed to prevent the Caribbean basin from becoming dominated by hostile regimes imposed by force, and maintaining their already considerable economic collaboration. How do these U.S. interests coincide with stated Venezuelan foreign policy objectives?

The first and foremost of Venezuela's foreign policy objectives is to safeguard and strengthen its own democracy. A second principal goal is to secure a long-term future for its oil exports while creating alternative sources of national income. The "sowing of oil" into national development to lessen Venezuela's dependence on the export of this single product has been a goal sought by all governments since 1936. Venezuela's third objective is to secure greater influence in critical global political and economic events that directly affect it, as well as to secure recognition as an independent and assertive actor on the international scene. Finally, Venezuela has legitimate geopolitical concerns in the Caribbean basin and insists on being an active and constructive participant in the determination of the region's future.[5]

The question of how U.S. and Venezuelan foreign policy objectives mesh is only one element in understanding the quality and extent of U.S. influence in the 1980s. To a very important degree, the possibility of a U.S.-Venezuelan convergence will be dependent upon Venezuelan interaction with a host of other nations and international forces. A considerable part of this chapter will deal with what has been called the challenge of Europe, Japan, and Brazil, and the impact of the Third World ideal on an alleged U.S. dominance in Venezuela. In addition, the Cuban factor will also be discussed.

Despite the fact that Venezuela has been considered to be the Latin American nation most favorably disposed toward the United States, there are potentials for divergence between the two nations. Their interests have not always coincided. With regards to the question of the New International Economic Order (NIEO) and the Venezuelan aspiration to be one of the vital and constructive voices of the Third World in general, and Venezuela's role in OPEC in particular, the two can be said to be adversaries. In a very real sense, starting in the late 1950s, and despite direct Venezuelan appeals, the United States also diverged from Venezuela as it preferred in that era of cheap oil to deal with the docile sheiks and monarchs of the Middle East.

It still annoys Venezuela's leadership to recall that in the late 1950s and early 1960s, it was they who tried to convince the United States of a mutual need to include Venezuela in the U.S. system of "hemispheric preference" in oil purchases.[6] This the United States refused to do, treating Venezuelan oil as if it were the same as Arab oil. Once again, in 1981, Venezuelans are becoming increasingly apprehensive about the United States intentions. The cause of their present alarm is the apparent downgrading of human rights considerations in U.S. foreign policy. Some Venezuelans suggested that the current drift of U.S. policy in Latin America may possibly threaten the continued survival of their own democracy.

There are four potential challenges to the continued dominance of U.S. influence in Venezuela. The most important of these is the European challenge, which brings with it the prospect that the European Community and Japan will replace the United States as Venezuela's principal trading partner. The second challenge is presented by a potential Brazilian hegemony in Latin America. A third and somewhat less probable challenge is that of the Third World ideal (tercermundismo). The final and most improbable one would have Soviet and Cuban influence increase in Venezuela to the detriment of U.S. interests.

THE EUROPEAN CHALLENGE

Europe, not the United States, has become the new world for Venezuela. Europe is the home of Venezuela's three primary political streams: Eurosocialism, Christian Democracy, and the Eurocommunism of Antonio Gramsci, all of which provide models of a purposive democracy. French indicative economic planning, British new towns and urban decentralization policy, and German industrial codetermination excite Venezuela's political, business, and cultural elites.

The governmental Christian Democratic-COPEI party and chief opposition party, Democratic Action (AD), have intimate ties to their respective German Social Democratic and Christian Democratic counterparts. Two public-supported German foundations, the Christian Democratic Konrad Adenauer Foundation and the Social Democratic Freidrich Ebert Foundation, have spearheaded this ideological penetration. Spanish-language publications of both foundations in Venezuela suggest that the populist, nonpurposive U.S. political model has exhausted its possibilities.

According to one Venezuela analysis, the "social democratic" push toward the Third World started in response to the 1973 oil crisis and has as one of its goals the displacement of the United States in critical import markets and energy production areas. European Christian Democrats and Social Democrats, according to this source, oppose Latin American military regimes in part because they are tied to the United States, and in part (as the case of Iran demonstrated) because they may disappear overnight, causing considerble turmoil and loss of oil.[7]

The Social Democratic political offensive in Latin America reflects Europe's search in the 1980s for political and economic solutions to the twin problems of internal socioeconomic stagflation and external energy dependence. An analysis of social democracy published in Venezuela suggests that the Keynesian welfare state programs adopted in Europe in the 1950s and 1960s will no longer perform satisfactorily in the 1980s.

Aided by detente, Europe will project a more assertive independent stance in the international arena as a means of securing new markets for its goods and new secure sources of energy.[8] The recent French election of a socialist government as well as continuing German insistence that the United States not ignore the reality of detente are illustrative of this new European assertiveness. Europe will stand with the United States to deter possible Soviet aggression; however, it may go its own way with regard to the Third and Fourth Worlds.

Willy Brandt, in his capacity as president of the Socialist International, and French Foreign Minister Claude Cheysson, seem to be projecting an activist socialist foreign policy toward Latin America. The Brandt Commission Report on North-South relations has been well received in Venezuela. The diplomatic initiatives of both regarding El Salvador have, however, caused some pain for Venezuela's incumbent Christian Democratic administration; previously, it had announced its "coincidence" with the United States concerning the nature of the preferred political solution for El Salvador.[9]

Francis X. Gannon, a senior U.S. adviser to the secretary-general of the OAS, recently wrote that "Europe's ability to act in its own self-interest can never be discounted, given the community's unparalleled record of post war achievement in regional integration and in reforming its international relationships."[10] Stating that Latin America will be "among the most dynamic regions of the world's economy" over the next decade, Gannon sees Europe not only exploiting the international ties of Europe's Christian Democratic and Social Democratic parties, but also the cultural ties of Spain (soon to be incorporated into the European Community) in its challenge to the United States in Latin America.

Political admiration and cultural goodwill lead to economic ties. In the late 1970s, Western Europe's share of the Latin American market rose to about 20 percent, while that of the United States declined to 30 percent. "Venezuelan purchases from the [European] Community, financed by ballooning oil revenues, expanded fivefold between 1970 and 1977, rising to almost $3 billion." A French government-sponsored consortium won the contract to provide the rolling stock for Caracas's multibillion-dollar subway project in 1978, beating out U.S. and Japanese competition. In 1980, despite European and Japanese competition, the United States continued its dominance of the Venezuelan foreign investment picture with 59 percent of the total.[11]

The European challenge to the United States also includes efforts by France and Germany to "define common areas of interest" with Venezuela regarding the development of the Orinoco Heavy Oil Belt. A recently formed state-financed German oil company (VEBA) has been working since 1978 with Venezuela's own Petroleum of Venezuela (PDVSA) and other German firms in advancing synthetic fuel technology. In July 1981 the state-owned French Petroleum Corporation (CFP) signed a similar accord with PDVSA.[12] A source in the U.S. Energy Department suggested that while French and German involvement in the Orinoco belt focuses more on refining oil as opposed to the U.S. technological interest in enhancing the quality of the Orinoco oil, there is an element of competition between the Europeans and the U.S. Franklin Tugwell, a U.S. scholar who has focused on energy issues, has suggested that with regards to managing the energy crisis, "the emerging Euro-Japanese model, involving extensive government support of large semiautonomous enterprises dependent on, and committed to, close partnership with the state," may be superior to our own disjointed, reactive, and fragmented policymaking orientation.[13]

Japan, without "a history of conflicting economic relations with Latin America" and a "still unobtrusive presence," has also rapidly expanded its sales and investments.[14] Japan's expanding economic bridgeheads transcend ideological frontiers, serving only Japan's needs for diversified sources of oil and new markets for its manufactured goods and technology. Japan may even finance a second Panama Canal in order to encourage its East-West economic penetration.

There are a number of indicators that if the 1980s do indeed become a decade of prolonged economic recession, the unity of the First World democracies, not only to sustain their alliance against the Soviet-dominated Second World, but also in its dialogue with the Third and Fourth Worlds, would shatter. Concerning the First World-Third and Fourth Worlds dialogue (the North-South dialogue), this projected intra-First World conflict will apparently be over competitive efforts to co-opt the Third World's strongest member states into either a European or U.S. partnership.[15] There is a concern expressed in Venezuela that the Reagan administration sees its natural targets for cooptation to be Mexico or Brazil. Democratic Venezuela (and its Andean Pact cosigners) may then have no alternative to seeking closer ties to Europe.

THE BRAZILIAN CHALLENGE

Venezuelans are increasingly aware of the success Brazil has had in "tropicalizing technology" and are impressed with that country's growth from 1965 to 1975. They are also aware of the costs of Brazil's authoritarian experiment in human terms, and that the luster of the Brazilian "miracle" has become quite tarnished since 1974. Recently, Venezuelans have become impressed with the record international debt of Brazil (estimated in 1980 to be in excess of $51 billion) and its record inflation rate of 100 percent in 1980.[16]

Brazil's role as a potential competitor of the United States was emphasized during the first official visit a Venezuelan president made to Brazil in 1977. During his stay in Brazil, former Venezuelan President Perez, "specifically noted . . . " that Brazil is producing "agricultural machinery . . . which [is] better suited to Venezuelan purposes and cheaper" than what Venezuela was importing from the United States.[17] Robert D. Bond also wrote that increased Brazilian influence in Venezuela might also imply an "undesired" diversion of Venezuela's Orinoco oil from U.S. markets to Brazil.[18]

Brazil's growing economic and technological power has already penetrated Venezuela. A Brazilian-managed joint Venezuelan-Brazilian construction consortium, BRASVEN, is currently constructing the huge Raúl Leoni-Guri Dam in the Guayana region of Venezuela. The tough attitude BRASVEN's Brazilian managers have taken with regards to labor questions has in democratic Venezuela resulted in much labor unrest and frequent strikes. The BRASVEN project is at least two years behind schedule.[19]

From 1965 to 1974, Venezuela was fearful of Brazil partly because that giant nation's military regime was then perceived to be a surrogate enforcer of U.S. hegemony. This fear of the Brazilian "green giant" was one of the primary reasons Venezuela joined the Andean Pact in 1973. However, following the OPEC oil shock of the same year, Brazil's foreign policy assumed a more open and "pluralistic" stance. As Brazil has acted more and more as a fellow Third World nation and as it returns to democratic rule, Venezuela's fear has lessened.

Venezuela appears to prefer balancing U.S., European, Japanese, and Brazilian interests in order to maximize its own political and economic freedom of action. Since Brazil is the proximate giant, Venezuela has had to respond with some diplomatic adroitness. The Brazilian initiative started in

1976 to organize an eight-nation Amazon River Basin Development Pact is a case in point. Venezuela fears that Brazil's proposal on the "physical integration" of the Basin might be used to legitimize aggression. Venezuela has also feared that the Amazon Pact initiative may be intended to weaken the Andean Pact with its democratic projection and its autonomous growth economic model. Strong interaction with the United States may be one reasonable response Venezuela can make to Brazil's hovering presence.

THE CHALLENGE OF THE THIRD WORLD IDEAL

Third-worldism would have the developing nations of Latin America, Africa, and Asia turn their backs on both "the rampant individualism of capitalist societies [the First World] and the grim collectivism of socialist societies [the Second World]."[20] Instead, third-worldism would have developing nations reflect upon their own cultural traditions in a search for a "genuine," "autonomous" "revolution of being not having," in which the national politics would be organized around the promise of communitarian integration.[21] A second key element of third-worldism is its call for a "spiritual solidarity" of all developing nations. In a less emotional sense, this has been called the promise of the South-South dialogue and South-South cooperation.

Much of the literature on the Third World ideal is polemical and aspirational. A discussion on the potential for a "spiritual solidarity" of all developing nations and for a unique "communitarian social integration" is beyond the scope of this chapter. However, Venezuela's contribution to the actual making of the New International Economic Order is second to none.[22] The late Juan Pablo Pérez Alfonzo, Venezuela's minister of mines in the early 1960s, has been acknowledge to be the "father" of OPEC. Dr. Manuel Pérez Guerrero, Venezuela's minister for international cooperation, has also been one of the most respected representatives of the Third World. Venezuela hosted a 1981 conference of the nonaligned Group of 77, chaired by Dr. Pérez Guerrero, considered to be a prelude to the North-South conference planned later in 1981 in Cancún, Mexico.

In the mid-1970s Venezuela was an active proponent of Third World solidarity in Latin America. It led the reincorporation of Cuba into the Latin American system, inviting that island nation to join the exclusively Latin, Latin American Economic System (SELA) created largely by Mexican and Venezuelan initiatives. The United States has been excluded from SELA. SELA was to provide the framework for a comprehensive Latin American economic integration by fomenting the exchange of technology and financial resources among Latin American nations. SELA has remained largely a planning or advocacy organization with little real budget or decision-making clout.

The smaller and more functional Andean Pact, which Venezuela joined in 1973, has had some initial successes in integrating the development programs of Bolivia, Colombia, Ecuador, Peru, and Venezuela. (Chile resigned from the pact following the military coup in 1973, and the status of Bolivia has been uncertain since its 1980 military coup.) Venezuela has been a strong supporter of the Andean Pact's "Decision 24." This decision established a strict regional code of conduct for foreign investment. The unity of the pact has floundered over the issue of integrating specific industries. With the exception of capital-intensive industries such as petrochemicals and automotive vehicles, Venezuela's industrialists retain a fear of "cheap" Andean imports flooding their national market.[23]

Venezuela must also face the fact that it and its immediate, democratic, and fellow Andean Pact neighbor, Colombia, have some highly emotional disagreements. It took Venezuela and Colombia 12 years to negotiate a draft agreement on disputed maritime boundaries in the potentially oil-rich Gulf of Venezuela. Unprecendented street demonstrations in Venezuela quickly forced the indefinite postponement of its consideration.

Venezuela's recent threat to commence deportation of a considerable number of the undocumented Colombians, who now comprise about 10 percent of its labor force, also strains relations. Colombian resentment over the treatment of its impoverished citizens in Venezuela, and Venezuelan fears of the "silent" Colombian invasion and its rumored connection with the drug industry, augur poorly for the future of Andean Pact solidarity.

Despite the fact the Colombia has broken off diplomatic relations with Cuba over alleged Cuban involvement with the M-19 guerrilla movement, Colombia has formally protested Venezuela's proposed purchase of a considerable number of advanced F-16 fighters. Venezuela insists that the F-16s are needed as part of its own national security concerns in the Caribbean and is in no way intended to pressure Colombia concerning their territorial dispute.

The role Venezuela has played in creating and maintaining OPEC since 1960, and the model it has developed for the successful nationalization of its critical natural resources such as oil and iron ore, have been its two major contributions to the pragmatic and rational implementation of the Third World ideal. Venezuela and the Saudis moved in 1960 to create OPEC out of their frustrations over "their inability to control the exploitation of their major and perhaps only asset, crude oil, and the realization that their political stability was entirely dependent on oil income."[24]

The primary goal of Venezuela's oil minister, Juan Pablo Pérez Alfonzo, in creating OPEC was to seek an international agreement among the producer nations that would regulate both production and prices as a means of overcoming their vulnerability to a market largely controlled by the powerful transnational oil companies. Throughout the 1960s, Venezuelan teams of experts toured the Middle East to increase the political awareness and technical knowledge of these nations regarding the control of the foreign oil companies. It was one such technical assistance team's finding of oil company abuse in Libya in 1969 that precipitated OPEC's first success in cutting back oil production. Finally, in December 1970, Venezuela's elected congress "galvanized OPEC" by pushing through a major increase in oil taxes over strenuous oil company resistance. This Venezuelan victory, and the Libyan production cutback, set the stage for the 1973 oil coup.[25]

Venezuela's role in OPEC may not have been the source of much joy in Washington; however, its role in OPEC has been that of a discreet and moderate force. OPEC never boycotted the United States in 1973, and Venezuela never denied the United States critically needed oil in either war or peacetime. In the late 1970s, at a time when U.S. relations with OPEC and the Third World were close to the breaking point, Venezuela assumed the role of being a conciliator and honest broker. In the face of "radical" opposition within OPEC, Venezuela, through its president, Carlos Andrés Pérez, insisted that oil would be an "instrument of negotiation and not of confrontation."[26] The importance of Venezuela's moderate position in the period immediately following the conclusion of the Vietnam war should not be underestimated.

In 1981, a time in which the demand for oil has proven to be quite elastic, Venezuela remains a defender of OPEC. Venezuela's minister of energy, Humberto Calderón Berti, at the 1981 OPEC meeting, pushed for a two- to three-year price freeze that would preserve oil's share of the world's total energy needs. Venezuela's proposal was midway between the $32 barrel asked by the Saudis and the $40 barrel asked by the radical "price hawks." While some Western sources are predicting the collapse of OPEC because of the Saudi refusal to raise its oil price, these sources ignore the Saudi decision to significantly cut back oil production by 10 percent. As long as OPEC remains united, the U.S. ability to influence Venezuela regarding oil prices should be minimal. The ability of the industrial democracies to substitute coal, nuclear power, and biomass energy for oil has been the primary factor moderating oil prices.

THE CUBAN AND SOVIET CHALLENGE

The Cuban Stalinist model has almost no possibility as a viable option in Venezuela, and only two most improbable developments can alter this reality. The first condition would be a sudden diminution of U.S. power in the Carribbean alongside an explosive surge of Soviet power there. The second would be the emergence of a political force in Venezuela that will both desire to emulate the Cuban experience and have the capacity to overcome resistance in the trade unions, business groups, political parties, and military. Since the attractiveness of the Cuban model is linked to the Soviet presence in the Caribbean, it would be of interest to discuss the growing Soviet influence in the Americas.

Soviet objectives in this hemisphere appear to be preeminently pragmatic. The Soviets seek to enhance their access to critical raw materials and at the same time to take advantage of the opportunity to "muck around" in the strategic rear of the United States. While some analysts such as Leiken suggest that the Soviet naval presence in Cuba may be part of a larger effort to develop a naval stranglehold on the South Atlantic sea lanes, this writer accepts the Domínguez thesis that the Soviet use of Cuban facilities is "modest" and largely symbolic.[27] According to Domínguez, the Soviet purpose seems to be to demonstrate a presence in the American "Mediterranean."

The Cuban experience may have made the Soviets less reluctant to take advantage of targets of opportunity that past U.S. folly or neglect presented them in Nicaragua and El Salvador. However, in both nations the breakdown of the old order was due to domestic developments rather than international intrigues. The long-standing Cuban involvement with the Sandinista guerrillas in Nicaragua may have been primarily defensive, since the late Nicaraguan dictator, Somoza, had been involved in the 1961 Bay of Pigs invasion and in several attempts to do away with Castro.

Regardless of its initial cause, Venezuela has moved to challenge Cuba's involvement in Central America. In doing so, Venezuela insists that it is not a "stalking horse" for the United States, but is defending its own vital interests in the Caribbean as well as advancing the ultimate development of democracy there. In Nicaragua, both the Democratic Action (AD) government (1974 to 1979) and the incumbent Christian Democratic (COPEI) administration have made respect for political pluralism a constant part of their dealings with the Sandinsta regime. Venezuela's Christian Democrats are also strong supporters of their fellow Christian Democrat in El Salvador, José Napoleón Duarte.

The turbulence in Central America illustrates that one key element of Soviet strategy in the Americas is to "lurk behind indigenous revolutionary elites" and would-be elites. However, nothing would suit Soviet interests better than to have the United States conclude that Soviet support automatically translates into Soviet control of these elites. The Soviets also support nationalistic right-wing military regimes such as that in Argentina. According to Duncan and Leiken, the Soviet "courtship of Argentina is proof of the pragmatic nature" of that nation's American involvement.[28]

Soviet strategists appear to be operating under a longer-term, two-prong assumption. Over the long run, they posit that the unrestrained overurbanization of Latin America will overwhelm the institutional capability of the existing order and create the "objective conditions" for their type of revolution. Their second assumption is that the United States will become more turbulent as it enters a "protracted phase" of profound economic difficulties. This will bring about heightened community conflicts among its diverse peoples and allow the Soviets considerably more room to maneuver around the world. The Soviets will pragmatically utilize Cuba and be utilized by it in achieving its purposes.

Cuba, despite the loss of some of its prestige in the Third and Fourth Worlds due to both its support of the Soviet invasion of Afganistan and its involvement in the violence that wracked Venezuela in the 1960s, retains a degree of attractiveness to certain elements of Venezuela's youthful populace. While the orthodox, Stalinist party of Venezuela, the Venezuelan Communist Party (PCV), known for its consistent pro-Soviet line, barely maintained its national status in the 1978 and 1979 elections, a number of other leftist groups gained 18 percent of the vote in 1979. These noncommunist leftist groups include Catholic radicals, Eurocommunists, and democratic socialists. While they do express a degree of sympathy for the Cuban revolution, they are also quite critical of its defects.

Cuba's natural allies in Venezuela and other Third World nations appear to be the youthful lumpenproletariat of the cities and the overflow of university graduates resulting from the revolution of rising expectations. It is the declasse intellectual and footloose urban youth who are often denied access to the protection of populist democracy's mediating structures, such as labor unions and peasant leagues. The myth of revolutionary violence serves these youths both as a welcomed therapy for their boredom and perceived disinheritance and as an instrument to be used to break into the system. Regis Debray, in the late 1960s, was accused of "developing the underpinning for Castro's political adventurism in Latin America." He advanced the notion that self-chosen, action-oriented revolutionaries could by themselves create a revolutionary situation; oppressed workers and peasants would not be needed.[29]

It is of interest to note that Venezuelan leaders of all political persuasions reject Debray's thesis. Given the reality of Venezuela's democracy and the climate of human rights existing in that nation, Venezuela's radical youth are active and reasonably successful participants in the democratic process.

An in-depth survey of Venezuelan political attitudes taken during that nation's 1973 election campaign revealed that the Venezuelan population overwhelmingly rejected both the ideal of communism and the Venezuelan Communist Party (PCV). Of the slightly over 1,000 responses to the question, "Is there a political party in Venezuela for which you would never vote," the PCV engendered by far the most antipathy. When the same survey asked, "Which of the three economic systems, capitalism, socialism or communism, is preferred," hardly anyone (28 respondents) indicated a preference for communism. However, the preferred economic system was socialism (615 respondents), nearly twice the number (324) who favored capitalism.[30]

There is a need for a reasoned and sophisticated U.S. response to the reality of Venezuela's political left. The expression of a degree of sympathy for Cuba, such as that recently made by the president of Mexico, should not be the sole criterion for judging these political groups. The growing force on Venezuela's left and among its university students, the Movement toward Socialism (MAS), is a case in point. While most of the leaders of MAS had been involved in the 1960s guerrilla effort and were members of the PCV, they insist that following the Soviet invasion of Czechoslovakia in 1968, they irrevocably broke with violence and Moscow. The MAS leadership constantly expresses its friendship for the United States and its recognition of legitimate United States hemispheric concerns.[31]

The party of the left that retains a significant voice in the labor movement is the People's Electoral Movement (MEP). While the electoral appeal of MEP has declined, this party of professed democratic socialist character contains some of Venezuela's most respected politicians who in the 1960s played critical roles in defeating Castro's violent intervention in Venezuela's politics.

An inflation rate of about 25 percent, a rising crime rate, and a growing awareness of government corruption have put the people in a pessimistic mood. However, rather than exploiting this situation by renewing violence or guerrilla operations, Venezuela's radical left seems to be on its best behavior. The fact that Venezuela's left is excited about its improved electoral possibilities in the 1983 elections may account for this. Whatever the reason, political violence in Venezuela in 1981 may be at its lowest level in years.

THE PROSPECTS FOR CONTINUED U.S. INFLUENCE

The prospects for the United States continuing to have considerable influence in Venezuela in the 1980s remain quite good despite the attractiveness to different Venezuelans of either a Euro-Japanese, Brazilian, or Third World alternative. The continuing political affinity and economic closeness between the two nations in large measure dates back to the legacy of the Kennedy years and the Carter administration. Venezuelans saw in President Carter a willingness to dialogue on terms of equality and fraternity. They applauded his human rights policy and his courage in resolving the festering issue of the Panama Canal. Carter's 1980 executive order ending Venezuela's exclusion from the Generalized System of Preferences (GSP) regarding U.S. tariffs opened the way for a number of exciting binational trade agreements.

Carter initiated his successful 1977 trip to strategic Third World countries by visiting Caracas. Before Venezuela's Congress, he promised active U.S. support for increased international cooperation in sharing technology, a vital concern to the Third World. His visit to Venezuela also focused on the fact that enhanced human freedom was the purpose of development and that the United States and Venezuela jointly shared in this belief. Carter's visit initiated a series of intense U.S.-Venezuelan consultations, which led in 1979 and 1980 to the signing of a number of bilateral agreements concerning joint energy research and the sharing of know-how concerning health and agriculture.[32] Vice-President Mondale also visited Venezuela to demonstrate U.S. interest in close relations with its sister democracy.

The 1980 U.S. elections and the violent heating up of the turbulence in Central America have influenced U.S.-Venezuelan relations. There is an overwhelming Venezuelan consensus concerning the maintainence of close political affinity and friendship with the United States which, as indicated above, includes the Eurocommunist MAS party. However, whereas the Christian Democratic administration of Luis Hererra Campíns has moved toward a "coincidence" with Reagan administration, Democratic Action, the principal opposition party, and the parties of the democratic left such as MAS and MEP, express some reservations about this bilateral collaboration.

Because of the dynamic quality of this complex political relationship, this chapter will deal first with the more long-term and consistent bilateral ties that focus on the oil linkage. It seems unlikely that the passions of the political moment will affect the natural economic linkages between the two nations.

THE OIL LINKAGE

A fall 1980 visit to Caracas of U.S. Energy Secretary Charles W. Duncan illustrated the willingness of both nations to move rapidly to implement terms of the Energy Research and Development Agreement. Six joint, oil-related research and development projects have started as the result of this visit, and mention was made of possible massive U.S. funding for developing Venezuela's Orinoco heavy oil belt. While the debate in the United States over synfuels policy continues, the U.S. Energy Security Act authorized the recently created Synthetic Fuels Corporation (SFC) to fund up to $2 billion in synfuel projects in the Western hemisphere. A speech Secretary Duncan delivered in Caracas perhaps best described U.S. attitudes:

We consider Venezuela an important international partner and a nation which shares the same basic values as those which we hold in such high esteem in the United States. It is a democracy respected for its interests in democratic values and human rights and it is a strong force for economic and social development throughout Latin America.[33]

Julio Sosa Rodríquez, former Venezuelan ambassador to the United States during the previous COPEI administration, wrote an article on the diplomacy of the oil connection between the two nations in mid-1981. He strongly hinted that Venezuela might link its future attitude regarding oil sales to the United States with favorable U.S. attitudes regarding human rights and an appreciation of Third World concerns. Sosa Rodriquez reiterated Venezuela's position that its oil will be used as an instrument of its comprehensive democratic development and not merely as a source of revenues.[34]

The hint of a "linkage" was part of Sosa Rodríquez's explanation of Venezuela's "cautious approach" to increasing its oil production. According to the article, the maximum production would be set at 2.8 million barrels per day (bpd), to be reached in the year 1988 and kept at this limit. While, "at first glance," this "seems to some contrary to the interests of the United States, we must not lose sight of the importance for the entire hemisphere of Venezuela's successful development model, based on the principles of liberty and the respect for human dignity".[35] Sosa Rodríquez concluded by suggesting that other countries of the Western hemisphere are going to need Venezuelan oil, that it would be unlikely for the United States to continue to receive two-thirds of Venezuela's oil exports.[36]

The energy diplomacy between Venezuela and the United States in the 1980s will not be confined to the relatively narrow limits of bilateral relations. There is the possible emergence of an "energy triangle," linking North America, South America, and the Euro-Japanese industrial democracies. Venezuela is also a charter member of OPEC. Any adequate description of U.S.-Venezuelan oil diplomacy must commence with a recognition of the complex nature of Venezuela's democratic management of this, its most vital industry. Similar to most democratic policymaking systems, there is an element of conflict and a system of checks and balances between the political and managerial roles. On one hand, the elected government has established a multifaceted system of political control over the industry, starting with the minister of energy and mines, who presides over the state-owned oil company's shareholders assembly.

On the other hand, the operational management of the industry has been given to an autonomous state-owned holding company, Petroleum of Venezuela. PDVSA and its affiliates have been granted considerable operational autonomy under the 1975 law that nationalized the industry.

PDVSA "has been structured and operates as a commercial company . . . which seeks to obtain maximum economic benefit for its sole shareholder, the Venezuelan State," according to President General Rafael Alfonzo Ravard.[37] Article five of the 1975 Organic Law for the industry explicitly enables PDVSA and its affiliates to participate in joint ventures with foreign companies as long as exclusive Venezuelan ownership is preserved.

The basic principle of democratic management of the industry is to allow the PDVSA management a maximum of administrative discretion within a set of broad guidelines established by the elected government. An increasingly active Joint Congressional Committee on Mines and Hydrocarbons and a potential "grand debate" in a National Energy Council are part of this oversight mechanism. A league of petroleum-impacted municipalities created in 1980 also provides grass-roots oversights on issues such as taxes, jobs, and pollution. However, there is an all-party agreement concerning the PDVSA "not to kill the goose that lays the golden eggs" with political intrigues.

This pragmatic awareness of the political parties to the needs of the industry not to have its management subjected to political intrigues, extends to the question of article five and joint ventures with transnational oil companies. One AD oil spokesman, Celestino Armas, recently stated that with regards to the huge investments and risks involved in guaranteeing a secure long-term future for its oil production, Venezuela would be foolish not to have the financial and technical know-how of these companies involved in the effort as long as PDVSA remains in charge.

A second important aspect of PDVSA's operational autonomy is the principle of financial self-sufficiency. This principle enables PDVSA to retain "ten percent of the net income from export sales . . . for the development of the oil industry."[38] The Venezuelan government has expanded this fiscal autonomy by allowing PDVSA to retain just about all its net income after paying taxes rather than having dividends declared to the nation. The investment program of the Venezuelan industry is expected to average "some $5 billion per year until the end of the century," which translates into about $25 to $40 billion for the decade of the 1980s.[39] Who gets what share of this prospective $40 billion Venezuelan investment, as well as the production level of Venezuela's oil industry, will no doubt determine much about U.S.-Venezuelan relations in the 1980s.

With regards to the policy assertion made by political leaders that the 2.8 million barrels per day production is to be reached in 1988 and maintained until the end of the century (the so-called cautious approach), one may not note a certain flexibility in PDVSA policy. Accepting the target of 2.8 million bpd as a "basic guideline" for the industry, "internal industry studies" mention the need to have a production cushion of an additional 500,000 bpd. This added production appears to result from a variety of technical and commerical considerations.[40]

This production cushion of an additional 500,000 bpd appears to be a factor in the planning to use advanced secondary and tertiary methods of oil recovery in the existing light of oil fields of the east coast of Lake Maracaibo. Because of the danger inherent in high-pressure steam injection, there is the consideration that an entire existing community, Lagunillas, may have to be relocated. Published studies mention the need to relocate upwards of 20,000 families in order to use the new technology in the existing fields of the east coast of Lake Maracaibo.[41] Added to the normal cost of oil production using secondary and tertiary recovery would be the costs of implementing a basic urban and agricultural redevelopment of this subregion. Having an integrated, democratic development has been a basic goal of Venezuela's management of its oil industry; however, to make this dream possible seems to require a production target from this subregion alone that should exceed the projected 200,000 bpd mentioned by some political figures.

Politicians too consider the fact that Venezuelan voters have grown accustomed to certain levels of expectations with regards to government services. In order to satisfy these expectations, the government will have to maintain its fiscal strength and resources. Presidential elections are, after all, scheduled for 1983 and 1988. Venezuela's government has become increasingly dependent on revenue from the oil industry in order to accomplish its necessary political tasks. The fact that the annual inflation rate of 20 to 25 percent affects government purchases and that the population continues to increase in excess of 3 percent per annum will also have an impact on the government's future revenue needs.

Domestic oil consumption at the end of the century has also been projected to reach one million bpd. Unless new production comes on board by the year 2000, Venezuela could hypothetically have no oil available for export; an impossible situation for the nation. Table 5.1 is concerned with the export implications of the cautious approach versus the production cushion approach. With regards to Orinoco heavy oil production alone, some have suggested that "Venezuela would have to produce enormous quantities to realize the same fiscal dividends" it was accruing from the easier to produce light oils.[42]

The United States has sought in recent years to encourage Venezuela to raise its oil production targets despite its adherence to OPEC. With regards to the Orinoco heavy oil, the United States in the 1970s considered offering Venezuela direct government guarantees regarding both a floor price and a fixed share of the U.S. market for ten years. The United States is anxious that the Venezuelan public appreciates that it is in their national interests to find new oil because of the progressive depletion of their existing reserves. Many Venezuelans, including respected oil experts such as Aníbal Martínez and Francisco Mieres of MAS, still insist that the decision to develop the Orinoco heavy oil at this time was premature and made only after

TABLE 5.1. Venezuela's End-of-Century Oil Statistics: Cautious Approach Compared to Need for Cushion (millions of barrels per day)

		2000	
	1980	*Cautious Approach*	*Production Cushion Approach*
Existing fields, using existing technology	2.45 (bpd)	1.10 (bpd)	1.20 (bpd)
Existing fields, new, secondary, and tertiary recovery	0.00	.20	.40
Off-shore	0.00	.50	.50
Orinoco heavy oil	0.00	1.00	1.20
Total Production	2.45	2.80	3.30
Domestic Consumption	.35	1.00	1.00
Available for Export	2.10	1.80	2.30

Sources: For the cautious approach: Julio Sosa Rodríquez, "U. S. and Venezuela: The Oil Diplomacy," *Latin American Times*, March 1981. The figure of 1 million bpd production from existing fields with existing technology results from calculations based on the figures mentioned by Sosa Rodríquez. For the cushion approach: *Daily Journal*, Caracas, Venezuela, May 30, 1980; "DJ Oil Supplement '80: The Orinoco Oil Belt."

considerable U.S. pressure was applied. The miniscule Communist party has called the Orinoco decision a "sellout" to the United States.

A second critical concern of the United States regarding the future of Venezuelan oil is that its companies not be discriminated against with regards to the estimated $25 to $40 billion investment PDVSA plans to make this decade. There is evidence to suggest that U.S. firms apparently have had to overcome an additional hurdle: their involvement in political controversy in bidding for contracts. This appears to be especially true with regards to the development of the Orinoco heavy oil belt. The fact that U.S. firms are more than holding their own in receiving contracts reflects the confidence PDVSA has in these companies. The ministry of energy and mines has also indicated its satisfaction with the six research and development projects it is undertaking with the U.S. Department of Energy, despite the feared "dependence" on the United States.

There is evidence to suggest that the giant U.S. engineering firm, Bechtel, which had previously been awarded "the lion's share of the feasibility studies in the Orinoco," may have been denied the first major production-oriented contract because of the political connections of some of its board of directors with various U.S. administrations. Bechtel Engineering has its headquarters in President Reagan's home state of California. However, a second U.S. firm was awarded the contract in question.[43]

The American connection with PDVSA includes its having two offices in the United States. In addition, BARIVEN, the affiliate of PDVSA created in 1980 with the responsibility of centralized purchasing of all materials, equipment, and goods for PDVSA and its affiliates, has created its own U.S. corporation, Bariven Corporation, located in Houston, Texas, the world capital for the oil industry.

The future for continued good corporate relations between the PDVSA and U.S. firms will apparently depend in large part on the ability of these U.S. firms to work alongside Venezuelan firms and to "buy Venezuelan" regarding material purchases and professional work. An increasing number of Venezuelans want to be part of the prosperous petroleum sector. Denying them access to contracts and jobs could become increasingly difficult.

The Venezuelans are especially interested in seeing a productive development of government-to-government cooperation, such as that in the field of energy research and development. Binational joint steering committees and a consultative mechanism govern the progress of these agreements. A Venezuelan embassy official interviewed in 1981 was explicit in stating that nation's purpose in signing these agreements: "a real transfer of technology . . . access to the basic blueprints and a real access to and participation in the initial generation of new technology as well as in its operational research and development." Venezuela apparently will continue to insist that no purchase "tie-in" commitment be part of any of these technology transfer agreements.

Venezuela has two interests regarding the progress of the technology transfer agreements it has with the United States and other nations. It insists that it should become a coproducer of the technology it needs and not just a consumer of other's know-how. There is evidence, for example, that Venezuela may pace the development of the Orinoco and off-shore oil reserves with its developing an autonomous, national technological capability regarding these two areas. In addition, it is going to insist that the technology that will be applied to both the redevelopment of the Lake Maracaibo area and the development of the Orinoco heavy oil belt assure a balanced growth of agriculture and small industry, and not just oil. All Venezuelans seem to oppose a repeat of the experience suffered by the east coast of Lake Maracaibo in the 1920s. The needs of the local population for a clean and livable environment and for a balanced economy will be a primary goal for all future oil development.

The Orinoco River Valley has an almost mystical hold on the Venezuelan people. It was the area of the El Dorado myth, and today there is even talk of moving the national capital there as proof of the nation taking its future in its own hands. PDVSA's president, Rafael Alfonzo Ravard, has formally stated that he would not allow an isolated oil-camp-style development of the Orinoco that could leave as its legacy slag heaps of contaminated debris, a polluted river system, and a devastated people. The grass-roots concerns of the people can no longer be ignored.

The balanced and ecologically sound development of the Orinoco oil reserve has become the supreme test of Venezuela's democratic management of its oil industry. An enhanced U.S. sensitivity to environmental concerns and an ability to demonstrate to Venezuela that development could be made consistent with environmental protection would increase U.S. influence with regards to both the Orinoco development and the Lake Maracaibo re-development. For example, Venezuela is quite excited about the possibility of using solar energy to help fuel its future heavy oil projects. This is the kind of technology Venezuela hopes to master through its various technology transfer agreements.

ECONOMIC RELATIONS

Oil has indeed brought a mixed blessing to Venezuela. Alongside the petrobillions has been a profound negative impact on agriculture, industry, and social relations. Venezuela's democratic leadership insists that these negative by-products of its oil will be lessened. It is precisely in moving beyond a mere oil linkage and in seeking broader imaginative links that U.S.-Venezuelan relations in the 1980s will face their most creative challenge. President Rafael Caldera (1969 to 1974) perhaps best articulated Venezuela's economic concern:

> In Venezuela, the percentage of the active population engaged in activities related to oil is less than 0.5% of the whole. This gives rise to an exceedingly grave problem: how and with what to provide sufficient economic activity for the remaining 99.5% of the population. . . . When oil development started, we were not a wealthy country, it is true, but we were exporting progressively larger amounts of coffee, cacao, and other vegetable items, cattle and animal articles—in other words, economic activity that offered job opportunities to the majority of the population. With the exploitation of oil that situation changed substantially.[44]

Venezuela, which in 1980 imported about 40 percent of its foodstuffs from the United States, has become particularly sensitive to the perceived threat inherent in Secretary of Agriculture John Block's assertion that U.S. food exports "can be the greatest weapon" the United States has in influencing other countries. Venezuela's own failure to maintain its agri-culture and its continuing difficulties in developing a viable industrial base may in a sense negate the advantage of its oil exports. After Mexico with its 70 million population, Venezuela is the largest customer of U.S. agricultural exports in Latin America.

The 1980 U.S.-Venezuelan agreement on agricultural development has demonstrated the willingness of the United States not to hold Venezuela "over the bushel," but to help that nation regain self-sufficiency in a number of basic food staples. United States agricultural exports to Venezuela may soon face stiff competition from Brazil with regards to rice, sugar, and soybeans. The goodwill earned as a result of the above-mentioned agreement may assist the United States in meeting this forthcoming Brazilian export drive.

With regards to industrial trade, the United States in the early 1980s is going to be concerned about its own economic redevelopment. Buffeted from both accelerating energy costs and the feared export of industrial jobs to Third and Fourth World nations under the terms of the special tariff privileges granted under the Generalized System of Preferences, one should anticipate much resistance in the United States to granting Venezuela, a member of that "sinister group" called OPEC, major concessions with regards to trade.

President Carter's ending the so-called anti-OPEC clause and granting participation to Venezuela and Ecuador enabled both Venezuela and the United States to maneuver around the mutually unacceptable bushels-for-barrels trade scenario. The dialogue initiated between the United States and the Andean Pact during the Carter administration granting each other reciprocal concessions through product-specific bilateral agreements, could develop into a major improvement of trade between the United States and the nations of the Andean Pact in the 1980s.

The tentative first steps toward cooperation between the U.S. public and private sector development of Rocky Mountain alternative energy systems and Venezuela's stated intention to have a comprehensive and integrated development of the vast Orinoco belt can blossom into a most creative economic symbiosis. American-made heavy duty construction vehicles can be assigned duty-free access to the Orinoco belt and other Andean Pact markets; in return, Venezuelan seamless oil pipes, made in Guayana City, can be given access to the Rocky Mountain projects. Coproduction agreements and joint ventures that satisfy the domestic-content and domestic-ownership requirements of both the Andean Pact and AFL-CIO scrutiny could become an innovative feature of this potential economic symbiosis.

The emergence of metropolitan Miami as a major bilingual commercial and financial center linking the United States and Latin America is one reason why talk of U.S.-Venezuelan coproduction is not totally visionary. Miami is no longer merely a Venezuelan gateway to the United States; it has become an integral element of Venezuela's social and economic "turf."

Estimates of Venezuelan investment in Miami, of real estate holdings, and of commercial purchases seem to suggest considerable pressure in Venezuela for an early annexation of metropolitan Miami as Venezuela's twenty-second state.[45]

The United States in 1980 emerged as the world's fifth largest Spanish-speaking nation, behind Spain, Mexico, Argentina, and Colombia. In a real sense, the long-term success of the increasingly intimate U.S.-Venezuelan economic connection will be dependent on how the United States faces up to the newly discovered reality of its emerging bilingualism. Issues such as statehood for Puerto Rico, the role of the Spanish language in the United States, and the delicate issue of undocumented Latin American migration can become as important to the future of U.S.-Venezuelan relations as any bilateral concern. Venezuela too has to face the question of hosting undocumented migrants and appreciates U.S. concern.

POLITICAL INFLUENCE

The political interaction between the United States and Venezuela in the 1980s will remain complex and multidimensional. On one level, there is a tremendous, diffuse feeling of goodwill in Venezuela toward the United States. There is, however, also a growing unease concerning U.S. political intentions with regards to the future of democracy in Latin America. Venezuela's awareness of the United States' increasingly weak economy and fragmented society has also caused an increasing number of its citizens to become disillusioned with it as a role model.

The extent of the existing political affinity between the two can be illustrated by the fact that, since 1968, U.S. media experts and campaign managers have played significant roles in Venezuela's election campaigns. Over 150,000 Venezuelans were tourists in the United States in 1979 and many thousands already consider Miami to be their weekend home. Thousands of Venezuelan students, many with government grants, are found in most U.S. universities, while U.S. commercial television serials and products are found in most Venezuelan homes.

Venezuela's political, economic, and cultural elites are frequent visitors to the United States. This includes some of the more radical personalities whose public role, more times than not, is directed at reducing the weight of U.S. influence in Venezuela. One radical political leader in 1980 gave an anti-imperialist television interview in his hospital room in Houston, Texas. A second radical politician, in an interview with this author, recalled with pride and affection the excellent care and education he received growing up as the son of a petroleum worker in a former EXXON (Creole Oil) camp.

His goal is to give every Venezuelan youngster the opportunities he had in his childhood.

The influx of billions of petrodollars in the 1970s may have caused Venezuela as many problems as it solved. The words of the late Juan Pablo Pérez Alfonzo that democracy in Venezuela "could die of indigestion as certainly as from hunger," have not been totally without an element of prophetic quality.[46] While by no means near death, the youthful Venezuelan democracy has found it difficult to manage its relative abundance.

Runaway inflation, a rising crime rate, and growing popular indignation at continuing government corruption and incompetence have led to a widespread feeling of frustration. There are indications that some among the general populace are yearning for the mythical "good and honest strong man" or for an allegedly efficient military government, but the vast majority continues to express strong support for their own brand of democracy.

The focus on Venezuelan fears about the United States, expressed to this author by some top Venezuelan officials, is that they sense their own democracy is being treated as a cultural mutant. Venezuela's political leadership fears that the United States erroneously perceives "moderately repressive" military regimes to be superior bulwarks against communism than is its own pluralist democracy. In addition to being horrified at an article written by an individual now in the Reagan cabinet suggesting that electoral politics in Latin America is a "Democratic facade ... modified by varying degrees of fraud, intimidation and a corruption,"[47] they were concerned by the tardiness of U.S. support for democracy in Spain in 1981. There is also the Chilean tragedy of 1973. Venezuelans of all political persuasions go out of their way to point out the great differences that exist between Venezuela 1981 and Chile 1973.

While there are some signs of popular discontent in this period of austerity and adjustment following a binge of petrodollars, there is every reason to state categorically that democracy in Venezuela will successfully meet the challenges of the 1980s. The conditions of internal partisan breakdown and hostility and external intervention that combined to destroy democracy in Chile in 1973 simply do not apply to Venezuela.

Venezuela's political parties have learned since 1958 to contain their natural antagonism within the confines of a democratic consensus. A tradition has evolved among the political parties to strive to arrive at a consensus regarding potentially provocative public policies prior to proposing these intiatives in the lawmaking process. Political debate in Venezuela is lively and often bitter, but no crisis has been allowed to break the bounds of what the Venezuelans call democratic civility.

Venezuela's business community since 1958 has also been a strong actor in the total democratic picture. Its top associations, the Federation of Chambers of Industry and Commerce (FEDECAMARAS) and PRO-

VENEZUELA are not a force for a reactionary turning back of the clock. While many businessmen are alienated by populist electoral politics, these same individuals share membership on numerous planning committees with elected politicians, government technicians, and labor leaders, which indicates that businessmen have a significant voice in public policy. In fact, the 1981 election of a new president of FEDECAMARAS demonstrated that business too enjoys a hard-fought electoral campaign when it concerns the selection of its own leaders.

There is also an institutional intimacy between the United States and Venezuela. This should prevent any U.S. misperception of the democratic game in Venezuela that might lead to a misadventure, such as trying to exercise a "veto" over a domestic political event (the events of Chile 1973 come to mind).

The strong business ties that have existed between U.S. and Venezuelan firms is a case in point. The former Venezuelan subsidiary of EXXON oil, Creole Oil Company, played a most creative and critical role in the 1960s in mobilizing the Venezuelan business community into a force committed to political democracy and the peaceful resolution of social problems. The work of the Creole Foundation, the philanthropic arm of Creole Oil, was crucial in organizing, based on the model of U.S. United Way Funds, a group called Voluntary Dividends for the Community (Dividendo). Businessmen are able to claim tax credits for up to 5 percent of their earnings, which are donated to the educational and social welfare programs of Dividendo. Rather than being a sterile force in the political life of their nation, Venezuelan businessmen have initiated a number of innovative adult education and community development programs financed through groups such as Dividendo.[48]

In addition, strong and intimate ties link the AFL-CIO and Venezuela's own Labor Confederation (CTV). Venezuelan Christian Democratic labor and peasant organizers are operating alongside a group organized by the AFL-CIO affiliate American Institute for Free Labor Development in El Salvador. Two U.S. agrarian reform officials associated with this AFL-CIO affiliate, Michael P. Hammer and Mark D. Pearlman, were murdered by right-wing assassins as was their Christian Democratic host, José Rodolfo Viera.[49]

Former Venezuelan President Carlos Andrés Pérez has suggested that the democratic compatibility between Venezuela and the industrial democracies of the First World can be further cemented by developing a stronger global sense of cooperation among the world's free labor unions. Global labor union cooperation, according to Pérez, could strengthen the voice of the working class in both the First and Third Worlds, and could be an important element of the future of U.S.-Venezuelan times.[50]

The extent to which the U.S. and Venezuelan political, cultural, and economic leaders have become sensitive to each other's concerns was illustrated by the November 20–22, 1980 United States-Venezuelan policy dialogue, organized by the Woodrow Wilson Center for International Affairs in Washington, D.C. While the two-day binational conference was organized prior to the U.S. elections, it did allow the Venezuelans the opportunity to meet members of the Republican transition team for energy and security matters.

The potential democratic convergence of Venezuela and the United States may be most striking regarding the complex interaction between the two as both have moved in parallel fashion to calm the turbulent politics of Central America and the Caribbean Islands. Venezuela, on its own and in conjunction with Mexico, sees itself as providing a friendly education of the Reagan administration regarding the reality of the Caribbean. Whereas the Reagan administration had identified the cause of the present unrest to be exclusively "communist subversion," Venezuela has hoped to redirect U.S. attention to problems such as the revolution of rising expectations, over-population, and the legacy of historic regional and communal conflicts. Whereas the Reagan administration had reportedly called for a military victory, Venezuela has suggested the need to develop strong civilian political institutions and a viable political consensus.

In many ways, Venezuela finds itself caught in the classic dilemma of navigating between Scylla and Charybdis with regards to the continuing political struggle in the Caribbean basin in general and in El Salvador in particular. In both his March 1981 address to Congress and in the April 1981 joint communiqué with Mexican President López Portillo, President Herrera Campíns has stated that Venezuela remains opposed to both the imposition by force of totalitarian regimes, and U.S. intervention in the internal affairs of Central America.

With regards to the Caribbean basin, Venezuela seems to be pursuing a dual policy that is consistent with achieving the prevention of a totalitarian victory and external intervention. Venezuela has acted with Mexico in reaching a consensus on which the oil-poor Caribbean nations have received oil at reduced prices. Both Mexico and Venezuela maintain diplomatic ties with the Sandinista revolutionary regime in Nicaragua, and both have economic aid programs under way in that nation. Venezuela has also provided aid to the Marxist government of Grenada.

Following a May 1981 meeting between Secretary of State Alexander Haig and two of President Herrera Campins closest advisers, Interior Minister Rafael Andrés Montes de Oca and Secretary to the Presidency Gonzalo Garcia Bustillos, the United States and Venezuela announced a "coincidence" regarding the policies of the two in the Caribbean. According to Montes de Oca, the United States will direct its policies "toward economic development with social justice" and the fostering of democracy.

Venezuelan officials interviewed by the writer regarding this coincidence were quite explicit in their support of the contention made by Robert S. Leiken that the United States "should consider crossing instead of burning" the bridges to the Central American left built by European Christian and Social Democrats.[51] In the ongoing geopolitical struggle, nothing could serve Soviet interests better than the United States allowing itself to become a captive ally of Latin America's right-wingers.

One apparent component of the emerging U.S.-Venezuelan coincidence is the increased U.S. commitment to social reforms and political democracy in the region, and a relative downplaying of the hard-line military approach. The friendship and open support Venezuela has demonstrated for the U.S. position in El Salvador has been of incalculable assistance, especially considering the recent French-Mexican initiative granting El Salvador's Democratic Revolutionary Front (FDR) "representative political status." Venezuela's own human rights record has recently been called "exemplary" by the Liberal-Left Council on Hemispheric Affairs, a group that opposes the Reagan administration's policy in Central America.[52]

This coincidence between two democracies should prevent U.S. policy in the 1980s from becoming the captive ally of the Latin right-wing that Leiken and others have feared. The formal visit to Washington of the President of the Salvadoran civil-military junta, José Napoleón Duarte, and his face-to-face meeting with President Reagan should protect Duarte from any right-wing intrigue in El Salvador. The strengthening of Duarte's own political position vis-à-vis the right-wing elements in the junta should also increase the possibility of a political solution to that nation's troubles.

The proposed Venezuelan purchase of a wing of F-16 fighter-bombers is a complex question. While there is good reason for justifying the need for modernization of Venezuela's air force and for Venezuela's own autonomous assertion of a greater role in Caribbean affairs, there are also many valid questions concerning the proposed purchase. The cost of buying and maintaining the aircraft will be a major fiscal burden even for oil-rich Venezuela. At a time of fiscal austerity, these costs could lessen support in Venezuela for the coincidence with the United States. The proposed sale may also start an unfortunate arms race between Colombia and Venezuela, heightening the tensions already plaguing relations between these two democracies.

The key to future U.S. influence in Venezuela may depend largely on internal developments in the United States. The degree of U.S. success in reindustrializing in the face of a determined European and Japanese export drive, as well as the emerging Brazilian competition, will affect its influence with Venezuela. In similar fashion, the active search for new domestic sources of oil, such as in the Rocky Mountain Overthrust belt, should impact on its increasing oil dependency. Finally, will the U.S. social fabric and political consensus hold together if the 1980s prove to be a decade of downward economic performance? Venezuelans are proud of their Hispanic culture, and any ugly incident in the United States that reveals a significant anti-Hispanic tendency may make the task of maintaining good relations with Venezuela more difficult.

Barring major changes in the political situation in the Middle East and a major domestic energy breakthrough, Venezuela should remain a provider of a significant share of U.S. oil needs. Assuming that the events of the 1980s prove to be relatively unspectacular regarding the energy situation, one might posit that in 1990 the United States will import from Venezuela between one to two million bpd of its oil, at a cost falling in the $40 to $50 range per barrel.

The question of the future of the close political affinity existing between the two nations is more problematic than that of the "natural" economic ties. Venezuela is a nation that is equally proud of its own democratic achievements and its adherence to the Third World principles of anti-imperialism and the right of all nations to autonomous development.

A number of valid reasons have led Venezuela's incumbent Christian Democratic administration to move toward coincidence with the United States in resisting the spread of Cuban-style authoritarianism in Central America. Venezuela's intent is a positive coincidence in favor of fostering democracy, and not merely a negative one opposing Cuban-style rule. Venezuelan Christian Democratic leaders have repeatedly stated that they reject the bizarre notion that there are "good" authoritarian dictatorships and "bad" totalitarian ones. Venezuela's Christian Democrats should not be expected to jeopardize their possibilities in the 1983 elections by becoming further entangled in El Salvador's bloodbath. Close U.S.-Venezuelan political ties could be damaged if the issue of coincidence becomes a factor in the 1983 election campaign now beginning.

A policy of a democratic-oriented coincidence with the United States will proceed in parallel fashion with that of a consensus on Third World issues with Mexico and the Andean Pact. A speedy political solution to the El Salvador tragedy would maximize U.S. influence with Venezuela. It would also allow for a broad and mutually beneficial meeting of the minds between U.S. and Latin American democratic movements. American-Venezuelan ties in the 1980s will be conditioned not only by the existing bilateral affinity, but also by the increasing attractiveness of Europe to Venezuela and the continuing appeal of the Third World ideal. To best influence Venezuela, the United States should be prepared to cross the bridges to dialogue with the democratic left and the Third World.

NOTES

1. The author sees the world loosely organized into four interrelated worlds of separate political-economic development. The First World comprises the advanced industrial demo-

cracies, while the Second is the Soviet-dominated states with their centrally planned economies. With all due respect to the Third World ideal, the writer separates those developing nations with a capacity for self-development and an autonomous international stance from those unable to achieve self-development and probably destined to need long-term massive external aid merely to survive. The Third World is a world of development, the Fourth World may tragically represent the damned. See Helio Juaguaribe, "The New Interimperial System," in *Problems of World Modeling: Political and Social Implications*, ed. Karl W. Deutsch (Cambridge, Mass.: Ballinger, 1977).

2. Franklin Tugwell, "The United States and Venezuela: Prospects for Accommodation," in *Contemporary Venezuela and its Role in International Affairs*, ed. Robert D. Bond (New York: New York University Press, 1977), pp. 218–19. See also his "Venezuela's Oil Nationalization" in the same volume, and *The Politics of Oil in Venezuela* (Stanford, Calif., Stanford University Press, 1975).

3. Committee on Energy and Natural Resources, United States Senate (Staff Report—Publication No. 96), *The Geopolitics of Oil* (Washington, D.C.: U.S. Government Printing Office, 1980), pp. 45–53.

4. Committee on Energy and Natural Resources, *The Geopolitics of Oil*, p. 76.

5. Charles K. Ebinger, "Caribbean Energy," *Washington Quarterly* 4, No. 2 (Spring 1981): 123. The writer's wording of Venezuelan objectives differs from that of Ebinger.

6. Julio Sosa Rodriquez, "U.S. and Venezuela: The Oil Diplomacy," *Latin American Times*, March 1981, p. 8.

7. Jesus Seguias, "El dilema actual de America Latina: La democracia cristiana y la social democracia se disputan el poder continental," *Diario de Caracas*, July 11, 1980.

8. M. P. Zenio Strong, "Latin American Connection: Europe Challenges ·U.S. dominance'," *Europe*, May-June 1980, pp. 48–49. See also Elio Lengrand, "Que Pasa con la social democracia?" *SIC* 44, No. 435 (May 1981).

9. *New York Times*, September 5, 1981, "Mexico Rejects Accusation on Salvador," and Op-Ed, Carlos Fuentes, "Salvador's Opposition," *New York Times*, September 16, 1981. See also Jeff Stein, "Interview: Robert E. White, Reagan and El Salvador," *Progressive*, September 1981.

10. Francis X. Gannon, "The European Community Looks toward Latin America," *Americas* 23, Nos. 11–12 (November–December 1980): 50.

11. *Latin American Times*, "Venezuelan Investment," August 1981, p. 46.

12. *Caracas Daily Journal*, March 8, 1980, "German Syn-Fuel Technology Advances for the Faja," and "PETROVEN Accord with France," *Latin American Energy Report* 3. No. 7 (July 2, 1981).

13. Franklin Tugwell, "Energy and Political Economy," *Comparative Politics*, October 1980, p. 105.

14. James D. Theberge and Roger W. Fontaine, *Latin America's Struggle for Progress* (Lexington, Mass.: Lexington Books, 1977), p. 7.

15. Roger D. Hansen, "North-South Policy—What is the Problem?" *Foreign Affairs* 58, No. 5 (Summer 1980): 1113.

16. *Wall Street Journal*, November 3, 1980, "Brazil's Debt Plight is Becoming Major Worry to its Global Lenders; Particularly U.S. Banks."

17. Venezuelan Ministry of Foreign Affairs, *Venezuela Now* (December 31, 1977) p. 73, "Meeting of Heads of State of Brazil and Venezuela to Benefit Both Countries."

18. Robert D. Bond, "Venezuela, Brazil and the Amazon Basin," *Orbis* Fall 1978, p. 650. See also Kim Fuad, "The Green Giant Comes Courtin': Brazil Woos Venezuela Oil," *Business Venezuela*, No. 64, November–December 1979.

19. *Latin America Weekly Report*, WR-18-37, March 27, 1981, "Brazil Exports its Engineering Know-How."

20. Gustavo Lagos, "The Revolution of Being," in *On the Creation of a Just World*

Order: Preferred Worlds for the 1990's, ed, Saul. H. Mendolovitz (New York: Free Press, 1975), p. 81.

21. Lagos, "The Revolution of Being," p. 85.

22. Luis Vallenilla, *Oil: The Making of a New Economic Order—Venezuelan Oil and OPEC* (New York: McGraw-Hill, 1975). See also Markos Mamalakis, "The New International Economic Order: Centerpiece Venezuela," *Journal of Interamerican Studies and World Affairs* 20, No. 3, (August 1978); Diego Luis Castellanos, "Venezuela en el Contexto de la Economia Mundial," *Nueva Sociedad* (Caracas), No. 49, (July–August 1980): 74.

23. John R. Pate, "Alarm Over Anpact," *Business Venezuela* (Caracas, published by the Venezuelan-American Chamber of Commerce and Industry), September-October 1979.

24. Alberto Quiros Corradi, "Energy and the Exercise of Power," *Foreign Affairs* 57, No. 3 (Summer 1979): 1146.

25. Kim Fuad, "Venezuela's Role in OPEC," in *Contemporary Venezuela and its Role in International Affairs*, pp. 134–35.

26. James Petras et al., *The Nationalization of Venezuela Oil* (New York: Praeger, 1977), p. 159.

27. Robert S. Leiken, "Eastern Winds in Latin America," *Foreign Policy* No. 42 (Spring 1981): 95; W. Raymond Duncan, "The Soviet Union in Latin America," in *The Soviet Union in the Third World: Successes and Failures*, ed. Robert Donaldson (Boulder, Colo.: Westview Press, 1981), p. 2; Jorge I. Dominguez, "The United States and its Regional Security Interests: The Caribbean, Central and South America," *Daedalus* 109, No. 4 (Fall 1980).

28. Duncan, "The Soviet Union," p. 6, and Leiken, "Eastern Winds," p. 98.

29. For an excellent socialist critique of the works of Chè Guevara, Frantz Fanon, and Regis Debray, see Lewis Coser, "Fanon and Debray: Theorists of the Third World," *Dissent*, 1968, reprinted in *Beyond the New Left*, ed. Irving Howe (New York: McCall, 1970).

30. Enrique A. Baloyra and John D. Martz, *Political Attitudes in Venezuela: Societal Cleavages and Political Opinion* (Austin: University of Texas Press, 1979), pp. 215, 228.

31. Steve Ellner, "Venezuelan Surprises," Op-Ed, *New York Times*, August 25, 1981.

32. Embassy of Venezuela, "International: Venezuelan-U.S. Relations," *Venezuela Up-To-Date* 21, Nos. 1–2 (Spring-Summer 1980). This article contains the English text of the U.S.-Venezuelan agreement on technology cooperation, energy research and development, agricultural cooperation, as well as the trade agreement and memorandum of understanding between the United States and the Andean Pact.

33. Embassy of Venezuela, "U.S. Secretary of Energy visits Venezuela," *Venezuela Up-To-Date* 21, No. 3 (Fall 1980): 7. This issue also contains the English text of the U.S.-Venezuelan agreement on health cooperation.

34. Rodriquez, "U.S. and Venezuela," p. 8.

35. Rodriquez, "U.S. and Venezuela," p. 9.

36. Rodriquez, "U.S. and Venezuela," p. 9.

37. Rafael Alfonzo Ravard, "The Venezuelan Oil Industry and Its Investment Plan (1980–1990)," speech delivered to Annual Joint Assembly of the International Bank for Reconstruction and Development, Washington, D.C., October 1980, p. 89.

38. Ravard, "The Venezuelan Oil Industry," p. 90.

39. Embassy of Venezuela, "Venezuela's Oil Industry and its Investment Plans," *Venezuela Up-To-Date* 21, No. 4 (Winter 1980-1981): 4.

40. *Daily Journal* (Caracas), May 30, 1980, "DJ Oil Supplement 80: The Orinoco Oil Belt."

41. Republica de Venezuela Ministerio del Desarrollo Urbano—Concejo Municipal del Distrito Bolivar, Estado Zulia, *Plan de Ordenacion Territorial de la Costa Oriental del Lago de Maracaibo* (vols. 1–4) February 1979.

42. Tugwell, "The United States and Venezuela," p. 204. Tugwell, using mid-1970s production cost and revenue estimates, suggested that Venezuela would need to produce up to 16 million bpd of Orinoco oil to maintain the same revenue levels it was gathering from light oil.

43. *Latin American Weekly Report*, WR-81-14, April 3, 1981, "Venezuela Takes a Major Step towards Oil Output in Orinoco."

44. Rafael Caldera, "Venezuela, the Oil Issue and the New International Economic Order," lecture at Liverpool University, April 21, 1977, p. 11.

45. Some estimate of the size of Venezuelan investment in Florida and of the Venezuelan government's concern for this awesome flight of its own national capital is provided by Mira Wilkins, "Venezuelan Investment in Florida: 1979" *Latin American Research Review* 16, No. 1 (1981).

46. Quoted in Jean-Pierre Clere, "The Difficult Art of Sowing Oil,' " *Venezuela Now* 2, No. 21 (May 30, 1977).

47. Jeane Kirkpatrick, "U.S. Security & Latin America," *Commentary* 7, No. 1 (January 1981): 34.

48. David Eugene Blank, *Politics in Venezuela* (Boston: Little, Brown, 1973), pp. 225–27.

49. AFL-CIO Department of International Affairs, "Labor Mourns Slain Heroes," *Free Trade Union News* 36, No. 1 (January 1981):1–3. See also William C. Doherty, Jr., "U.S. Labor's Role in El Salvador," *Free Trade Union News* 36, No. 2 (February 1981).

50. Carlos Andres Perez, "El Dialog Norte-Sur," *Neuva Sociedad* (Caracas), No. 51 (November–December 1980): 44–45.

51. Leiken, "Eastern Winds," p. 111.

52. Council on Hemispheric Affairs, "Human Rights Report for Venezuela: 1980–1981," *Washington Report on the Hemisphere* 1, No. 21 (July 28, 1981).

6

Colombia:
Cool Friendship

Daniel L. Premo

Unlike Venezuela or the United States (or Argentina, Brazil, and Chile under civilian rule), foreign policy issues have not played a prominent role in Colombia's party politics. For most of this century, the dominant factions within Colombia's Liberal and Conservative parties have consistently agreed on the limited goals of foreign policy, although different administrations have varied in the means of pursuing them. Politics in general and elections in particular tend to focus on personalities and domestic problems rather than foreign policy issues. The result is that foreign policy formulation and execution have developed along sectorial lines, especially over the past quarter century, which has seen Colombia's economy evolve from a largely rural and agricultural base to a more integrated urban-industrial and services orientation.

Various economic ministries, semiautonomous government agencies, and economic interest groups from the private sector have become involved in the foreign policy process. Problems related to international loans and finance, for example, are handled by the Ministry of Finance. Policy considerations related to coffee are dealt with by the Federation of Coffee Growers in New York, not by the Foreign Ministry in Bogotá. Similarly, commercial matters are handled by the Export Promotion Fund (PROEXPO), also located in New York, or the Colombian Foreign Trade Institute (INCOMEX), which establishes import policies and is the official representative of the Colombian government to the Andean Pact Commission. The Colombian military maintains a separate network of informaton and communications, while the Colombian official assigned to serve as liaison in coordinating drug policy does not work out of the Colombian embassy in Washington, but through the U.S. Drug Enforcement Agency. In brief, the Ministry of Foreign Relations exerts relatively little control over the implementation of various major policy issues affecting relations between Colombia and the United States.

Colombia's historical uninvolvement in international or even inter-American affairs has had an adverse effect on the development of an administrative-bureaucratic structure essential for the effective conduct of bilateral relations with the United States. One needs only to compare the size of the diplomatic staffs maintained at the countries' respective embassies to realize the disadvantage from which Colombia operates. Colombia presently has five officials assigned to its Washington embassy, excluding military attachés and clerical staff, while the United States has over 200 officials working out of its embassy in Bogotá. The Colombian embassy lacks the fundamental bureaucratic mechanisms and personnel to develop the independent sources of information necessary to represent effectively the nation's interests. The embassy is unable to serve as a coordinator of overall policy, much less exert more than token influence on the conduct of relations. Under such conditions, it is not surprising that Colombia's ambassadors to the United States tend to concern themselves more with Colombian presidential politics than representational problems during their period of appointment.[1] It is even less surprising that the two countries make use of the more functional embassy in their bilateral relations; issues are essentially "resolved" at the U.S. embassy in Bogotá, although agreements may be signed with appropriate diplomatic fanfare at the Foreign Ministry or the State Department, depending upon their content. The imbalance in the administrative-bureaucratic capabilities of each country underscores Colombia's fundamental weakness and perhaps the major source of U.S. influence in the foreign policy arena. This problem, as yet inadequately studied, affects the entire scope of U.S.-Colombian relations.

To be properly understood, U.S.-Colombian relations should be viewed within the context of big power–small power relations. A constant in such a relationship is that, from Colombia's viewpoint, the United States operates with great concern for diplomatic courtesy as long as questions of substance vital to the big power's interests are not involved or compromised. Throughout the course of their relations, the United States has demonstrated repeatedly, especially during the early decades of the twentieth century, that it will not hesitate to act unilaterally with little or no regard for Colombian reaction.

Issues involving a big power–small power relationship can seldom, if ever, be negotiated or reconciled on the basis of equality. At best, Colombia is a junior partner in the hierarchy of hemispheric importance to the United States, lumped with Chile and Peru behind Brazil, Mexico, Argentina, and

Venezuela, whose influence as a major oil producer is sufficient to elevate it in rank to the highest level of priority. At worst, Colombia is treated by the United States as little more than a client-state whose internal and foreign problems are of concern only when they impinge on the policy considerations of the dominant power.

Although ardent Colombian nationalists might disagree, since the Panama Canal episode at the beginning of the century the United States has been guided in its relations with Colombia more by a sense of paternalism than imperialistic design. United States territorial and security considerations gave way in the 1920s to a diplomacy of investment and finance in which the United States sought to penetrate the Colombian marketplace, especially through the promotion of American enterprise in the development of Colombia's petroleum and banana industries. However, even before the international rivalry to obtain petroleum concessions, the United States had already established its economic influence by becoming Colombia's principal customer for coffee, which remains the country's leading export and source of legal revenue.

CURRENT AREAS OF CONTROVERSY

Although the present status of U.S.-Colombian relations is generally cordial, there exist several areas of disagreement that deserve special attention. The issues are of mutual concern insofar as they affect the interests of both countries. However, their relative importance to each is subject to different perceptions and interpretations, affected by such factors as the time, source of information, and policy priorities. The three areas of controversy singled out for study have all featured prominently in bilateral relations over the past decade. They relate to the issue of drug trafficking; the 1972 treaty between the United States and Colombia concerning the status of the Quita Sueño, Roncador, and Serrana reefs; and trade policy issues.

Drug Trafficking

The illegal export of marijuana and cocaine from Colombia ranks among the most important issues in bilateral relations dating back to the early 1970s. Certainly no other policy issue has received more widespread attention in the United States. The "Colombian connection" has been the subject of feature articles in leading news magazines and television news programs and documentaries.[2] The impact of drug trafficking on the domestic economies of Colombia and the United States has been the topic of congressional hearings in both countries and the subject of numerous executive memoranda. No other policy has been more widely misperceived and, at times, exploited for political purposes.

Until the late 1960s, most marijuana entering the United States came from Mexico. However, a successful U.S.-backed operation to eradicate marijuana (and heroin) in Mexico led to increased production in Colombia, where an elaborate smuggling network already existed along the country's extensive Caribbean coastline. Colombia increased its production of marijuana to the point where it now supplies an estimated 70 percent of the illicit traffic in the United States. In addition, Colombia is the source of an estimated 70 percent of the cocaine market. Although the coca leaf is grown principally in Peru and Bolivia, processing facilities are concentrated in Colombia.

While marijuana remains the single biggest drug problem in the United States, it was the increasingly serious traffic in cocaine that led to political recriminations between Colombia and the United States in the mid-1970s. During a state visit in September 1975, President Alfonso López Michelsen accused American interests of turning Colombia into a "drug smuggler's den." He expressed the official view that Colombia was simply "a country of transit" due to its geographical location and that the smuggling of cocaine and marijuana into the United States was essentially a problem for U.S. authorities.[3]

United States allegations of high-level corruption in Colombia in relation to drug trafficking produced a minor diplomatic incident in 1978. López described the "Bourne Memorandum" as "the biggest diplomatic blunder by the United States in Latin America."[4] The U.S. embassy hastily assured prominent Colombian officials and politicians that charges of their implication in cocaine smuggling were groundless.

Colombia's perception of the drug trade began to change following the inauguration of Julio César Turbay Ayala as president in August 1978. An agreement on drug control was signed with the United States involving additional security measures in the Guajira peninsula, where most of the traffic originates. For the first time the Colombian armed forces took over responsibility for drug interdiction from the national police and soon placed the Guajira region under virtual military jurisdiction.

Turbay's crusade against trafficking was not uniformly supported, however, even within the Colombian government. The president of Colombia's Supreme Court attacked the United States, charging it with responsibility for controlling the drug traffic. He accused the United States executive of "following the path of least resistance" by urging Colombia to stop the illicit trade, "even with the armed forces."[5] The country's minister of development stressed that Colombia was "an innocent victim" of drug trafficking because it was "neither Colombia's desire nor intention to become the supplier of drug addicts in the United States."[6]

By the end of 1979, the disruptive effect of the drug trade on the Colombian economy, combined with evidence of an alarming increase in drug addiction at all levels of Colombian society, prompted officials in both the public and private sectors to accept drug trafficking as a Colombian problem and address the issue with a greater sense of urgency. In May 1980, at the military's urging, Colombia's national police once again assumed primary responsibility for drug interdiction. More recently, drug enforcement officials in both countries have expressed concern over the rapid increase in the volume of cocaine traffic. According to U.S. drug authorities, the cocaine trade has doubled since 1978 and now has an estimated market value in the United States of $25 to $35 billion.[7] The traffic is dominated by Colombian organized crime operating out of Miami.

For its part, the United States has been singularly unsuccessful in formulating a coherent and consistent drug policy. It is difficult to fault Colombia for accusing the United States of hypocrisy in demanding more effective enforcement procedures when the move in this country is toward liberalization of existing drug laws, the criminal justice system operates inefficiently, and the use of cocaine is alarmingly commonplace. According to the former director of the U.S. Drug Enforcement Agency, drugs must be stopped at the source, as is the case with marijuana and heroin production in Mexico. This will require a stronger international commitment from countries such as Colombia to deal with the drug distribution problem.

If the optimum form of drug control is to attack the problem at its source, that is, the producing or processing countries, then one must seriously question the low level of U.S. funding for international narcotics control, and especially that portion destined for Colombia. With worldwide appropriations for FY 1981 planned at approximately $50 million, Colombia's allocation—for a country that provides the United States with 70 percent of its marijuana *and* cocaine—is only $3.6 million, slightly over 7 percent of total funding.[8] Moreover, according to a former U.S. ambassador to Colombia, Colombia's interdiction effort in 1979 actually surpassed that of the United States. Colombia was seizing marijuana at roughly three times the rate as in the United States, and cocaine somewhere in the area of six times the rate.[9] Considering the fact that domestic narcotics law enforcement at all jurisdictions cost the United States about $1 billion in 1979, and the United States provided Colombia with only $3.8 million under the international narcotics control program, the Colombian government should be commended for its efforts in drug interdiction.

While both Colombia and the United States now appear to be in agreement on the need to eliminate drug trafficking, there still remains the difficulty of working out the complex details of narcotics cooperation. Despite Colombia's access to more advanced equipment, technology, and special training, smuggling interests are thus far proving equal to the challenge. Cooperative efforts are also weakened by the fact that the United States is not presently using all of its administrative, technological, and financial resources to combat the drug traffic. Congress, for example, has refused to lift the ban on the sale of paraquat through the foreign assistance program. Sophisticated communication equipment deployed by the United States military could be put to use in the Caribbean to assist drug enforcement officials in the detection and apprehension of smugglers. The State Department has failed both to provide a consistent, long-range program for dealing with the drug distribution problem and to establish the level of funding necessary to attack it more efficiently.

In view of recent budgetary and personnel cuts in the Drug Enforcement Agency, the Reagan administration has chosen not to make an issue of the drug problem at the present time, either domestically or in bilateral relations with Colombia. As long as the potential for exorbitant profit far outweighs the risk of swift and certain punishment, marijuana production in the United States and Colombia will expand to meet demand. In the final analysis, the effectiveness of either government's actions to combat marijuana traffic in Colombia will be severely impaired by the relatively low level of concern in the United States about the availability and use of marijuana.[10] Much the same could be said for the dramatic increase in Colombia's illicit trafficking in cocaine, although its importance in the trade is being challenged by increased competition from Peru and especially Bolivia.

There is no clear perception that drug control occupies a high priority in either the United States or Colombia, although the latter now recognizes that drug production and trafficking is no longer a unilateral concern of the former. The shift in Colombia's official positions since the López administration is probably due to the destabilizing effect of the drug traffic and domestic consumption on Colombia's economic and social life than any political pressure brought to bear on the problem by the United States.

Apart from the unsettling and still unpredictable consequences on Colombia's economy, drug-related problems have led to disturbing increases in common crime, lack of personal security, and the general impression that the quality of life in Colombian society is deteriorating. If the United States wants to contribute to the stability of a democratic government in Colombia, it must as a first step reassess its own position on drug control and establish more realistic priorities in working out a program of cooperative enforcement.

The Quita Sueño Treaty

A second major issue affecting current U.S.-Colombian relations centers on the status of a treaty signed on September 8, 1972, in which the United States renounced all claims to sovereignty over three uninhabited outcroppings of coral reefs in the Caribbean: Quita Sueño, Roncador, and Serrana.

The purpose of the treaty is to settle long-standing questions concerning the status of the reefs, which are located between 380 and 460 miles from the Colombian mainland. Following discovery of the reefs by an American citizen in 1869, the United States claimed them in the late nineteenth century under the terms of the Guano Islands Act of 1856. In 1890 Colombia protested the extraction by U.S. nationals of Guano, claiming that Colombia had inherited sovereign title to the reefs from Spain in 1803. In a formal exchange of notes on April 10, 1928, the United States and Colombia recognized the existence of their dual claims and agreed to maintain a status quo situation. Negotiation of the treaty in 1972 emerged in response to Colombia's desire to establish its sole claim to sovereignty.

The treaty assures that the fishing rights of each government's nationals and vessels in the waters adjacent to Quita Sueño will be free from interference by the other government or by its nationals or vessels. Colombia also agrees to guarantee to U.S. nationals and vessels a continuation of fishing in the waters adjacent to Roncador and Serrana, subject to reasonable conservation measures applied on a nondiscriminatory basis. The treaty further stipulates that the continued maintenance of navigational aids on the three reefs will be determined in a separate exchange of notes between the two parties. The treaty does not affect the position or opinion of either government with respect to the extent of the territorial seas or the jurisdiction and rights of coastal states on any matter not specifically dealt with in the treaty.[11]

The status of the 1972 treaty would normally constitute little cause for diplomatic concern. However, the situation was complicated considerably by a revival of Nicaragua's claim to sovereignty over the reefs in 1972.

The dispute between Colombia and Nicaragua over the sovereignty of the reefs dates back to 1803, when the reefs and the islands of San Andrés and Providencia were taken away from the captaincy-general of Guatemala and placed under the viceroyalty of New Granada in Bogotá. In 1828 Colombia and Nicaragua signed a treaty in which Colombia recognized Nicaragua's claims to its eastern seaboard, which under the 1803 agreement had also been transferred to New Granada. In return, Nicaragua accepted Colombian sovereignty over several keys, including those now under dispute. Colombia, however, bases its claim on the more recent Esguerra-Barcenas

Treaty of 1928 in which Nicaragua ceded to Colombia the islands of San Andrés and Providencia, while Colombia renounced any claims west of meridian 82. Nicaragua ratified this agreement in 1950. The 1928 treaty did not mention the three keys, which are east of meridian 82, because they were at that time the subject of litigation between the United States and Colombia. This was resolved by the 1972 treaty in which the United States renounced all claims to sovereignty over the reefs. At this point, the Nicaraguan government issued a formal statement reiterating its claim to sovereignty over Quita Sueño, Roncador, and Serrana. It contended that the water surrounding the reefs does not exceed 200 meters in depth and therefore they comprise part of the continental shelf over which Nicaragua has rights. Colombia responded to Nicaragua's claim by sending its defense minister and senior military officers to conduct a formal ceremony on the reefs confirming Colombian sovereignty.

Colombia ratified the treaty in 1973. However, the United States Senate ignored President Nixon's request to act favorably on the treaty "in the near future." In fact, the treaty was not brought to the Senate floor for a vote of ratification until July 31, 1981, when it was approved unanimously. For reasons not entirely clear, the United States elected to ignore Colombia's request for approval of the treaty for almost nine years. One can speculate that for much of the 1970s the Somoza lobby was more effective than Colombia's representation in dealing with the White House, the Senate leadership, and members of the Foreign Relations Committee. It is also possible that the Senate was responding to the interests of multinational corporations that were speculating on the existence of oil deposits on the continental shelf. At one point in 1978, President López thought he had gained leverage with the United States as a result of his personal support for the Carter administration's efforts to negotiate and secure the ratification of a new Panama Canal Treaty. The large number of U.S. senators who visited Colombia led López to believe that he had developed a close relationship between himself and Congress, especially the Senate Foreign Relations Committee. Observing that "usually governments deal with each other through their presidents, ministers, secretaries or ambassadors," López stated confidently:

> With good reason now we expect another small treaty—to be ratified. It has been six years since the U.S. Senate last debated this issue, and we feel we now have enough friends for this matter to be discussed by the committee and possibly approved.[12]

The long failure of the United States to ratify the treay may have emboldened the Sandinista government to revive Nicaragua's long-standing claim to the reefs in 1979. The announcement on August 14 produced no official response from Colombia's Foreign Ministry. However, Nicaragua's decision in December to reassert its claim over the islands of San Andrés and Providencia produced a violent reaction in Bogotá, where a government spokesman called the action "an act of international treachery."[13]

Nicaragua contends that its 1928 treaty with Colombia is invalid because it was signed "under duress" during the U.S. military occupation of Nicaragua. Notwithstanding Nicaragua's assurance that it intends to pursue its claims through judicial means, the Colombian armed forces view the situation as a serious problem. Colombia has increased its naval and air patrols of the reefs, and a new military base has been constructed on San Andrés to serve as naval headquarters in the Caribbean.

Although State Department officials believed that the treaty issue was blown out of proportion in Colombia and especially Nicaragua, the seriousness with which Colombia views the matter should not be under-estimated. The nine-year delay in the ratification of the treaty attests to both Colombia's weakness in attempting to influence the United States, and the lack of good faith on the part of the latter for failing to press forward with a commitment that should have been carried out much sooner. If the United States had reservations about ratifying the treaty, they should have been aired and a new agreement negotiated. The delay simply gave credence to the view that withholding ratification has been politically expedient to the United States, both as a carrot and a threat, in its relations with Colombia and Nicaragua.

While ratification of the treaty is a significant step by the United States toward improving its relations with Colombia, an additional and perhaps more compelling motive for acting on the treaty at this time is a desire on the part of the Reagan administration to signal its disapproval of the Nicaraguan regime.

Trade Policy Issues

Since the 1960s, Colombia has pursued a development policy in which the principal objectives have been to reduce the economy's dependence on coffee through export diversification, and to alter the traditional pattern of its trade relations by actively seeking new markets in Latin America and Europe.

The United States is still Colombia's leading trading partner, although its relative share of foreign trade has been decreasing as Colombia has successfully developed new markets. The proportion of exports going to the United States dropped from a high of 62 percent in 1962 to a low of just over

22 percent in 1979. Colombia's imports from the United States have declined less sharply, from 48 percent in 1966 to a recent low of 33.9 percent in 1977.[14]

Colombia's shift in the late 1960s from a development strategy emphasizing import substitution to one stressing export promotion resulted in the rapid expansion of nontraditional exports such as fresh flowers and leather goods. With the penetration of new exports in U.S. and European markets, Colombia has joined the ranks of the more vocal Latin American countries in urging the developed nations to avoid applying restrictive trade measures against alleged unfair trade practices on imports coming from Latin America.

Private groups within Colombia, such as the National Association of Financial Institutions (ANIF) and the National Association of Industrialists (ANDI), tend to view U.S. protectionist policy as a "dangerous political weapon" whose measures have unfavorable repercussions on Colombia's economy. In December 1977, ANIF's president described U.S. trade law as "a new, subtle and complex form of intervention that dangerously conditions trade relations." He claimed that the implementation of a protectionist tariff policy was "a step backward in the traditional policy of privileged trade relations as occurred during the time of the Good Neighbor Policy and the Alliance for Progress."[15]

In a campaign designed to influence the trade policies of the Carter administration, Colombia's foreign minister joined the public sector's criticism of growing protectionism against the sale of Colombian products in the U.S. market. He deplored U.S. restrictions on imports of flowers, leather bags, shoes, and textiles, and called for a relationship based on "friendly free trade."[16]

The Colombian Export Promotion Fund (PROEXPO) is another vehicle through which Colombia has channeled its demands for more eqitable treatment in its commercial relations with the United States. When the United States threatened to impose a tariff surcharge on Colombian textiles in 1978, PROEXPO noted that Colombia's export policy had been defined at the urging of the United States within the initial programs of the Alliance for Progress. Colombia denied that its incentives for certain export items in the form of Tax Allowance Certificates (CAT) constituted a subsidy, and were therefore subject under U.S. trade law to compensatory levies. However, in order to avoid import levies on textiles, Colombia's trade negotiators ultimately agreed that CAT incentives paid by the Colombian government to textile exporters could not exceed 5 percent.[17]

Bilateral trade issues have been resolved amicably for the most part, especially since December 1979 when Colombia announced its decision to join the General Agreement on Tariffs and Trade (GATT). Although Colombia, like most Latin American countries, was generally disappointed by the outcome of the GATT multilateral trade negotiations in Geneva, agreement was reached in April 1979 on a code governing subsidies and countervailing duties. In return for promises of a phasing out of export subsidies by some developing countries, the United States agreed to conduct "injury tests" to determine whether subsidized imports are harmful to domestic competitors before imposing countervailing duties on them. For Brazil, Colombia, and the Andean Pact countries in general, the code represented the major achievement of the negotiations. Although Colombia had already begun to phase out export subsidies, it was felt that U.S. acceptance of injury tests would improve prospects for Colombian exports of cut flowers, leather goods, and textiles, which were previously threatened by countervailing duties.

On May 14, 1981, President Turbay signed the documents of ratification, completing Colombia's process of adhesion to GATT. The chief benefit of membership to Colombia is allowing it to take advantage of tariff concessions granted to full members of GATT. As an immediate responsibility Colombia will have to reduce its common external tariff as it applies to 36 specific products. More important than the act of ratification is the question of whether Colombia will now sign the code on subsidies and countervailing measures.[18] It is clearly in the interests of the United States for Colombia to do so, since the code establishes the conditions for levying countervailing duties. Colombia, on the other hand, is reluctant to give up export subsidies, an instrument of economic policy that it may need, along with other trade promotion measures, as part of its development program. While Colombia's membership in GATT is likely to involve it more in multilateral trade issues, the United States will still seek bilateral agreements, even assuming Colombia signs the subsidies code.

Promotion of nontraditional exports has been a major factor in accelerating the process of Colombia's development. While protectionist sentiments in the United States are not likely to diminish in the immediate future, trade issues between Colombia and the United States are primarily a question of Colombia seeking to improve the competitive position of its exports on the world market. For its part, the United States must deal with increasing competition for the Colombian market from Europe and Japan. A recent report on U.S. trade prospects in Colombia concluded that despite some slowdown in the economy, Colombia should remain an important and expanding market both for U.S. consumer goods and imports to further Colombia's development efforts.[19]

The United States lost a major instrument for exercising economic and political influence in its trade relations with Colombia when Colombia relinquished U.S. economic assistance after 1975. As a major recipient of aid during the early years of the Alliance for Progress, Colombia received a total of almost $1.4 billion from the United States from 1960 to 1974, most of it in the form of loans administered through the United States Agency for International Development (AID). While emphasizing the existence of cordial economic relations with the United States, President López explained that "foreign aid breeds an unhealthy economic dependency and delays or undermines measures that should be taken for development."[20]

As one of two giants in the coffee-producing world, Colombia wants the United States to support a reasonable base price for coffee. As the world's largest consumer of coffee, the United States is in a position to play a role in the negotiations that precede the expiration of the present International Coffee Agreement in September 1982. Coffee supplies on the world market have returned to their pre-1975 abundance, increasing the desire for international price-support measures on the part of exporters and reducing the incentive for cooperation on the part of consumer nations. There exist some fears among the former that the free-market philosophy of the Reagan administration could result in a general weakening of the United States commitment to international price agreements, which, if certain, would have effects vital to Colombia's economy.

As Colombia's trading patterns become more diversified, including trade with the Soviet Union and Eastern European nations, its economic dependence on the United States will continue to decrease. The United States will remain Colombia's single most important economic partner, certainly as long as coffee is the country's principal export. However, the latitude of U.S. influence in bilateral trade relations will steadily diminish in direct proportion to the success of Colombia's development program.

OTHER ISSUES

While the problems of drug trafficking, treaty ratification, and trade policy have been singled out because of their prolonged impact on bilateral relations, there exist a number of issues of lesser controversy and occasional incidents that have produced periods of tension between the United States and Colombia. For the most part, the examples selected suggest a general decline of U.S. influence in Colombia.

The role of the Summer Institute of Linguistics (SIL) in Colombia has had definite political, cultural, and religious overtones that carry over into the foreign policy arena. The SIL, linked with the Wycliffe Bible Translators, has been the target of nationalist attacks since it began operating in Colombia in 1962. It has variously been criticized for the allegedly poor quality of its linguistic work, the destruction of Indian cultural values, the dissemination of political propaganda, religious proselytization, and for acting as an information network for the CIA. The Colombia government has repeatedly threatened to revoke the SIL's contract. The foreign minister of the Turbay administration announced in 1978 that the establishment of the SIL had been a "serious mistake" on the part of previous administrations, and "detrimental" to the national interests in the vast Amazon territory. He declared that the government would cancel the institute's activities "by the end of the year."[21] However, in 1981, after an SIL official was killed by guerrillas who demanded the expulsion of the organization, the government announced there was no reason for the institute to leave the country, since "nothing has been decided on the matter."[22]

On occasion, diplomatic emissaries, appointments, or even nominations have provoked dissent. According to one source, Colombia's political establishment has been widely regarded in the State Department's Bureau of Inter-American Affairs as "one of the more snobbish in the hemisphere." In 1977 the Foreign Ministry stalled for weeks on Washington's request for the acceptance of a native Puerto Rican as U.S. ambassador to Colombia. Although President López denied that the Colombian government had vetoed the appointment, formal agreement to accept the nominee was not issued until the eve of Rosalynn Carter's arrival in Bogotá, by which time he had withdrawn his name from consideration.[23] According to a Bogotá daily, the government's refusal to grant its approval was "in retaliation" for the State Department's refusal to accept a former finance minister in the López administration as Colombian ambassador to Washington.[24]

Since the reestablishment of diplomatic relations with the Soviet Union in 1968, Colombia has signed a number of commercial, scientific, and educational cooperation agreements with the USSR and other socialist countries. Although limited in volume by the reduced list of products, Colombia has encouraged reciprocal trade with the Soviets in an attempt to expand the market for Colombian exports. In 1976 the two countries signed an agreement for the construction of several hydroelectric plants in the department of Córdoba. The Soviet Union is to design, supply, and install the generators and automatic control equipment. At the protocol signing ceremony of the contract, López called the construction of the Urrá dams "an ambitious pilot project . . . which will serve as a showcase in Colombia of the economic and technological achievements of the USSR."[25] Colombia expects to finance Soviet investments with increased exports of coffee, beef, and other agricultural products. In negotiating terms of sale for Colombian beef, the government encountered the opposition of the United States, which feared another breach in its grain and beef embargo on the Soviet Union. Colombia accepted a temporary suspension, but urged the United States to put pressure on Venezuela to reopen its market to Colombian beef. When Venezuela subsequently refused to lift its embargo, the Colombian government announced that it had rejected the United States request to join the food boycott against the USSR, asserting its economic and political sovereignty to conclude the sale of beef to the Soviet Union.[26] The two countries formalized a commercial agreement in May 1980 under which 12,000 tons of Colombian beef would be exported to the USSR. A Soviet delegation visited Colombia in October 1980 to explore the possibilities of increasing bilateral trade.

In addition to trade, the Soviet Union and its Eastern European allies have expanded their educational links with Colombia in recent years. Of the 5,010 students from Latin America being trained in communist countries as of December 31, 1979, 1,035 (20.6 percent) were from Colombia. This represents a significant increase since 1976, when an estimated 400 Colombians were studying in communist countries—less than 10 percent of Latin America's total.[27] It should be of some concern to U.S. policymakers that the increase in the number of Colombian students studying in communist countries has occurred since the United States agreed to phase out its technical assistance program with Colombia, which was previously administered through AID. The Organization of American States (OAS) and the Inter-American Development Bank (IDB) continue to administer modest grant programs, but the Reagan administration's commitment to continue present levels of funding to international and hemispheric lending institutions is highly tenuous. As work on the Urrá dam projects advances, one can anticipate a further increase in the availability of scholarship opportunities for Colombians in communist countries, as well as the increase of Soviet technicians in Colombia.

In another area, Colombia recently criticized the United States for selling sophisticated weapons to some Latin American countries. The country's foreign minister termed the policy "imprudent" and "a source of tension" between countries in a region that has been more or less moderate in its military spending. In commenting on Venezuela's decision to purchase fighters from the United States and Nicaragua's negotiations for planes from the Soviet Union, he cautioned that "Latin America must be kept free from the fatal germ of the arms race."[28] Earlier, it had been announced that the Reagan administration had requested $92.6 million in military aid for Latin America for FY 1982, a 60 percent increase over the last Carter budget. Colombia was expected to be the second largest recipient after El Salvador, with $12.7 million in equipment credits and $850,000 in training. Despite a visit to Washington by Colombia's defense minister in March, the military has not yet received what it wants from the United States in the way of assistance. In the absence of a firm promise of support, Colombia may threaten to turn to other sources of supply. On the whole, however, harmonious relations are believed to exist between Colombian military personnel and their U.S. counterparts. Given Colombia's long-standing boundary and immigration disputes with Venezuela, Nicaragua's contentious claims, and an internal security problem with rural and urban guerrilla groups, the United States' greatest influence in the immediate future may lie precisely in the area of military aid.

PROSPECTS FOR FUTURE RELATIONS

On balance, the evidence presented thus far indicates declining U.S. influence and the means potentially usable to shape events in Colombia. However, despite the attention given to issues of recent controversy, there exists an underlying affinity of interests between Colombia and the United States.

Both countries, for example, are concerned with maintaining stability in the Caribbean, and Colombia has become one of the most vocal critics of Cuban interventionism. After advocating the lifting of sanctions against Cuba for much of the López presidency, Colombia rather abruptly broke diplomatic relations with Castro on March 23, 1981. Although careful to note that Colombia's action had "nothing to do" with the ideology of the Cuban government, President Turbay could not ignore the military's charge that Colombian guerrillas who invaded the country had been trained in Cuba.

The United States is also concerned with Colombia as one of the few surviving democratic systems in Latin America. It is widely believed that the United States exerted a positive influence in the area of human rights during the Carter administration. Torture and disregard for individual rights had become a real issue following Turbay's implementation of a controversial security statute in 1978. The emphasis on human rights had a salutary effect on reinforcing Colombia's adherence to the principles of due process of law at a time when the military was assuming a greater role in the administration of justice. United States policy had a supportive effect that is evident in Colombia's subsequent initiatives within the Andean Pact to strengthen the democratic system as a "essential means" to obtain the subregion's economic, social, and cultural development. Both the Panama Declaration of October 1979 and the Santa Cruz Declaration of January 1980 reaffirm the conviction that "representative, social and participatory democracy is the most appropriate means for the realization of Latin America's development."[29]

Economically, Colombia is important to the United States because of its proximity to Venezuela and also because it is probable that Colombia will become the third largest coal exporter in the world by the end of the decade. Moreover, Colombia is the fourth most populous nation in Latin America after Brazil, Mexico, and Argentina, as well as the continent's fourth largest country, two facts that in themselves call attention to its economic importance as a market for U.S. goods. The United States supports

Colombia's goal of economic development, although there is occasional disagreement over the most suitable means to accomplish it. The United States should continue to be Colombia's major trading partner; however, American industries must become more competitive. Colombia's current investment code welcomes foreign capital, subject to regulations established by Andean Pact codes and certain guidelines set forth in the country's national development plan. There has never been an expropriation in Colombia of a foreign investment, and there are no outstanding investment disputes between American companies and the Colombian government.

Underlying many bilateral issues is the feeling on the part of some Colombian officials that the press in the United States frequently represents only a "populist" point of view, advocating facile, radical solutions to complex problems. They argue that Colombia's praiseworthy initiatives in support of human rights concerns, democratic institutions, and the country's fundamental commitment to international organizations as a means of ensuring international peace and hemispheric security have been over-shadowed by the coverage of guerrilla activity and drug-related violence.

The United States has dissipated much of the goodwill it generated immediately following the ratification of the Panama Canal Treaty. In retrospect, President López may have been overly optimistic when he viewed the approval of the treaty as the beginning of a new era in relations between the United States and Latin America:

> I would describe what has just taken place as a thawing, because by renouncing the rights specifically obtained by the 1903 treaty, the United States proves that equality between Latin American countries and the United States does exist. I hope that this will extend to other fields, such as trade relations, especially modification of the protectionist position often adopted by the United States toward our products.[30]

Since the Good Neighbor Policy, each U.S. president has imprinted his own personal concept—within certain general guidelines—on relations with Latin America. However, policy cannot consistently be reduced to simple words of affection that are divorced from reality. The basis of mutual understanding and some measure of predictability of response in relationships eventually require that deeds become more important than slogans and symbols. Latin Americans still remember how President Eisenhower spoke in cordial terms and made almost daily overtures toward them. However, this did not keep him from supporting dictatorial regimes and ignoring pleas for economic assistance. In some respects, "the wine is still bitter." The foreign policy positions adopted by the Reagan administration, particularly the linkage between security considerations and economic assistance, are somewhat reminiscent of the attitudes that prevailed during the Eisenhower era.

The United States does not have a "Colombian policy" as such, but tends to view the country in the broader context of relations with Latin America as a whole. As a consequence, the United States continues to appear insensitive to Colombia's importance to its security and trade interests in the hemisphere. Colombia is not presently in a position to offer economic assistance on a level with Mexico, Venezuela, or Canada. However, its exclusion from the Caribbean basin consultative meeting of foreign ministers with Secretary of State Haig in Nassau in July 1981 was a diplomatic oversight on the part of the United States that typifies its bilateral relations with Colombia. Colombia warranted an invitation to participate in the discussion not only for its strategic location, but, more importantly, in recognition of its basic adherence to democratic principles at a time in history and in a region of Latin America where support for the simplest of rights is routinely classified as subversion.

NOTES

1. Two of Colombia's last three presidents, Misael Pastrana Borrero and Julio César Turbay Ayala, served as ambassadors to the United States.

2. See, for example, the issue of *Newsweek* for February 9, 1981, and *Time's* feature article on cocaine, July 6, 1981.

3. *New York Times,* September 21, 1975, p. 10.

4. *El Tiempo,* April 4, 1978, p. 1. The memorandum was prepared by Peter Bourne, a narcotics expert during the Carter administration.

5. *El Espectador,* January 29, 1979, p. 4.

6. *El Siglo,* January 27, 1979, p. 2.

7. No one knows the amount of Colombia's cash flow from the illegal drug traffic. Colombia's total legal exports in 1980 were approximately $3 billion, of which coffee exports accounted for $1.8 billion. Estimates of illicit drug exports range from $1.6 billion to $4 billion, of which an estimated $600,000 stays in Colombia for local investment in such areas as real estate and construction. A portion of foreign currency receipts from contraband activities enters into official channels through the "open" window of the Central Bank, labeled as tourism or other such services. Much of what returns to Colombia is spent on conspicuous consumption. While contraband activities in general and the drug trade in particular have contributed to Colombia's current balance of payments surplus of $5.4 billion, the inflow of illicit funds has also had serious inflationary effects on the economy.

8. Total funding for FY 1972–77 was $6 million, with $2.5 million allocated in FY 1978 and $3.8 in 1979. Colombia received $16 million in FY 1980 as the result of special concern by members of Congress representing districts heavily affected by the drug traffic, for example, Representative Lester Wolff, chairman of the House Subcommittee on Narcotics. This unusually large appropriation was directed for use in training and the purchase of small aircraft, patrol boats, and telecommunications equipment for narcotics interdiction. Colombia had been using World War II surplus radar equipment, which in 1979 was operational for only 45 days.

9. Cited in testimony by former ambassador Diego Asencio before the U.S. Senate Permanent Subcommittee on Investigations of the Committee on Governmental Affairs, July 12, 1979. Asencio's prepared statement on the corrosive effects of illegal narcotics profits on the economic and social structures of Colombia is an invaluable starting point for anyone wishing to

pursue the topic. It is reproduced, along with the ambassador's testimony, in the *Congressional Record* for July 12, 1979, pp. 201–19.

10. For a recent article on the profitability of growing marijuana in California and the casual attitude of drug enforcement officials, see Jay Mathews, "California Growers Find Raising Marijuana Nets Them a Pot of Gold," *Washington Post*, July 6, 1981, p. A2.

11. The text of the treaty and accompanying documents are still under an injunction of secrecy. The content of the former with respect to the protection of fishing rights and the maintenance of navigational aids was ascertained from the presidential message requesting ratification, transmitted to the Senate and printed in the *Congressional Record* for January 9, 1973, pp. 587–88. The content of additional articles pertaining to the extent of the territorial seas and the rights of coastal states was translated by the author from a copy of the treaty in Spanish provided by the Colombian Foreign Ministry.

12. *El Tiempo*, March 17, 1978, pp. 1, 8.

13. *El Tiempo*, December 21, 1979, p. 1.

14. The percentages are taken from data provided by the Colombian Administrative Department of National Statistics (DANE) and the Colombian Foreign Trade Institute.

15. *El Tiempo*, December 31, 1977, p. 8.

16. *El Siglo*, January 16, 1978, p. 2.

17. *El Tiempo*, October 19, 1978, p. 6; *Latin America Economic Report*, November 24, 1978, p. 367.

18. For an explanation of the code and also a concise summary of the U.S. Trade Agreements Act of 1979, see *Subsidies and Countervailing Measures*, Vol. I (Washington, D.C.: U.S. Department of Commerce, 1981).

19. *Foreign Economic Trends and Their Implications for the United States: Colombia* (Washington, D.C.: U.S. Department of Commerce, May 1981), pp. 5–6.

20. H.J. Maidenberg, "Colombia Explains Aid Refusal," *New York Times*, October 4, 1975, p. 40.

21. *El Tiempo*, November 9, 1978, p. 8.

22. *El Espectador*, June 10, 1981, p. 6.

23. Graham Hovey, "Hispanic-American Turns Down Envoy's Post Amid Controversy," *New York Times*, June 13, 1977, p. 1.

24. *La República*, July 8, 1977, p. 1.

25. *El Tiempo*, January 6, 1978, p. 1.

26. *El Tiempo*, February 22, 1980, p. 4.

27. The data are taken from *Communist Aid to the Less Developed Countries of the Free World* (Washington, D.C.: CIA, 1976), p. 10; and *Communist Aid Activities in Non-Communist Less Developed Countries, 1979 and 1954–79* (Washington, D.C.: CIA, 1980), p. 22. The figures represent minimum estimates of the number of students present for a period of one month or more. Approximately half of Colombia's students receive training in the Soviet Union. The rest are scattered throughout Eastern Europe.

28. *El Espectador*, June 9, 1981, p. 1.

29. *El Tiempo*, January 16, 1980, pp. 1, 8.

30. *El Espectador*, April 19, 1978, p. 1.

7

Panama: Restive Client

Steve C. Ropp

Many recent analyses of U.S. power and influence in Latin America stress economic sources and the maintenance of a "neocolonial" pattern of relations in which the politico-military dimension of influence is derived from an underlying structure of capitalist domination and exploitation. This perspective may have some utility for relations with specific countries during specific historical periods; however, it is not an adequate framework for understanding either historical or contemporary patterns of U.S. influence in Panama. While Panama has been (and continues to be) a magnet for U.S. investment, prior strategic interest and the attendent application of military power nurtured such an economic climate.

In pursuing these military and strategic interests during the nineteenth and early twentieth centuries, the United States created a set of politico-military relationships with Panama that insured the successful exercise of influence. During the late 1970s, changes in the conception of U.S. strategic interests led to the passage of two new canal treaties. These treaties contain seeds for modification of traditional politico-military influence patterns. With modification of these traditional patterns, the exercise of U.S. influence during the 1980s becomes more problematic.

TRADITIONAL POLITICO-MILITARY INFLUENCE PATTERNS AND THEIR RECENT MODIFICATION

United States influence in Panama originally derived not so much from what was bestowed through mechanisms such as investment and foreign aid, but from what was denied. Most importantly, the United States prevented the development of two domestic institutions critical in the process of establishing national political and economic autonomy. First, the Panamanian armed forces were disbanded and only gradually replaced by a national guard. Second, labor unions were divided into "domestic" unions and those associated with the canal and banana enclaves. Given these limitations placed on the development of domestic institutions (limitations that persisted through the 1960s), a power vacuum was maintained that facilitated the exercise of U.S. influence.

At the time of the 1903 Revolution, the Colombian army garrison was commanded by General Esteban Huertas. By switching to the side of the revolutionaries, he became a national hero and was retained as commander-in-chief of the first Panamanian army. However, Huertas was neither a native-born Panamanian nor a member of the urban upper class. Thus, his potential ability to mobilize a mass-based following was viewed with suspicion by the members of the Conservative party who initially controlled the government. From the standpoint of the United States, the existence of any army presented a potential challenge to the U.S. military forces that were brought in to defend the newly created Canal Zone. Consequently, the armed forces were disbanded in November 1904 through mutual agreement between U.S. representatives and members of Panama's urban commercial elite.[1]

With the disbanding of the armed forces, a critical power imbalance was created that facilitated the exercise of U.S. influence until quite recently. The national police force that replaced the Panamanian army was extremely small and was kept under the watchful eye of U.S. authorities. Police units were directly under North American control because their superintendent was a U.S. citizen. Their total subjugation to outside authority came in 1913 after a number of incidents involving Panamanian and Canal Zone police. At that time, the Springfield rifles of the Panamanian police were shipped to the Zone and they were left with only a few rifles with bolts removed.

Many Panamanians believe that their government concluded a formal or informal agreement with the United States to ensure that the National Police would never become larger than half a division.[2] Whether true or not, the National Guard emerged during the 1950s as an expanded and more highly trained successor to the police. By 1978, the Guard contained 9,000 men, 2,000 of whom were members of military combat units. Due to the advent of the cold war, the U.S. government facilitated this growth. However, military aid was not given to Panama at levels commensurate with the high levels of economic aid granted after World War II. Panama ranked only ninth among Latin American recipients of U.S. military sales (per capita) between 1946 and 1975, and tenth in military grants.[3]

Following Panamanian independence in 1903, the growth of domestic labor unions was similarly inhibited by U.S. action if not intention. A major factor contributing to the weakness of organized labor was the origins of the urban laboring class. During the late nineteenth century, this work force was expanded as part of the foreign-directed effort to upgrade the Isthmian transit route through the construction of a railroad and later a canal. Laborers were imported by the French and North Americans from the Antilles, and this class remained racially and culturally isolated from the rest of the Panamanian population. When the Canal Zone was established, the predominantly Black Antillean work force was brought under U.S. jurisdiction. As unions were formed during the 1940s and 1950s, they were incorporated into U.S. confederations; thus, the Panamanian labor movement remained jurisdictionally divided.

United States influence in Panamanian labor organizations was based on the existence of clearly delineated labor enclaves. Antillean workers in the Canal Zone were paid lower wages than their North American counterparts and segregated from the white population. Nevertheless, they had more in common with the white Zone population than with their fellow Panamanian citizens. Enclave relationships with Panamanian labor also extended into the banana zones near the Costa Rican border. Here, the laboring class was drawn either from Antilleans or from Indian tribes in the area that had minimal ties to the national government.

These historical constraints on the Panamanian armed forces and labor movement created a domestic political context in which U.S. influence could be more easily exercised. The local urban commercial elites who controlled the government were racially, culturally, and socially isolated from the urban working class and vulnerable to unrest within this class because of the small size of the National Police. Unable to adequately protect themselves, they had to rely on officials in the Canal Zone for such protection.[4]

Recent events have eroded this traditional power imbalance and hence weakened U.S. influence. The National Guard emerged during the 1970s as a key political actor, capable of challenging U.S. interests on occasion, and intent on restructuring the domestic political relationships between various classes and institutions. When Omar Torrijos seized power in 1968, the Guard systematically set about limiting the influence of the urban commercial elite that retained close ties to the United States. As a counterbalance to the influence of both the elite and the U.S. government, Torrijos also began to develop closer relations with organized labor. In 1970 he established a major new labor confederation called the National Central of Panamanian Workers (CNTP). Control of CNTP allowed the regime to offset U.S. and elite influence by diminishing the traditionally central role of the Confederation of Workers of the Republic of Panama (CTRP) (see Table 7.1), which had been formed in the 1950s under conditions that made it quite responsive to elite and U.S. interests.

Table 7.1 Panamanian Labor Confederations (1978)

Name	Number of Members	
Confederation of Workers of the Republic of Panama (CTRP)	22,101	Influential in enterprises controlled by the urban commercial elite (e.g., meat processing and beverages) and in the Canal area
National Central of Panamanian Workers (CNTP)	21,629	Strength is in the banana zones; controlled by the government through the Communist party
Panamanian Central of Transport Workers (CPTT)	4,690	Established in 1975; controlled by the government
Isthmian Central of Workers (CIT)	3,906	Allied with the Christian Democrats; most influential in commercial activities and the service sector
Authentic Central of Independent Workers (CATI)	2,775	Independent; not officially recognized by the government

Source: Sección de Estadísticas Laborales, Ministerio de Trabajo y Bienestar Social, "Las organizaciones sindicales en Panamá," 1978, p. 11.

Another development that could lead to a further loss of U.S. influence within the Panamanian labor sector was ratification of new Panama Canal treaties in 1978. While treaty-implementing legislation makes it clear that the U.S. government is intent on retaining direct administrative control over the labor force of the Panama Canal Commission, the long-run impact of the treaties may be to pull these workers into the Panamanian orbit.[5] The Republic of Panama may at some future point challenge U.S. rights to organize and control labor organizations within its sovereign territory. Some labor leaders representing commission employees believe that closer ties with the Panamanian labor movement would increase their bargaining leverage within the commission.

The traditional pattern of U.S. influence based on the limited role played by Panamanian military and labor organizations was thus drastically altered during the 1970s. The National Guard emerged as an institution not only intent on controlling organized labor, but also willing to use it as a counterweight to the urban commercial elite and the United States. The power vacuum that existed in previous decades is now largely filled, and the Panamanian political system has come to more closely resemble its neighbors in Latin America, with a full complement of military and civilian institutions. The one remaining constant in this altered pattern of politico-military relations is the continued presence of U.S. troops at a number of military installations within the Canal Area. As long as these troops remain (i.e., until the year 2000), the potential for exercising the most direct form of international "influence" remains.

SOURCES OF ECONOMIC INFLUENCE

Examining Panama's pattern of economic relations with the United States since independence, the most striking feature is the extremely high level of U.S. participation in the economy. There have been massive U.S. direct private investments, intensive trade, and relatively large amounts of foreign aid. However, it should be kept in mind that it was the prior emergence of U.S. strategic interests that led to the present economic configuration rather than the reverse.

Using data on direct investment, trade, and aid patterns from 1950 to 1973, Neil R. Richardson concludes that Panama's economic dependence on the United States during this period was higher than that of any other country in the world.[6] Richardson's data also indicate that Panamanian dependence, while fluctuating considerably over the years, experienced an overall decline. Nevertheless, a strong prima facie case is presented for the existence of considerable U.S. influence (see Figure 7.1). Perhaps Richardson's most important finding is that this high level of economic dependence did not translate into support for the United States in the United Nations on cold war issues. He calculates coefficients of compliance for U.N. votes during this period and discovers that Panama's compliance level is lower than that of many other Third World countries.[7] Richardson's general conclusion is that nowhere in the Third World does economic dependence on the United States make much difference in terms of compliant voting in the United Nations.

Several observations concerning Richardson's study are in order. First, it could be argued that United Nations voting would not be the ideal place to discover compliant behavior if in fact it exists. United Nations voting by its very nature is a highly public form of activity, and thus compliance can prove internationally and/or domestically embarrassing to the dependent country. Second, the dominant power might feel that it could regularly tolerate noncompliance in the marginal arena of U.N. voting in exchange for compliance in more important (yet less visible) ways.

Regardless of whether the U.S. economic presence in Panama

Figure 7.1 Four Cases of Unstable Dependence

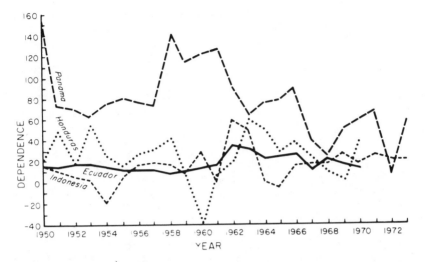

Source: Neil R. Richardson, *Foreign Policy and Economic Dependence* (Austin, Texas: University of Texas Press, 1978), p. 111. Reprinted with permission. Copyright © The University of Texas Press.

influences behavior, it should be noted that this presence is extensive. By 1978 Panama ranked third among all Latin American countries in terms of absolute level of U.S. direct investment (see Table 7.2). Direct investment in 1978 equalled total investment in all the rest of Central America and Peru combined. On a per capita basis, U.S.-Panama investment led all Latin American countries with over $1,300 per person. This level was eight times higher than that of its nearest competitor (Venezuela), and twenty times that of per capita investment levels in Brazil and Mexico.[8]

The rapid growth of U.S. direct investment during the 1960s and 1970s was largely the result of Panama's emergence as a center for export by multinational corporations of goods and services to Latin America. Panama became the center of an expanding "Latindollar" market. Since the U.S. dollar served as Panamanian currency, and since the Isthmus operated within the same time zone as major New York banks, Panama could service dollar transactions overseas profitably (beyond the reach of United States regulations). By 1979 there were 33 U.S. banks operating in Panama with combined assets of $12 billion.

Although direct private investment and its attendant banking and commercial activities are the most obvious components of the U.S. presence in the Panamanian economy, there are several others that deserve attention. During the 1970s, both Panamanian imports from and exports to the United

Table 7.2 U.S. Direct Investment in Latin America, 1929 to 1978 ($ millions)

	1929	1943	1950	1960	1970	1978
Total Latin America	3,519	2,798	4,576	9,249	14,760	32,509
Brazil	194	233	644	953	1,847	7,170
Mexico	682	286	415	795	1,786	3,712
Panama	29	110	58	405	1,251	2,385
Venezuela	233	373	993	2,569	2,704	2,015

Sources: *Multinational Corporations in Brazil and Mexico: Structural Sources of Economic and Noneconomic Power*, Report to the Subcommittee on Multinational Corporations of the Committee on Foreign Relations, U.S. Senate (August 1975), p. 36; *Survey of Current Business*, Bureau of Economic Analysis, U.S. Department of Commerce (August 1979), p. 27.

States and the Canal Zone remained important, although declining as a percentage of total Panamanian world trade. Imports from the U.S. declined from 40.1 percent in 1970 to 33 percent by 1978. Exports to the U.S. dropped during the same period from 65.9 to 55 percent, with most of the slack being picked up by neighboring Latin American countries.[9]

Another potential source of influence is U.S. public economic assistance. Examining the pattern of U.S. government aid to various Latin American countries since World War II, one can see that Panama has been very favorably treated. To bolster its security position and influence, the United States has given a country with a relatively high per capita income large amounts of per capita economic assistance.[10]

THE MYTH OF CULTURAL INFLUENCE

The need to rationalize dominant-subordinate relationships often leads to a myth of cultural influence, the feeling that the demonstrated merits of a "higher civilization" will be apparent to the weaker partner. This belief has been particularly appealing to residents of the former Canal Zone, whose most frequent point of contact with "Panama" was with the English-speaking Antillean workers in the canal area. The temptation to blur the line between military-economic and cultural sources of influence can even be seen in the writings of sophisticated diplomatic observers of U.S.-Panamanian relations:

Through the years of the digging of the Canal and since the opening of that great waterway in 1914, Panama has lived in a symbiotic relationship with its huge hemispheric neighbor to the North. It sells most of its products there ... and buys most of its imports from U.S. suppliers .... And U.S. colleges and universities remain the academic Mecca for the vast majority of Panamanian students studying abroad—especially in the technical fields of medicine and dentistry, engineering, architecture, as well as in law and business administration.[11]

This temptation to believe that Panamanians are culturally attracted to U.S. education must be tempered by an understanding of Panama's past struggle to achieve political and cultural autonomy, first from Colombia and later from the United States. With the influx of North American and Antillean workers into the urban area during the late nineteenth century, Hispanic Panamanians began to feel overwhelmed by English culture. They were resentful not only of the job displacement that occurred but also of the creeping inroads made by the English language. As early as 1914, a law was adopted to encourage the preservation and strengthening of the Spanish tongue. Under this law, all locations with only English names were given Spanish ones and these were to be taught in the public schools.

By the early 1920s a movement called Community Action had been formed that aimed specifically at restoring the paramount position of Spanish culture. This movement eventually came to be led by Arnulfo Arias, who gained a huge following among residents of the interior and former rural dwellers who had migrated to Panama City and Colón. Arias was elected president on three separate occasions, the last time in 1968. During his first presidential term (1940 to 1941), his firebrand cultural nationalism became such a threat to the United States and the urban commercial elite that he was overthrown by a force of arms.

While the overwhelming urban presence of North Americans and Antilleans encouraged a strong cultural backlash during these decades, it is also true that a relatively large number of high Panamanian government officials were influenced by U.S. education. If one examines the educational background of Panamanian presidents since 1903, two distinct periods stand out. For several decades, Colombian degrees were predominant. However, beginning in 1924, U.S. and Panamanian degrees replaced them. Of the 12 constitutional presidents between 1924 and 1978, five received at least part of their education in the United States (see Table 7.3).

If there was in fact a "golden age" of U.S. education for Panamanian government officials, it is rapidly coming to an end. When Torrijos came to power in 1968, he ceased to rely exclusively on the urban commercial elite as a pool of administration talent. Since it was this elite whose educational ties were closest to the United States, the links of top leadership with the United States have become increasingly tenuous in recent years. This trend becomes clear when one looks at the educational background of high-ranking National Guard officers and of those who have recently occupied high government positions (see Table 7.4).

Unfortunately, the idea of North American cultural influence rests upon

Table 7.3 Constitutional Presidents of The Republic of Panama: 1903 to 1981

President	Education	
1. Manuel Amador Guerrero	Colombia	
2. José D. de Obaldía	Colombia	
3. Belisario Porras	Colombia	1903 to 1924
4. Ramón Valdés	Colombia	
5. Belisario Porras	Colombia	
6. Rodolfo Chiari	Panama	
7. Florencio H. Arosemena	Germany	
8. Harmodio Arias Madrid	England	
9. Juan D. Arosemena	Panama	
10. Arnulfo Arias Madrid	United States	
11. Domingo Díaz Arosemena	United States	
12. José Antonio Remón Cantera	Mexico	1924 to present
13. Ernesto de la Guardia Jr.	United States	
14. Roberto F. Chiari Remón	Panama	
15. Marco Aurelio Robles	Panama	
16. Arnulfo Arias Madrid	United States	
17. Demetrio Lakas	United States	
18. Arístides Royo	Spain	

Source: Joaquin A. Ortega C., *Gobernantes de la Republica de Panama: 1903–1960* (Panamá: 1960).

Table 7.4 Educational Background of National Guard and Government Leaders (1975)

Country/Area where highest degree obtained	National Guard	Government	Total
United States	0	4	4
Latin America	16	2	18
Western Europe	0	4	4
Panama	6	12	18

Note: Leaders of the National Guard include members of the General Staff and troop commanders. Government leaders include all cabinet officers and heads of autonomous government agencies.

Source: Renato Pereira, *Panamá: Fuerzas Armadas y politica* (Panamá: Ediciones Nueva Universidad, 1979), pp. 142–47.

a dangerous tendency to equate power with cultural virtue. The strong politico-military and economic presence of the United States has often led Panamanian leaders to put on their North American "face." There are also many superficial aspects of U.S. culture that have been adopted in a faddish fashion by Panamanians and can give the impression of deeper cultural ties. It is a mistake to assume that such cultural influence translates directly into political influence.

CASE STUDIES OF RECENT U.S. INFLUENCE

The purpose of the following section is to examine the nature of contemporary U.S. influence in Panama by studying a number of cases of foreign and domestic policymaking. A major working premise of this section is that there is often an inverse relationship between the importance of the policy being pursued and the diplomatic visibility it is given. It should be kept in mind that such influence is being discussed in relation to a particular regime. Influence vis-a-vis the regime cannot be assumed to reflect U.S. influence with the numerous dissenting counterelites or among Panamanians as a whole. This observation is particularly important in light of General Torrijos's death in July 1981 and the heightened probability of regime change.

Panama's Activities within the Caribbean Basin

One of the most important arenas for U.S. and Panamanian foreign policy decision making during the past several years has been the Caribbean basin. Beginning in 1978 with the concerted effort launched by the Sandinistas to overthrow the government of Anastasio Somoza, there has been an ongoing struggle to determine whether the countries in and around the area would be controlled by regimes responsive to the strategic and economic interests of the United States or responsive to hostile powers such as Cuba and the Soviet Union. From the start, Panama played a role in this struggle. To what extent were its actions influenced by the attitudes and perceptions of U.S. government officials?

At the outset, it must be recognized that General Torrijos and the Panamanians had an independent perception of the problem in Nicaragua. For Torrijos, the problem was largely Anastasio Somoza himself. Since the early 1970s, Somoza had treated Torrijos as an authoritarian neophyte whose ideological credentials were also suspect. One action that greatly angered Torrijos was the Nicaraguan dictator's effort to convince U.S. financiers to bankroll construction of a new sea-level canal through Nicaragua. After the extremely thorough U.S. government study of alternative canal routes was released in 1970, there was little real hope that Nicaragua would be selected. However, the possibility of that construction was used by certain U.S. members of Congress to argue against a new Panama Canal treaty.

Thus, when the September 1978 uprisings occurred, Torrijos was more than ready to contribute to the Sandinista cause. His first step was to contract with suppliers in the United States for $4 million worth of small arms. Working through the Panamanian consul in Miami (who was a former officer in military intelligence), seven arms shipments were arranged. These arms were sent to the Panama Hunting and Fishing Club, whose principal stockholder was the head of the Panamanian Intelligence. Torrijos formed a semiclandestine military unit called the Victoriano Lorenzo Brigade.[12] As leader, he chose Hugo Spadafora, who had served in the government as vice-minister of health. Spadafora had also been a volunteer medical doctor in Guinea-Bissau during the mid-1960s. There he had worked with the guerrilla army of Amílcar Cabral, which was attempting to liberate this former Portuguese colony.

In October 1978 Spadafora traveled with a number of volunteers to a penal colony run by the Panamanian National Guard on the island of Coiba. After three weeks of training, 65 of these volunteers were infiltrated through Costa Rica into Nicaragua. Apparently, this initial contingent (expanded by the time Somoza was overthrown to approximately 200) contained a number of National Guard personnel. These troops "retired" from the Guard prior to volunteering, and were most likely included to handle the heavy weapons.

After the overthrow of Somoza in July 1979, the Panamanian regime continued its military involvement in Nicaragua but with quite different results. Since the Victoriano Lorenzo Brigade was partially composed of military personnel, Torrijos volunteered the services of 43 members for training of the Sandinista militias and police. In September 1979, 100 Nicaraguan policemen were graduated from the new César Augusto Sandino Police Training Center in a ceremony that was attended by the Panamanian personnel who had trained them.

However, by December 1979 the honeymoon period between the Sandinistas and the Torrijos regime was over and Panamanian advisers were sent home. Sandinista leaders such as Tomás Borge had most likely concluded that allowing Panama too extensive a training role risked strengthening the hand of moderate Social Democrats such as Eden Pastora, whom Torrijos supported. By January 1980 the Panamanian advisers had been replaced by Cubans. This turn of events apparently led Torrijos to conclude that the "ideological pluralism" being espoused by the Sandinistas was somewhat narrower than he had been led to believe, and that Fidel Castro constituted a new Nicaraguan problem created in the wake of Somoza's demise.

How (if at all) was U.S. influence brought to bear on Panama in this rapidly developing situation? First, it would seem that Torrijos was prevented from engaging in a more open military intervention against Somoza due to pressures directly exerted by President Jimmy Carter. By fall 1978 the new canal treaties had been ratified by the Senate, but the crucial implementing legislation had not been passed by the House. Some House members (who felt that they had not been given their say in the ratification process) believed that this implementing legislation could be used to undermine the treaties. Given this fact, the U.S. executive branch felt that any attempt by Torrijos to intervene in Nicaragua would have a disastrous effect on congressional action. In September Torrijos was directly warned by the White House of the pending problem.[13]

There is thus good evidence that the U.S. government had an impact on the style of Panamanian intervention in Nicaragua. The government may have had an impact on substance, although this is more difficult to document. Some of the evidence suggests that Torrijos may have been partially responding to U.S. interests by intervening in Nicaragua on the side of the Social Democrats within the Sandinista coalition. Through such intervention and the subsequent training of Sandinista police, U.S. weapons could be supplied and the Cubans presumably denied access. It is certainly difficult to believe that the Carter administration was unaware of the arms shipments from Miami and the purpose to which these arms might be put.

After Panama's displacement by Cuba as the major source of Sandinista military and police training, there is clearer evidence of Panamanian support for the U.S. position in the Caribbean basin. Perhaps as a response to growing concern over Cuban influence in Central America, or as a means of personally getting even with Castro, Torrijos began to direct more attention to the island nations. In February 1980 the National Guard contracted to train police from Grenada. It is important to keep in mind not only that the Grenadian government had recently fallen under the influence of the left-leaning New Jewel Movement, but also that the U.S. government was prevented by Congress from training police contingents in Latin American countries.[14]

Another critical arena for recent U.S.-Panamanian foreign policy interaction has been El Salvador. By October 1979 the Salvadoran armed forces became sufficiently alarmed by the overthrow of Somoza and the rising tide of guerrilla activity in their own country to remove General Carlos Humberto Romero from the presidency. With the support of the United States, a sweeping land reform program was implemented that undermined the position of the traditional oligarchy. Nevertheless, the violence continued and El Salvador became a regional focal point for U.S. attention under the incoming Reagan administration.

From Torrijos's standpoint, El Salvador was a quite different case from

Nicaragua. For one thing, the second Salvadoran junta (installed just two-and-one-half months after the first) included two members of the Christian Democratic party. To support the junta meant indirectly supporting the Christian Democrats, and this created domestic political problems for the regime. Not only was the Panamanian Christian Democratic party a strong opponent of Torrijos's policies, but it was also beginning to show signs of real electoral strength. It did particularly well in the "training elections" held in September 1980.

Discussing Panama's support for the U.S. position in El Salvador is particularly difficult because of the paucity of reliable information.[15] It would appear that Torrijos attempted to maintain his ties with the Social Democratic Left in El Salvador while at the same time remaining unwilling to supply substantial military aid to their guerrilla cadres. Although there were hints in late 1980 and early 1981 that Panama might send an international brigade to El Salvador under the leadership of Spadafora, and a Panamanian airplane loaded with ammunition was seized in 1980 by the Salvadoran army, there was little evidence of direct military involvement.

However, Torrijos's diplomatic involvement was more extensive. Because of his contacts with Latin American and West European Social Democrats and his familiarity with Salvadoran military officers (from his academy days), Torrijos was uniquely qualified to play the role of mediator in the search for a long-term negotiated settlement. For example, in December 1980 he met in Panama with former Venezuelan President Carlos Andres Pérez, former Bolivian President Hernán Siles Suazo, Secretary-General of the Dominican Revolutionary party José Francisco Peña Gómez, and the Secretary-General of the Spanish Socialist party Felipe Gonzáles. Also on hand were a former member of the Salvadoran junta (Colonel Adolfo Majano) and representatives of the Sandinistas.[16]

Was Torrijos influenced by the United States in his behavior toward El Salvador? First, it can be noted that he was willing to play the role of intermediary for the Carter administration between the United States and leaders of the Salvadoran Social Democratic left such as Guillermo Ungo and Adolfo Majano. Second, the Panamanian government was willing to tolerate the use of U.S. military bases in the Canal Area for the training of Salvadoran military personnel. Panama may have had little choice in this matter, given the U.S. treaty rights, but it could have made things considerably more difficult.

There is also some evidence to suggest that Torrijos may have been successfully pressured by the Reagan administration on El Salvador. According to Colombian writer Gabriel Garcia Márquez, Torrijos was given a note in February 1981 from Secretary of State Alexander Haig that criticized Panama for maintaining friendly relations with Cuba. The letter also alleged that Panama had allowed itself to be used as a conduit for arms shipments from Cuba to the Salvadoran guerrillas.[17] Although the Panamanian government publicly criticized this U.S. meddling in its affairs, the advice on Cuba seems to have been taken to heart. Following Colombian accusations in March that Cuba was arming and training M–19 guerrillas, Panama announced that it was reviewing its relations with the Castro government. Diplomatic relations were not completely severed, but Torrijos clearly indicated that he was displeased with the continued Cuban role in Central America and with Castro's opposition to negotiate political solution to the conflict in El Salvador.[18]

Viewing the evidence from the Nicaraguan and Salvadoran cases, one can conclude that Panama has been more inclined toward being "influenced" when its own foreign policy positions parallel those of the United States.[19] In Nicaragua, Panama was willing to modify its style of intervention to suit the needs of the Carter administration and to extend its military support to the Sandinistas after the revolution, in partial reflection of U.S. interests. In the Salvadoran case, the domestic political problems created for the Torrijos regime by Christian Democratic participation in the second junta made it impossible (ideology aside) to fully support the U.S.-sponsored government. Nevertheless, Panama did not go as far as it might have in supplying military aid to the left.

With the advent of the Reagan administration, Panama moved even further toward a foreign policy in the Caribbean basin that paralleled U.S. interests. However, it should be recognized that this shift to the right responded as much to Panamanian perception of the evolving situation in Central America as to U.S. pressure. Torrijos was angered by the covert Cuban support given to Salvadoran guerrillas for their "final offensive" at a time when he was still working toward a negotiated solution. Panama's perception of the Cuban threat was further heightened during spring 1981 by the attack on U.S. embassy marine guards in Costa Rica and by the above-mentioned M-19 guerrilla operation that was launched from Panamanian territory.

Panama's Behavior in International Forums

To what extent has the United States been able to influence Panamanian foreign policy behavior within international forums? Has Panama generally been supportive of U.S. policy initiatives and goals? As with issues affecting the Caribbean basin, the answers to these questions are complex, with Panamanian behavior and levels of support contingent upon a host of often case-specific factors. There is, for example, little evidence that Panama has systematically supported U.S. positions on Latin American issues in the United Nations General Assembly since 1975. The two countries voted in tandem on only 4 of 17 resolutions concerning the area between 1975 and 1979.[20]

However, if one looks at Panama's global pattern of diplomatic relations, a different picture of U.S. influence emerges. Panama considers itself to be a member of the nonaligned movement and thus theoretically balanced in terms of its relations with the superpower blocs. Yet, while Panama has diplomatic relations with all of the major capitalist powers, it has none with either the Soviet Union or the People's Republic of China. In Eastern Europe, Panama recognizes Czechoslovakia, Hungary, Romania, Poland, and Albania, but not East Germany and Bulgaria. It is clear that this particular "nonaligned" country has a pattern of diplomatic relations that is skewed toward the West.

Numerous specific cases of behavior in the international arena can be cited as examples of Panamanian support for, or opposition to, clearly stated U.S. policy positions. Lack of influence (not only by the United States but also by a number of other Western powers) is demonstrated by Panamanian behavior following the hijacking of a Honduran passenger plane in March 1981 by leftists. The airplane first flew to Nicaragua, where it remained for 34 hours and then left for Panama. Although the Panamanian government received strong notes of protest from the United States, West Germany, France, and Canada arguing that the hijackers should be prosecuted according to international agreements, they did not proceed as recommended. In this particular case, Panama's perception of itself as an asylum for political figures of all ideological persuasions probably conditioned the negative reaction.

In spite of such obvious cases of lack of influence, the overall pattern appears to be as follows: Panama will support the United States in regional and global arenas on critical matters and do what it pleases on marginal issues. For example, it is clear that one of the basic goals of the United States in the Central American region has been to preserve the institutions through which security can be collectively pursued. At the Sixth Nonaligned Nations Conference held in September 1979 in Cuba, an effort was made to abolish the Central American Defense Council (CONDECA) and the Inter-American Reciprocal Assistance Treaty (TIAR). Panama strongly opposed this effort. Similarly, Panama has consistently supported the United States regarding the issue of Puerto Rico. It argues that Puerto Rico should retain its right to choose its own destiny. An example of a cold war issue where Panama was willing to fall in line with the United States at some cost to its self-esteem was the 1980 boycott of the Olympic Games following the Soviet invasion of Afghanistan. President Arístides Royo at first publically declared that Panama would attend, and then reversed his decision.

There can certainly be no more dramatic example of Panamanian support for the United States than its behavior during the Iranian hostage crisis. Immediately after the hostages were seized, General Torrijos and President Royo stated in a letter to Carter that they were willing to do everything in their power to help get the hostages released.[21] It was through Panamanians who visited Iran in December 1979 that the first U.S. negotiating contacts were established with the Iranian government. After the Shah moved from the United States to Panama in January 1980, the Panamanian government systematically attempted to negotiate with Iran, offering to "arrest" the Shah in exchange for a transfer of the hostages from the militants to the Iranian government.[22] And there can be no gainsaying the political cost to the Panamanian government incurred by accepting the Shah in the first place.

This particular case is instructive because it highlights a subtle yet significant aspect of influence. The Panamanians were willing to help the United States at the outset of the Iranian crisis precisely because they were not pressured to do so. For a change, the shoe was on the other foot and it was the United States that needed Panamanian help. Also important was the fact that both Carter and his aide Hamilton Jordan had established good personal relations with Torrijos. While Torrijos did not particularly respect Carter, he felt that he was an honest man who had negotiated in good faith on the canal treaties. Influence in this particular case was more a function of human relations than of the calculus of power.

Influence in Panama's Domestic Politics

During the latter half of the 1970s, the Panamanian government took a number of steps that seem to have brought certain domestic policies more in line with the wishes of the Carter administration. In the human rights area, the record of the Torrijos regime during the early 1970s was less than spectacular. The best publicized violation occurred in July 1971 when Father Hector Gallego disappeared from Santa Fe, Veraguas Province. The Catholic church and several other groups believe that this young Colombian priest (who was organizing a peasant cooperative at the time) crossed paths with a large landowner who happened to be a personal friend of Torrijos. For many, these suspicions were confirmed when a government investigation found no signs of foul play.

By the late 1970s, some of the regime's blatantly repressive activities had been curbed. While many observers attributed this change to pressure from the Carter administration (particularly within the context of the treaty negotiations), other factors need to be kept in mind. It is often the case that the most overt and extensive human rights violations occur while a new regime is consolidating its power. At this point, such brutal shows of force are deemed necessary, and they sometimes coincide with the period when the new regime has little control over its own security forces. Later, the machinery of repression is more carefully calibrated through measures such as press control and reliance on intelligence activities.

One can also ask to what extent the U.S. government was instrumental in influencing Panama in moving toward a more open political system during the late 1970s. In 1978 Torrijos gave up the extraordinary political powers that he had been granted and "returned to the barracks." He was replaced by an appointed "civilian" government headed by President Arístides Royo. The traditional parties were to be allowed to participate once again in the political process through direct presidential elections to be held in 1984.

During the late 1970s, the Carter administration did all within its power to encourage this democratic opening as part of its human rights program and effort to move Latin America away from reliance on military forms of government. As with broader human rights policy, additional leverage was available to the United States prior to passage of the treaty implementing legislation in late 1979. However, if U.S. pressure was the only determining factor in the democratic opening, a narrowing of that opening could have been expected to occur during 1980 and 1981.

The fact that the democratic opening has persisted suggests that the Torrijos regime was motivated as much by domestic considerations as by U.S. pressure. By 1975 it had become clear that the Panamanian economy was experiencing difficulties that were likely to continue for some time. This in turn raised the costs to the military leadership of direct control of the political system, and they began to search for ways to turn their problems over to the civilians. United States influence appears to have played an important but less than central role in the process of democratization not only in Panama but also in countries such as Peru.

Influence as a Two-Way Street

The above discussion would not be complete without recognition of the fact that influence flows in both directions. While it is true that the United States possesses resources that allow it to influence Panamanian decision making, the reverse is also the case. In spite of the decline in the relative strategic value of the Panama Canal, the Isthmus remains important to the United States in a number of ways.

As has been pointed out by a number of observers of international relations, the weaker partner in a dominant-subordinate relationship often paradoxically retains subtle psychological forms of bargaining power. Cal Clark and Donna Bahry have argued that there is a tendency for the Soviet Union to treat its weaker satellites more leniently than the stronger ones, not only for fear of stirring up political trouble, but also due to the belief that having to bully a small client state demonstrates ineptitude and lack of real influence.[23] In such a context, the smaller East European satellites have often been able to extract considerable economic concessions. Past U.S.-Panamanian relations reveal somewhat similar patterns. After the riots of 1964, the United States engaged in an extended process of negotiations with the Panamanian government, which culminated in the economically concessionary terms of the 1978 Panama Canal Treaty.

In addition to this psychological source of influence, Panama remains important to the United States as a strategic ally. For example, a large portion of the U.S. Effective Control Fleet is registered there. United States defense strategy since the late 1940s has assumed the availability in times of international crisis of a large number of merchant ships operating under international flags of convenience. During the 1970s the two major flags of convenience used by the United States were the Liberian and the Panamanian. However, several events occurred during the decade that made the reliability of the former seem increasingly questionable. On November 2, 1973 Liberia issued an executive order specifying that their shipping could not be used to transport materials of war to the Middle East. This measure was clearly aimed at preventing the use of U.S.-owned ships in the massive resupply of Israel. The April 1980 military coup in Liberia served to further heighten U.S. concern with that country's reliability and hence further strengthened the position of the Panamanians.[24]

Panama is also playing an increasingly important role in supplying oil to the continental United States. The oil crisis of the mid-1970s led to increased U.S. reliance on the new North Slope fields of Alaska. Since this oil was "sour" crude with a high sulphur content, most of it could not be refined in West Coast facilities geared primarily to low sulphur oil. Given the hesitancy of Canada and the western states to construct new pipelines that could transport this oil to eastern refineries, one alternative was to send it through the Panama Canal. United States merchant marine fleet owners and shipbuilders lobbied heavily to insure that the only other available option (shipping the oil to Japan in exchange for Middle Eastern oil) was not exercised.

Most analysts believe that Panama will remain important through the 1980s as a transit point for North Slope oil. Even if the contemplated North Tier pipeline is financed and completed by 1985, there is a large anticipated oil surplus that will have to be moved across the Isthmus. At present, this oil is shipped from Alaska to Panama in supertankers, where it is then transferred to medium-range tankers that can transit the canal. A $45 million onshore transshipment facility that is jointly owned by the Panamanian government and U.S. oil companies has been built in Chiriquí Province. In addition, $250 million is being spent to construct a pipeline running from this facility to the Atlantic Ocean.[25]

Beyond the obvious strategic chips that Panama has to play in the influence game, there are some not-so-obvious factors that may continue to enhance Panama's appeal as an ally. In a world where the perception of revolutionary legitimacy is an important element of influence, Panama can project such legitimacy with the best of them. Although the Torrijos regime was by no means revolutionary in political or economic terms, it managed to maintain such a global image through negotiation of the 1978 Panama Canal treaties, participation in the nonaligned movement, and in the overthrow of the Somoza dynasty. The Carter administration was particularly adept at using the Panamanian regime's legitimacy to create triangular arenas of negotiation for matters such as the Iranian hostages.

CONCLUSIONS: U.S. INFLUENCE IN THE 1980s AND BEYOND

United States influence in Panama has historically derived from the pursuit of strategic goals rather than the search for economic advantage. Thus, in evaluating future influence patterns, it is important to note changes that have occurred recently in the strategic equation. The canal treaties ratified in 1978 reflect a reduced U.S. concern for the value of the Isthmus and hence for the necessity of preserving a direct military presence. All troops will be withdrawn by the year 2000. Not only will the removal of these troops reduce U.S. influence in Panamanian affairs, but also the fore-knowledge of their removal affects current Panamanian decision making.

The Neutrality Treaty of 1978 gives the United States the right to "protect" Panama from domestic disturbances. In the 1980s Panama will respond to the perceived threat of future U.S. military intervention by adding more signatories to the protocol of the Neutrality Treaty. At the same time, the ongoing political crisis in Central America will give the regime, or any moderate successor, good reason to continue relying on the United States for direct military protection.

As for Panama's domestic policies, the major changes that have occurred in organized labor and the military leave the United States with less direct means of exercising influence. Organized labor can be expected to act more independently during the decade, and labor turbulence could at some point affect canal operations. The National Guard will probably continue its relatively independent course in both domestic and international affairs. Recent activities in the Caribbean basin indicate that Panamanian foreign policy will respond most readily to U.S. interests when it suits Panamanian purposes. Influence will be most easily exercised in specific circumstances that temporarily increase U.S. leverage.

Although U.S. influence in Panama has in the past been the product of strategic considerations, investments followed in the wake of the battleships. During the 1970s, U.S. direct private investment grew rapidly and the multinational corporations began to develop perspectives concerning the Isthmus that differed from those of U.S. government officials. Thus, although the U.S. private investment is extensive, this will not necessarily translate directly into U.S. government influence. At any rate, various measures of U.S. economic influence show a sustained decline since the 1950s. Economic sources of influences will probably continue their decline through the 1980s unless reversed by large infusions of U.S. aid.

The myth of U.S. cultural influence may be brought into sharper focus during the 1980s as Panamanian students return from the highly developed countries of Latin America, Western Europe, and the Soviet bloc. A particularly crucial factor affecting U.S. influence will be the locus of training for coming generations of Panamanian military officers. Torrijo's generation (which includes most members of the general staff and troop commanders) received semiprofessional training in the military academies of Central America during the 1950s. The successor generation will most likely be drawn from officers who were trained in Latin American academies during the 1960s and 1970s. Such generational change will gradually increase even further the psychological distance between the Panamanian military leadership and the United States.[26]

These changes, coupled with the passing of Omar Torrijos, are likely to make the 1980s a difficult time for the United States. With such dramatic shifts in the structural base for exercising influence occurring in the 1970s, increased attention will have to be devoted to the nuances of influence. In examining this process, it is hoped that the human dimension will not be ignored. If too much attention is devoted to the naive calculus of raw military and economic power, little success can be anticipated in molding a climate of influence.

NOTES

1. Ernesto J. Castillero Reyes, *Historia de Panamá* (Panamá: Impresora Panamá, S.A., 1962), p. 159.

2. Renato Pereira, *Panamá: fuerzas armadas y política* (Panamá: Ediciones Nueva Universidad, 1979), p. 21.

3. David Scott Palmer, *Peru: The Authoritarian Tradition* (New York: Praeger, 1980), p. 86.

4. Alexander Cuevas, "El movimiento inquilinario de 1925", in Ricuarte Soler (Ed.), *Panamá: dependencia y liberación* (San José, Costa Rica: Editorial Universitaria Centroamericana, 1974). A classic case occurred in 1925 when U.S. troops were brought in from the Canal Zone to supress a renters' riot.

5. A key provision of the Panama Canal Act that implements the 1978 treaties states that "Labor-management and employee relations of the Commission . . . shall be governed and

regulated solely by the applicable laws, rules, and regulations of the United States." "Panama Canal Act," in *The United States Southern Command News* (no date), p. 14.

6. Neil R. Richardson, *Foreign Policy and Economic Dependence* (Austin, Texas: University of Texas Press, 1978), p. 105.

7. Richardson, *Foreign Policy*, p. 139.

8. Inter-American Development Bank, *Economic and Social Progress in Latin America: 1978 Report* (Washington, D.C.: 1979), p. 415; and U.S. Department of Commerce, *Survey of Current Business*, August 1979, p. 27.

9. United Nations, *Yearbook of International Trade Statistics: 1979* Vol. I (New York: United Nations, 1980), p. 745.

10. Panama deviates considerably from the rest of Latin America in the receipt of U.S. aid. Not counting Panama, there is a clear tendency for the largest amounts of aid per capita to go to the poorest countries (presumably the most in need). If Panama were a "normal" Latin American country, it would be expected to receive $59 per capita in U.S. aid, approximately one-sixth of its actual aid.

11. William Jorden, *Panama Odyssey* (Austin, Texas: University of Texas Press, forthcoming).

12. For further details on activities of the Brigade, see Pedro N. Miranda M., *El pueblo que asombra al mundo* (Panamá: Talleres Diálogo, 1979); and Hugo Spadafora, *Experiencias y pensamiento de un médico guerrillero* (Panamá: Centro de Impresión Educativa, 1980).

13. *Miami Herald*, January 2, 1979, 3AW.

14. This, of course, was also true of Nicaragua.

15. The best source is Marcel A. Salamin C., *El Salvador: sin piso y sin techo* (Panamá, 1980).

16. It might be argued that Torrijos's role as a mediator in El Salvador has been somewhat exaggerated. His closest contacts within the Salvadoran military were either with senior officers who were removed from their high-ranking positions following the October 1979 coup, or with junior officers possessing little real influence in the current context (for example, Majano). Furthermore, his strongest political allies within the Caribbean basin were out-of-power politicians such as Carlos Andres Pérez.

17. *Latin American Weekly Report*, February 20, 1981.

18. *Diálogo Social*, No. 134 (May 1981), p. 11.

19. For a good theoretical treatment of the concept of parallel interests, see James A. Morris, *United States Foreign Policy in the Caribbean Basin: New Relations and Parallel Interests* (New Mexico State University: Central American Working Group, 1981).

20. These issues were ratification by the Soviet Union and France of protocols to the Treaty of Tlatelolco and establishing a United Nations trust fund for Chilean exiles; *Index to Proceedings of the General Assembly* (New York: United Nations, 1975–1979).

21. ABC Television Program "Nightline" (January 21, 1981).

22. Terence Smith, "Putting the Hostages' Lives First," *New York Times Magazine* (May 27, 1981), pp. 85–86.

23. Cal Clark and Donna Bahry, "Dependency in the Soviet Bloc: Reversal of the Economic-Political Nexus," Paper presented at the 1979 Annual Convention of the International Studies Association, Toronto, Canada.

24. For an account of recent developments affecting U.S.-Liberian-Panamanian relations, see Rodney Carlisle, "Liberia's Flag of Convenience: Rough Water Ahead," *Orbis* 24, No. 4 (Winter 1981).

25. *Business Week*, March 9, 1981, pp. 27–28.

26. It is one of the ironies of U.S.-Panamanian relations that the largely U.S-equipped and U.S.-trained National Guard has so few points of personal and diplomatic contact with the United States. It is one of the most insular military institutions in all of Latin America.

8

Nicaragua:
The Rock that Crumbled

Charles D. Ameringer

The United States has lost the overwhelming influence it once exercised in Nicaragua. Many North Americans are perplexed by this loss, particularly because U.S. policy helped to bring it about. The United States contributed to the overthrow of a repressive regime in Nicaragua, with which it had long been associated, but could no longer support without change. As should have been expected, it was easier to cause a tyranny to fall than to replace it with a government that might be forgiving, much less grateful. One could exaggerate the role of the United States in the ouster of Anastasio Somoza Debayle, but neither should one minimize it. The Sandinista National Liberation Front, dominant in Nicaragua today, prefers to ignore the part the United States played and the fundamental change of policy that took place. Fortunately, there are elements of Nicaraguan society who think differently. For this reason, it is important to review former U.S.-Nicaraguan relations, in order to understand what went wrong, and to examine more recent relations, in order to be aware of the opportunity for a new, healthy relationship.

The Nicaraguan Revolution has been an evolutionary process. The violence of the guerrillas, commencing in 1975 and climaxing in 1979, was abetted by over 40 years of institutionalized violence on the part of the regime of the Somozas. The struggle was against the exploitation of the mass of the people and the repression of the middle and upper sectors by Anastasio Somoza Garcia and his sons, Luis and Anastasio, from 1936 to 1979. It also had an anti-American aspect, because of the widespread belief that the Somoza dynasty was "made in the U.S.A."

Ever since the Hise Treaty of 1848, by which, if it had been ratified, the

United States was to receive exclusive rights for a canal across Nicaragua in return for a guarantee of Nicaraguan sovereignty, the United States has been the dominant foreign power in Nicaragua. The Grant administration enhanced the relationship by conducting surveys in Central America and declaring that Nicaragua was the best site for the construction of an isthmian canal. The United States might have built the canal in Nicaragua, except for the extraordinary efforts of Philippe Bunau-Varilla and William Nelson Cromwell, who delivered the prize to Panama.

With the construction of the Panama Canal, one might expect that Nicaragua would be resentful and that U.S. influence would diminish; but such was not the case. Nicaragua was still a possible alternate route, and it was too close to Panama to permit it to fall under anyone else's influence. Many of the policies that the United States developed to establish its hegemony in the Caribbean and to protect the approaches to the Panama Canal focused upon either Nicaragua or Cuba. The problems plaguing Central America today involving guerrilla incursions from neighboring states and the international trafficking in arms are not new. They have been chronic in the region, where political rivalries ignore national boundaries, and the ins of one state frequently assist the outs of another.

In an effort to control this violence and thereby reduce any excuse for outside meddling, the United States tried a number of schemes. It promoted the Central American Court of Justice in 1907 and encouraged U.S. private investment ("dollar diplomacy"). When all else failed, it intervened militarily. Varying numbers of U.S. marines occupied Nicaragua almost continuously from 1911 to 1933. To establish a native constabulary force to maintain law and order and to uphold constitutional government, the marines helped to train the Nicaraguan National Guard, which, after the marines left, became the personal force of a caudillo, not the defender of constitutionality.

Anastasio Somoza García used his position as commander of the National Guard to seize the presidency in 1936 and begin the Somoza dynasty. Even though the United States did not foresee this use of the Guard, Somoza was grateful and steered a decidedly pro-United States course. If the outcome was unexpected, it was not unwelcome. "Tacho" Somoza was aware of this and played the "American card" with skill. He had studied business administration in Philadelphia and sent his sons to the United States to be educated. His younger son, Anastasio ("Tachito"), was graduated from the United States Military Academy in 1946. Somoza named the principal avenue of Managua, running from Lake Managua to Tiscapa Hill, Avenida Roosevelt (for Franklin, not Theodore). Atop Tiscapa sat the presidential residence, dominating the city both physically and psychologically. Below was an open space for several hundreds yards, broken only by the Roosevelt Monument, the Officers' Club, and, later, the Inter-Continental Hotel. Abroad, Somoza was described as a dictator who had the blood of the patriot, Augusto César Sandino, on his hands; at home, he depicted himself as the friend of Franklin Roosevelt and the favorite of the world's greatest democracy.

The United States had a firm ally in Nicaragua. During World War II, it had no fear of subversion or attack in its own backyard. When the cold war came, Somoza made clear his hatred of communism. The United States could rely upon the support of Nicaragua in the Organization of American States and the United Nations. Somoza's Nicaragua aided the Central Intelligence Agency in the overthrow of Jacobo Árbenz of Guatemala in 1954, and Nicaragua provided the staging area for the Bay of Pigs episode in 1961. When Lyndon Johnson intervened in the Dominican Republic in 1965 and called for an OAS peacekeeping force, Nicaragua was one of only three states to provide troops. During this time, the relationship between Somoza and U.S. Ambassador Thomas Whelan was so close and cordial that critics labeled the period "the era of Tommy and Tacho."

Although U.S.-Nicaraguan relations appeared to be mutually beneficial, the United States exhibited discomfort from time to time. Somoza's reputation as a dictator tarnished the image of the United States as a free-world leader and undermined its moral authority. Not only did the Somoza regime deny Nicaraguans political freedom, but Somoza and his heirs also treated Nicaragua as a private estate and amassed one of the world's largest fortunes. By sharing this corruption with selected political and business leaders and with the chiefs of the National Guard, the Somozas created an economic system that relied upon their exclusive political control. The United States helped to keep the system going by providing Nicaragua with nearly $300 million in economic and military assistance between 1949 and 1979. United States policymakers must have asked at some point, "Who is using whom?" As a North American businessman residing in Managua told the House Subcommittee on Inter-American Affairs in 1979, the Somozas "robbed us blind."[1]

To its credit, the United States tried to head off this situation early on. In 1946 it opposed Somoza's plans to run for a third term. When Somoza subsequently removed his hand-picked successor in a dispute, the United States refused to recognize the illegal situation and blocked Nicaraguan participation in the 1947 Inter-American Conference in Rio de Janeiro. Eventually, after Somoza held new elections and restored a modicum of constitutionality, and with cold war exigencies weighing heavily, Somoza overcame the crisis. Still, his nation was not originally included in the Mutual Security Program, but was brought in later in the context of the action against Guatemala in 1954. Even while Nicaragua was participating in the CIA's anti-Castro movement in 1960, opponents of the regime were benefitting from CIA covert funding to various organizations of the noncommunist left in the Caribbean and Central America. The United States was not certain which way events might go following the assassination of the senior Somoza in 1956. The dynasty seemed to be holding up, but dictatorships in Latin America were definitely on the decline in the late fifties.

Luis Somoza Debayle succeeded his father in the presidency and enabled the dynasty to weather a dangerous period. Harvard-schooled and civilian-oriented, Luis displayed reformist tendencies and recognized the changed attitude of the Eisenhower administration brought about by the experience of Vice-President Richard Nixon in Caracas in May 1958 and the rise of Fidel Castro in Cuba. He pursued more moderate policies and kept his word to serve only one term in the presidency. The Kennedy administration attempted to mediate between the Somozas and the opposition Conservative party for the conduct of free elections in 1962, but the dynasty had limits on accommodating the United States and imposed its own candidate, René Schick.

The experience of the immediate post-John Foster Dulles years demonstrated the dynasty's vulnerability to shifts in U.S. policy, but it proved adaptive. Schick gave the regime a civilian cast, but Luis kept a sharp eye on the economic front, and the junior Anastasio assumed command of the national guard. Anastasio Somoza Debayle was more authoritarian than his brother, but he was not reckless and possessed a keen insight into Washington politics. Moreover, Nicaragua demonstrated its loyalty in the Bay of Pigs affair and the Dominican intervention, and a grateful Johnson administration rewarded it with the abrogation of the 1916 Bryan-Chamorro Treaty. (The treaty, which gave the United States exclusive canal rights, had rankled Nicaraguan nationalistic sentiments.) The election of Anastasio as president in 1967, and the death of Luis from a heart attack in the same year, making the new "Tacho" the sole head of the dynasty, did not bring out the worst in him immediately. He knew the value of the "American card" as well as his father. He faithfully attended reunions of his West Point class and carefully cultivated friends in the U.S. Congress, particularly his West Point classmate Representative John Murphy of New York and Annapolis graduate Representative Charles Wilson of Texas. The dynasty's performance during the sixties had been encouraging. Even José Figueres of Costa Rica, who had been the archenemy of the dynasty's founder, noted the improvement and declared, "We are not conspiring. We are not going to hold the son responsible for what his father did or did not do."

The improved image that Anastasio Somoza Debayle had taken pains to create came undone by an act of nature on December 23, 1972. The great earthquake leveled Old Managua in minutes, killed 10,000, and left 450,000 homeless; it also cracked the democratic façade of the Somoza regime. The reconstruction effort, if done properly, might have earned for Somoza the gratitude of Nicaragua forever. Instead, Somoza turned it into a spectacle of insatiable greed, in which he and his minions compounded the suffering of the victims. The United States, other governments, and international agencies provided millions of dollars and tons of relief supplies, which ended up in Somoza's warehouses for resale on the black market. Somoza profitted from the sale of even the barest necessities, including plasma, which put him on a par with Count Dracula in the minds of the people. Somoza properties were selected for relocation sites, and Somoza-owned construction firms made scandalous earnings in the task of rebuilding. Perhaps in an economy where Somoza owned so much, such conflict of interest was unavoidable; but important elements of the private sector, which had gone along before, became alienated in the face of such avarice. United States Ambassador Turner Shelton tried to cover up these abuses, but the embassy's political office, James Cheek, used the Dissent Channel to report the truth to Washington. Somoza would not recover from this self-inflicted wound.

It was not easy to oppose Somoza, even during the 1960s when the dynasty tried to appease the United States. In deference to the United States, Somoza permitted some opposition, but it was contained within tolerable limits. The safest place to oppose Somoza was in exile, but within the country one man managed to dissent and survive. Pedro Joaquín Chamorro, editor and publisher of *La Prensa* and leader of the Conservative party, had over the years endured imprisonment, torture, and exile, but he also enjoyed periods of relative freedom in Nicaragua. His international reputation probably protected him. He was a close friend of José Figueres and other leaders of the Democratic Left of Latin America, who could rally international public opinion in his behalf. His membership in the Inter-American Press Association and service as chairman of the Freedom of the Press Committee provided him with an influential international forum. He was also a member of an important family. There were a number of dynastic families in Nicaragua: Argüello, Borge, Cardenal, Chamorro, Fonseca, Lacayo, Rivas, Sacasa, Solórzano, and others whom the Somozas tried not to antagonize. One should not overlook the role of these families in Nicaraguan politics even today. By the time of the earthquake, Chamorro and Somoza had reached a standoff: Chamorro knew that his situation was precarious, but Somoza knew the penalties he faced if he harmed him. Nonetheless, Chamorro was determined to take advantage of the discredit the regime had brought upon itself.

Chamorro denounced Somoza's behavior in *La Prensa* and undertook to organize the growing opposition to the regime. In a circumstance that confused outsiders, Chamorro headed the Conservative party in opposition to the Liberal party of Somoza. The Conservative and Liberal parties originated in the nineteenth century during the Central American Federation, reflecting traditional/centralist and anticlerical/federalist concepts, respectively. In Nicaragua Pedro Joaquín Chamorro shucked off the dynastic trappings of the Conservative party of the old patriarch, Emiliano Chamorro, and transformed it into a reformist party of the opposition, whereas the Liberal party became a meaningless label for Somoza's personal electoral vehicle. In 1974 Chamorro formed the Democratic Union of Liberation (UDEL), a coalition made up of the Conservative party and Independent Liberals, along with emerging Christian Democratic, Social Christian, and Social Democratic elements, joined by several labor unions. In the past Chamorro had engaged in revolutionary activity, including leading an airborne invasion from Costa Rica in 1959, but now he recognized his value as a responsible leader of the political opposition within Nicaragua. Somoza harassed him and threatened him with arrest for defamation, but Chamorro persevered in the belief that the momentum was with him. Chamorro was encouraged when the United States replaced Somoza's friend, Shelton, with a less sympathetic ambassador, but the actions of the Sandinista National Liberation Front (FSLN) dramatically upstaged him.

Chamorro had been following a nonviolent course, but the FSLN perceived the time as ripe for radical action. Daniel Fonseca Amador founded the FSLN in exile in Havana in 1962 in the hope of imitating in Nicaragua Castro's successful guerrilla warfare. Cuba's sponsorship of the group was open, but Castro did not recruit it; he simply had to be there, and they came to him. Exile politics were not new in the history of Nicaragua. During the forties and fifties refugees from Somoza's tyranny found haven in Mexico City and San José, as well as other places. In the sixties Havana was the place to go, especially for those bent on revolutionary activity. The Sandinista Front did not make much headway in the first ten years of its existence; as late as 1974, it had fewer than a hundred members. It conducted guerrilla operations in remote parts of Nicaragua and occasionally made headlines by hijacking a commercial airliner. Few took the FSLN seriously, and Somoza had been wise to ignore it, but in the context of his other woes, the Sandinistas managed to provoke him.

On December 27, 1974, a small group of Sandinistas stormed a farewell party in honor of Ambassador Shelton in suburban Managua. The ambassador had already departed, but the raiders seized as hostages 45 of the elite of Somoza society, including Somoza's brother-in-law, Guillermo Sevilla Sacasa,the long-time Nicaraguan ambassador to the United States. Taken by surprise, Somoza yielded to the Sandinistas' demands for $1 million in ransom, the release of 20 imprisoned comrades, including Daniel Ortega Saavedra (presently a member of the ruling Junta), and an aircraft to fly them to Havana. The event incensed Somoza, who seemed to lose all sense of perspective. He determined to destroy the FSLN and ordered a National Guard offensive into the three rural provinces where Sandinista guerrillas had been active. Somoza's troops pillaged the countryside for two years. Finding few Sandinistas, the Guard committed acts of barbarism against the peasants of the region. In January 1977 the bishops of the Catholic church of Nicaragua issued a pastoral letter denouncing the guard's "shocking brutality" and accusing it of "torture and rape," among other crimes. In the meantime, Somoza declared a state of siege, installing military tribunals and imposing press censorship.

Although Somoza was radicalizing the Nicaraguan people and building up the FSLN in the process, the Sandinistas were also hurt, and seemed unsure as to how to proceed. The organization's founder, Fonseca Amador, was killed in the fighting in November 1976, bringing to the surface existing differences over political ideology and military strategy. The FSLN's predominantly Marxist leadership opposed cooperation with the bourgeoisie. Among them, two so-called tendencies emerged: the Prolonged Peoples' War, which was resigned to a lengthy guerrilla struggle in the bush, and the Proletarian Tendency, which favored an urban movement involving the unions. However, a third group (Tercerista) took shape, comprised of non-Marxists and elements with social democratic leanings, which perceived an opportunity for a broad-based insurrection against the Somoza regime. The Insurrectional or Tercerista faction provided the bridge between the Sandinistas and the moderate opposition. By assuming a democratic character, the Terceristas brought the Sandinistas into the larger movement against Somoza. This strategy bore fruit in October 1977, when a group of respected Nicaraguans, known as Los Doce (The Twelve), issued a statement in exile in Costa Rica demanding Somoza's resignation and acknowledging that the FSLN had earned a place in the future government of Nicaragua.

Meanwhile, Somoza's relations with the United States deteriorated. Somoza's dismay at losing Turner Shelton was compounded by the new U.S. ambassador, James Theberge, who, he alleged, was instructed "to keep his distance."[2] Somoza blamed everybody but himself for his troubles. He associated Washington's changed attitude with the fall of his friend, Richard Nixon. He blamed the reporting and activities of James Cheek. When the U.S. House of Representatives conducted hearings in June 1976 dealing with human rights in Central America, he blamed the Washington Office for Latin America (WOLA), a human rights activist organization, for lining up critical witnesses and influencing the thinking of certain members of Congress, particularly Clarence Long of Maryland and Edward Koch of New York. He blamed the "bleeding heart" press for turning American public opinion against him, mentioning specifically Jack Anderson, who pinned upon him the label "the world's greediest ruler," and Dan Rather, Mike Wallace, Alan Riding, and Karen DeYoung. Most of all, he blamed Jimmy Carter. Although Somoza was slipping badly before Carter became president, Somoza charged that "the Carter Administration contrived to hand Nicaragua over to the Sandinistas and, in this contrivance, used deceit, duplicity, and outright lies."[3]

The human rights policy of the Carter administration brought ill upon many governments of force. Jimmy Carter set the course of his foreign policy in his inaugural address, affirming, "because we are free we can never be indifferent to the fate of freedom elsewhere." Secretary of State Cyrus Vance, during his confirmation hearing, explained what the president meant: "we must have policies based upon fundamental values. In particular, we must stand for human rights." The commitment of the Carter administration to human rights was deep and consistent, which one may observe by paging through the U.S. State Department *Bulletin* and reading the statements of Carter, Vance, and Warren Christopher, among others. The policy created controversy, with foreign leaders asking what right the United States had to sit in judgment of them, and labeling the action of a new type of U.S. interventionism. At home, critics expressed dismay over a policy based upon morality when only one side was willing to play fair, and insisted that the ignoring of geopolitical considerations would undermine the cause of freedom in the long run.

In some respects, this criticism was misdirected because the U.S. Congress had already mandated that foreign aid and assistance be linked to human rights performance. The Foreign Assistance Act of 1961 stated that "a principal goal of the foreign policy of the United States is to promote the increased observance of internationally recognized human rights by all countries." In the appropriations for the State Department for fiscal year 1978, Congress directed the secretary of state to report on measures designed to strengthen human rights and created the position of assistant secretary of state for human rights and humanitarian affairs. The activities of Patricia Derian, the first person appointed to that post, were less a new departure than a vigorous implementation of existing standards. Secretary Derian stated: "[Arms] transfers may link the United States with regimes that violate basic human rights and fundamental freedoms and thereby undermine our traditional support for those ideals, conflict with our international obligations, tarnish our reputation, and damage our long-term national interests."[4] Such comments were associated with the "born-again" philosophy of Jimmy Carter, but were, in fact, reaffirmations of American liberal thought, which had long objected to U.S. ties with dictators such as Anastasio Somoza Debayle.

Because Somoza's human rights violations were then among the grossest in the world, the Carter administration could not ignore the situation in Nicaragua if its policy were to be credible. Somoza complained that the Carter administration picked on him because his nation was small and strategically unimportant; but, in point of fact, Nicaragua was a major recipient of U.S. economic and military assistance, which provided the United States with particular leverage in dealing with it and made unavoidable decisions that affected it.

Within two weeks after assuming office, the Carter administration suspended arms transfers to Nicaragua, pending a review of its human rights performance. In April the administration created the Interagency Committee on Human Rights and Foreign Assistance, chaired by Deputy Secretary of State Christopher and made up of senior officials of the departments of agriculture, commerce, defense, and treasury, and AID, among others. The so-called Christopher Committee was charged with ensuring "consideration of human rights aspects in the conduct and administration of [United States] foreign assistance policy." The Congress also acted. Under the leadership of Representative Koch, the House Appropriations Committee voted in May 1977 to remove Nicaragua from the list of countries eligible to receive U.S. military assistance in FY 1978. However, Somoza's Nicaragua lobby, with Representative Wilson as spokesman, managed to restore Nicaragua to the list of recipients when the full House acted upon the measure. In reviewing the relations between the Carter administration and Nicaragua, one is led to the conclusion that Congress frequently tied the hands of the executive and made it very difficult to maintain an effective and consistent policy. Still, despite the House vote, the Christopher Committee, acting upon broad congressional mandates, prevented the shipment of any military equipment to the Nicaraguan government in 1977.

These actions came at a bad time for Somoza. In July 1977 he suffered a severe heart attack, which required several months of convalescence. While recovering, he consulted with friends in the U.S. Congress, such as Representative Murphy, and decided to try to appease the Carter administration. He recognized that it would be dangerous to follow the example of other governments, such as Guatemala, which had informed the United States they would not accept aid with conditions. In September Somoza lifted the state of siege and removed restrictions upon the press. These measures improved the situation a bit, but the Carter administration did not ease the pressure. It sought to create a political climate that might enable the democratic opposition to work for an electoral solution to Somoza's succession. This policy acquired an urgency when the Terceristas carried out simultaneous raids upon scattered National Guard posts in October, which though repelled, earned the recognition of the FSLN by Los Doce. The link between the Terceristas and Los Doce was fast overcoming the image of the Sandinistas as a small Fidelista band of terrorists and was making them an integral part of the anti-Somoza movement. The Carter administration demanded that Somoza state publicly that he would not run for the presidency again and would relinquish control of the National Guard when his term expired in 1981. This strategy received a serious setback with the assassination of Pedro Joaquín Chamorro on Janaury 10, 1978.

The assassination of Chamorro removed the most effective leader of the democratic opposition and deprived the Carter administration of an acceptable alternative to Somoza. Somoza denied any part in the murder of Chamorro. Somoza insisted that, because of his visibility and usefulness in demonstrating freedom of the press in Nicaragua, "Chamorro was the last man [he] wanted to be killed."[5] The public reaction, however, was violently anti-Somoza, and resulted in two weeks of rioting in Managua and a general strike led by the Chamber of Commerce. Viron Vaky, who subsequently became assistant secretary of state for inter-American affairs, observed that the assassination of Chamorro, "more than any other single factor, catalyzed opposition to the regime."[6] Nonetheless, Somoza held on.

In the aftermath of Chamorro's death and the violence that followed, 16 opposition groups and parties banded together to form the Broad Opposition Front (FAO), with the single purpose that Somoza must resign without delay. The FAO consisted of UDEL, with its component parts, business and professional groups organized through the Chamber of Commerce, and Los Doce. The Sandinistas were associated through the link between Los Doce and the Terceristas, but an ambiguity persisted. Moderate elements continued to distrust the FSLN and appeared to be awaiting a move by the United States. The Carter administration, however, dampened these hopes by exercising caution and refusing to call for Somoza's immediate resignation. Through the new U.S. ambassador, Mauricio Solaun, it induced Somoza to announce his intention to step down in 1981 and to resign from the National Guard at the same time. Solaun, a Cuban-American, represented a gesture to the Hispanic community in the United States, but was not a known human rights activist. The administration persuaded Somoza to permit Los Doce to return to Nicaragua and to invite the OAS Human Rights Commission to visit the country. It continued to withhold economic and military assistance, although it encountered resistance from Somoza's friends in Congress, who threatened to retaliate against other Carter programs and raised doubts about the authority of the Christopher Committee. Finally, in June Carter wrote a personal letter to Anastasio Somoza in which he noted "heartening signs" with regard to the respect for human rights in Nicaragua.

The Carter letter may have been a tactical blunder, but it was not intended to "prop up" the Somoza regime, as was charged. On the contrary, it sought to establish the basis for free elections and peaceful transition in Nicaragua and to let Somoza know what was expected of him. It endeavored, in essence, to buy time for the democratic opposition to evolve new leadership and achieve effective organization. It was recognized that a Chamorro was not replaced overnight. Despite its good intentions, the letter was terribly misunderstood. Although Somoza later characterized it as "a ruse and a ploy" to get him to "cooperate with those forces which were determined to destroy [him],"[7] he was able to use it at the moment as a political plus by revealing the existence of the letter, but not its contents. It had the effect of undermining the democratic opposition, by giving the impression that Carter was backing off in his opposition to Somoza, and of strengthening those groups, such as the Terceristas, which were demanding immediate action against Somoza. The initiative slipped from the moderate to the radical elements, which became irreversible with the events of August 22, 1978.

On this date, the Tercerista faction of the FSLN seized the National Palace in Managua. There were approximately 1,500 persons in the building at the time, including the Nicaraguan Congress, officials and staff of various government offices, and ordinary citizens on routine business, such as paying taxes. The boldness of the operation, carried out smoothly by just 14 Sandinistas under the command of Eden Pastora ("Comandante Cero"), captured the imagination of the world. They demanded several million dollars in ransom, the release of 59 imprisoned comrades, the publication and broadcast of a prepared manifesto denouncing Somocismo, and safe conduct from the country. Somoza had little choice but to surrender; he was capable of killing, but his cousin, Luis Pallais Debayle, and scores of close personal friends were also among the hostages. Through the mediation of three Nicaraguan bishops, the Sandinistas obtained their demands (except that they accepted $500,000 in cash, but the amount was unimportant) and departed for Panama and Venezuela in a little over 48 hours after the event began. As the Sandinistas went from the National Palace to Las Mercedes airport (now Augusto Sandino International Airport), thousands of cheering Nicaraguans lined the route. Somoza was humiliated, and the Sandinistas had taken over as the leaders of the Nicaraguan Revolution.

The revolution had begun. In September the Sandinistas launched an offensive, attacking National Guard posts in a number of cities across Nicaragua. This time they were not alone, because thousands of persons took up arms and gave the movement an insurrectional character. Somoza struck back in terrible fury, ordering the National Guard to use every weapon in its arsenal to put down the rebellion. His ruthlessness shocked the international community, as National Guard planes bombed and strafed Nicaraguan cities. Somoza won another round militarily, inflicting a toll of 3,000 lives and leveling a number of cities, such as Chinandega and Estelí; but politically he was beyond redemption.

The carnage in Nicaragua and the rapidly changing political situation there spurred another initiative on the part of the United States. The Carter administration recognized that Somoza had to go, but it had no intention of seeing its human rights policy result in a takeover by the FSLN. Already there were assertions that Nicaragua was another Cuba. Seventy-eight members of the U.S. Congress said as much in a letter to Carter on September 22, 1978, but the Carter administration persisted in the search for a democratic alternative. Besides, in crushing the September offensive, Somoza demonstrated that he was still a dangerous foe, and the Carter administration believed that the Nicaraguan people had sacrificed enough. It decided to try to mediate between the FAO and Somoza for the purpose of restoring peace and creating a climate in which the democratic process might function.

Working within the Organization of American States, the United States secured the passage of a resolution creating the International Commission of Friendly Cooperation and Conciliation for Achieving a Peaceful Solution to the Grave Crisis of the Republic of Nicaragua. The long title told much, and, after preliminary negotiations, three countries comprised the OAS commission: the Dominican Republic, Guatemala, and the United States. The U.S. representative was William G. Bowdler, an experienced Latin American specialist, who during a foreign service career beginning in 1951 had served as ambassador to El Salvador, Guatemala, and the Union of South Africa and was then director of the department's Bureau of Intelligence and Research. Bowdler also had been political officer in the U.S. embassy in Havana from 1956 to 1961, so that he experienced déjà vu upon arriving in Managua. He knew that there was a broad coalition of forces in opposition to the dictator, but had seen that in a revolutionary situation the people with the guns prevailed. The main outline of the commission's plan, which was, in essence, U.S. policy, was to secure Somoza's acceptance of, and the FAO's cooperation in, an internationally supervised election of an interim government of national reconciliation. The interim government's principal purpose would be to prepare the legal framework for free elections for a new president and congress, giving political parties and groups time to organize and conduct effective campaigns. The plan also included a reorganization of the National Guard, purging it of political officers and placing it under the jurisdiction of the interim government, and, as a concession to Somoza, guarantees of his personal fortune.

The mediation effort encountered resistance from the beginning because of the failure to demand Somoza's immediate resignation and the exclusion of the FSLN from the talks. Critics further charged that the National Guard could never be "cleansed" of Somocista elements and that the entire process was a carbon copy of Henry L. Stimson's mission of mediation in the civil war of 1927, which, in effect, took the present crisis full circle.[8] The United States considered the reform of the Guard critical. It counted upon its essential professionalism and believed that only the top echelon of officers and some NCOs, readily identifiable, were beholden to Somoza. It reasoned that numerous competent officers resented being passed over by Somoza's favorites, as exemplified by the rapid rise of Somoza's son, Anastasio Somoza Portocarrero, only 28 years old at the time. Thousands of officers and enlisted men had received training at U.S. installations over the years, during which important contacts were made and friendships established. Somoza boasted that this training was evidence of U.S. support of his regime, but it was a two-edged sword that the United States hoped to use in reshaping the Guard.

In the end, Somoza wrecked the mediation effort. He did not intend to relinquish power and played for time to strengthen the guard. He made a counterproposal in which he suggested a plebiscite to determine whether or not he should be permitted to complete his term of office. The plebiscite proposal had some merit, but Somoza frustrated every effort to implement it in a way that he could not control. The policies of the Carter administration influenced events in Nicaragua, but they could not influence Somoza when it really counted. Somoza, in fact, was more effective in exerting pressure on the Carter administration by playing on the theme "either Somoza or another Cuba," which his friends in the U.S. Congress trumpeted. By prolonging the negotiations, Somoza also cracked the unity of the FAO. Los Doce was the first to go, perceiving that Somoza was insincere and suspecting that the United States, given its past performance, was conducting a charade. The failure to set any time limit on the negotiations, plus the concessions to Somoza with reference to the Guard, the Liberal party, and Somoza's properties, strengthened these suspicions and led to additional defections. By the time that the mediation effort collapsed in December, those elements of the FAO that continued to cooperate with Bowdler were severely compromised and virtually shorn of political influence.

Despite the failure of the efforts of the OAS commission for a peaceful resolution of the crisis, Bowdler found some comfort in the three months of labor. In his report to Secretary Vance, Bowdler pointed out that the presence of the mediators in Nicaragua restored calm and brought "relief to a population that had been under tension for more than a year." He noted that the mediators had induced Somoza to lift the state of siege and restore constitutional guarantees. He felt generally that while the mediators were in Nicaragua the repressive conditions and restrictions upon free expression had eased significantly. He felt also that the exchange of opinions and identification of issues had been salutary. He had no illusion, however, that the situation would stay the same, and placed the blame for the breakdown of the negotiations squarely upon Somoza. He was angered by Somoza's rigidity and warned that "the absence of alternation in power of different political groups and the loss of confidence in existing electoral procedures . . . has brought about a growing discontent and frustration which has become so widespread that unless other opportunities or alternatives become available, they can lead to a growing tendency to seek or sympathize with violent solutions."[9] In view of the direness (and accuracy) of this prediction, it is difficult to understand the failure of the United States to undertake any new initiative from January to May 1979. As Alfred Stepan observed, the United States entered "a period of policy inertia."[10]

The Carter administration seemed to experience a failure of nerve.

Despite Somoza's intransigence, the crisis in Nicaragua had abated. The Carter administration appeared to hope that Somoza might yet serve out his term, and that it could monitor his human rights performance in the meantime and strive to establish effective guarantees for free elections in 1981. It rejected the suggestion that it demand the resignation of Somoza and threaten to rupture relations if he refused, out of concern that it would provoke renewed violence. This rejection caused Ambassador Solaun to resign in disgust, but the Carter administration reasoned that Somoza possessed formidable firepower and that he was not afraid to use it. Of course, the spectre of a Sandinista victory haunted Carter, but his wish to spare the Nicaraguan people further suffering and bloodshed was genuine. Nor could Carter ignore the actions of Representatives Murphy and Wilson, who were threatening to block legislation affecting the Panama Canal treaties if the United States continued to withhold aid from Somoza. Viron Vaky, the assistant secretary of state, candidly admitted the consequences of this state of affairs:

> When the U.S. Government failed to react to Somoza's rejection of the mediators' last proposal, the opposition, the Sandinistas and the oppositions' supporting patrons in Venezuela, Costa Rica, Panama and elsewhere concluded that either the U.S. was not serious or in any event that there was no solution to the crisis except by force of arms.[11]

Other governments, indeed, stepped into the vacuum created by the U.S. policy inertia, and the opposition forces organized for an armed uprising. The political groups governing Costa Rica and Venezuela had a long history of opposition to the Somoza regime, during which they fashioned alliances with the Christian and Social Democratic leadership of Nicaragua, in particular. They understood the socio-political roots of the crisis and determined to render aid to those closest to them ideologically, on the basis of principle and security. The "elsewhere" to which Vaky referred was Cuba. Castro played a critical role in the months before the final assault against Somoza by informing the FSLN that it must achieve unity if it expected to receive aid. As a result, the FSLN announced in March that the three tendencies had organized a unified military command. The FSLN entered the final struggle against Somoza still divided politically, although it endorsed the program of the United People's Movement (MPU), a new coalition of leftist groups that had broken away from the FAO. This program spoke of profound political and social change, but retained a decidedly democratic character with reference to the new Nicaragua. The impression existed that the Tercerista strategy of a popular insurrection of all forces against Somocismo had prevailed. As Thomas Walker observed, the victory over Somoza was "a victory of the Nicaraguan people as a whole."[12]

After months of preparation, the final attack against Somoza began in May 1979. Somoza responded, as expected, with the full terror at his command, but this time the rebels were better organized, better armed, and better led. The Sandinistas unified the Nicaraguan people, who had been convinced by Somoza himself that there was no alternative to armed insurrection. As Somoza's fortunes ebbed, he depicted himself as the victim of an international conspiracy. He charged that the rebels were receiving vast amounts of modern weapons from Cuba, Panama, Costa Rica, and Venezuela, while the United States had cut off all military assistance to him and prevented him from purchasing arms elsewhere. He decried that the OAS ignored these violations of international law, including the operations of rebels from "sanctuaries" in Costa Rica, but the OAS threatened to impose sanctions upon him if he retaliated. By June it was clear that Somoza was going to lose, even if he made a wasteland of Nicaragua in the process.

Faced with the inevitability of Somoza's collapse and the senselessness of further killing, along with the fear of a radical takeover, the United States again tried to influence events in Nicaragua. The United States requested the OAS to convoke a meeting of consultation for the purpose of ending the fighting in Nicaragua and negotiating a political settlement. On June 21 Secretary Vance presented a six-point proposal to the meeting, including the "replacement" of Somoza, an end to the flow of arms, a cease-fire, the creation of an OAS peacekeeping force, and a program of "humanitarian relief." The meeting endorsed the call for Somoza's resignation, but refused to organize a peacekeeping force. The proposal for such a force was the most radical aspect of the U.S. initiative, designed to deny the Sandinistas a monopoly of military power in post-Somoza Nicaragua. Throughout the crisis, Carter had ruled out the use of military force, but now, in the eleventh hour, when it would be extremely costly, he was prepared to resort to it. The Carter administration knew beforehand that it would be rebuffed, but felt it was essential "to sensitize" other nations as to the depth of its concern.[13]

With the fighting continuing, the United States believed that it still had a chance to effect a solution that would prevent excesses and preserve a role for the democratic opposition in the political process. Acting on the basis of the OAS watered-down resolution, the United States undertook to negotiate Somoza's replacement with the Junta of Government of National Reconstruction, which had been organized in San José, Costa Rica, as the political arm of the revolutionary movement. The Sandinista commanders, busy with the fighting in Nicaragua, had approved the composition of the five-person Junta in mid-June, which included representatives of various opposition groups: Violeta Barrios de Chamorro (the widow of Pedro Joaquín), Alfonso Robelo (FAO), Sergio Ramírez (Los Doce), Daniel Ortega (FSLN/Tercerista), and Moisés Hassan (MPU). Despite the fact that Ramírez and Ortega represented Social Democratic tendencies, the United States felt that they, along with Hassan, gave the Junta an overly radical cast, and it endeavored to have the Junta enlarged to include additional representatives of the democratic opposition. This effort failed, in part because of time constraints, but the Junta pledged to observe the principle of pluralism in the appointment of the new cabinet and of a 33-member Council of State. Ambassador Bowdler conducted these negotiations with the Junta in San José and Panama, while Ambassador Lawrence Pezzullo (Solaun's replacement in Managua) dealt with Somoza.

By mid-July the two envoys had worked out an agreement for the resignation of Somoza and the transfer of power to the Junta, which included a plan for the creation of a new security force through the merger of a reformed national guard and the Sandinista command. The Junta also agreed to avoid reprisals and call for free elections. Somoza submitted his resignation to the Congress on July 17, 1979, and departed Managua. The Congress elected a new president, Francisco Urcuyo, who was supposed to turn over power to the Junta. At this point the agreement broke down, because Urcuyo tried to remain in power. Allegedly, Warren Christopher demanded that he surrender power to the Junta in 24 hours, under threat of returning Somoza (then in Miami) to Nicaragua, with no guarantee of Urcuyo's personal safety. Urcuyo yielded, but the harm had been done. The confusion lasted two days, during which the almost leaderless National Guard, not apprised of the formula for its merger with the revolutionary forces, literally fell apart, and the Junta assumed power on its own. What had happened in Cuba 20 years earlier had reoccurred in Nicaragua: the most radical elements of the antidictatorial coalition had a monopoly of arms. The United States had managed to remove Somoza while he still had the power to inflict heavy casualties, and it had established the right of all forces in opposition to Somoza to shape the future of Nicaragua; but the action of Urcuyo thwarted its goal of depoliticizing the military power and placing it under the jurisdiction of the Junta.

When the Junta began functioning in Managua, the Sandinista commanders, organized as the Sandinista National Directorate, continued to exercise control over the military. As a result, the Sandinista National Directorate comprised a shadow government in competition with, and, in many respects, superior to, the Junta of Government. The actions and decisions of the Junta depended to a large extent upon the goodwill of the Sandinista National Directorate. Clearly, the Sandinistas were by then a legitimate and popular force in the Nicaraguan Revolution and might have controlled the course of events in any case, but the military weapon gave them supremacy. Given the fact that the United States had done much to try to prevent this state of affairs, its relations with Nicaragua were not going to be easy.

The legacy of the past and the unfavorable attitude of the United States toward the FSLN hampered U.S. efforts to promote democracy and pluralism in Nicaragua. The Carter administration knew that economic and social inequities were at the heart of the anti-Somoza movement and it sympathized with democratic elements seeking change. Nevertheless, it was concerned about Marxist influence in the Nicaraguan Revolution and the Sandinistas' close ties with Castro. The Carter administration faced many problems simultaneously, not the least of which was the accusation that it had "lost" Nicaragua.

The Carter administration did not believe that Nicaragua was "lost," nor that cold war rhetoric applied in this case. It understood that the Nicaraguan Revolution sprang from internal causes and that the situation was fluid, with the interplay of many forces. It was not oblivious to the fact that what happened in Nicaragua affected U.S. interests, but believed that these interests, along with good neighborliness, dictated the development of a "positive" relationship with the new Nicaragua. Indeed, it felt that a position of indifference or hostility on the part of the United States would undermine the democratic leadership of Nicaragua and provide the opportunity or pretense for radical elements to strengthen ties with Cuba and the Soviet Union. The Carter administration did not want "another Cuba" anymore than its critics, but felt that errors on the part of the United States would influence such an outcome as much as Cubans might do. It proposed economic aid to Nicaragua as the best means to avoid such errors, but had a difficult time implementing this policy; conservative members of the U.S. Congress were opposed to social revolution in Nicaragua and argued that American assistance would only enable the Marxists to succeed.

The Carter administration won the first round, because of the dire need for emergency and humanitarian aid for devastated Nicaragua. The armed struggle in Nicaragua had been extremely costly. Forty-five thousand persons were killed in the fighting, many more were maimed, wounded, and left homeless, and the economic loss approached $2 billion. The Nicaraguan treasury was almost empty, the country was saddled with a $600 million debt, and agricultural production was at a standstill. Joining a number of countries that provided relief assistance, the United States made available $7 million in food, medicines, and other supplies. In explaining the decision to provide this aid, Secretary Vaky told the House Subcommittee on Inter-American Affairs in September 1979 that the political and economic situation in Nicaragua remained "unclear," and that "many outcomes and scenarios" were still possible. He did not try to mislead anyone by promising that U.S. aid would produce a favorable outcome, but stressed that the risks were greater if the United States failed to act:

While it is true that Marxist elements are well-positioned to exert power, they do not yet dominate the situation. Moderate democratic elements capable of exerting influence and power of their own also exist in key places in the Government and in society generally. . . . The course of the Nicaraguan revolution can thus be affected in no small way by how the U.S. perceives it and relates to it.

Vaky conceded that Cuban influence was strong, but pointed out also the influence of Colombia, Venezuela, Costa Rica, and Panama. He concluded: "It is conceivable, if you did everything right, it might still go sour. One never knows. But certainly, if you do not help, it will almost surely push the revolution out of desperation into radical authoritarian molds."[14]

Appearing at the same hearing, Ambassador Pezzullo estimated that up to that time, U.S. aid was 20 times greater than that of Cuba. He noted that the Soviet Union had flown in "two Aeroflots," each carrying 30 tons of food. The United States, he related, was bringing in an average of 250 tons a day.[15] The relief assistance which the United States provided came from the reprogramming of foreign assistance funds already appropriated. The real test of Carter policy came in December, when the president called for $70 million in loans and $5 million in grants to assist the economic reconstruction of Nicaragua.

The Carter administration attempted to convince Congress that the same reasons that made it advisable for the United States to provide relief assistance to Nicaragua applied to making available funds for economic reconstruction. It acknowledged that Sandinista leaders were traveling to Havana and Moscow and that Cuban teachers, medical personnel, and security advisers were present in Nicaragua, but appeared encouraged by the openness of Nicaraguan society and the generally good record of the revolutionary government in the area of human rights. Displaying greater confidence, State Department officials were anxious to play a dynamic role in Nicaraguan affairs and to assist the moderates and private sector, which, they affirmed, had also opposed Somoza and had "earned the right to share in the nation's future." Bowdler, who had succeeded Vaky as assistant secretary, told the House Subcommittee on Inter-American Affairs in May 1980, "We are in a competitive situation in Central America between those who want a democratic, pluralistic system and those who think in other terms. . . . There are contending forces, and it is very important for us to be an active participant in this competition."[16] Ambassador Pezzullo supported this position: "The country needs help too badly and the moderates need our support too badly for us to be sitting on the side of the road waiting for things to happen."[17] Nonetheless, despite these vigorous assertions, the debate on economic assistance for Nicaragua dragged on.

An example of the difficulties the Carter administration encountered on Capitol Hill occurred in hearings of the Senate Foreign Relations Committee on April 16, 1980. The Senate had already approved the $75 million economic support fund for Nicaragua, but the House had yet to act. Senator Jacob Javits was angry over the "hangup" in the House, but also scolded Secretary Bowdler for not doing more to reprogram funds in the meantime. "We will defend you up here," he told Bowdler. "I will and I think others will. There is no dearth of standing up for you over here if you are bold. This is one issue that deserves and demands boldness. Seriously, . . . it breaks your heart, having started right, to end up so wrong on this Nicaraguan situation."[18] Bowdler needed this pep talk, because Senator Jesse Helms examined him next and sharply criticized U.S. policy in Nicaragua. Senator Helms expressed entirely different opinions about the leadership of Nicaragua and asked Bowdler why we wanted to send "the taxpayers' money down there to that crowd."[19]

Six months later, State Department officials were still trying to persuade Congress that the policy of providing economic assistance to Nicaragua was the correct one. In September, in yet another hearing of the House Subcommittee on Inter-American Affairs, J. Brian Atwood, assistant secretary of state for congressional relations, pleaded:

Our friends in the free labor unions, the church, and the media need to know the United States will stand with them. They have told us that delays in moving forward with this aid undermine their role and serve the interests of the elements in Nicaragua who would shed no tears if U.S. relations with Nicaragua were to be harmed.[20]

In all, it took ten months to achieve approval of the $75 million in economic assistance for Nicaragua, meaning that the funds were hardly available before the end of Carter's term. In the meantime, his administration had managed to provide $71.8 million in assistance to Nicaragua through reprogrammed funds and by tapping Public Law 480 and AID appropriations; but the delay in winning approval of the $75 million request, plus the accompanying publicity, seriously hampered its efforts to influence events in Nicaragua.

It is difficult to determine how different the situation would be in Nicaragua today if the Carter administration had not attempted to maintain a positive relationship with the revolutionary government. The political situation in Nicaragua following the overthrow of Somoza was in a state of flux, and the democratic and private sectors might have survived in any case. Moreover, the FSLN, including the most radical elements, recognized the need for the cooperation of all anti-Somoza elements in the task of reconstruction and the restoration of peace. Even Castro advised the Sandinistas to take a pragmatic approach to the solution of problems. Nonetheless, the Carter administration, by displaying a sympathetic understanding of the dynamics of the Nicaraguan Revolution and by offering economic assistance without offensive conditions, contributed to a higher level of tolerance. Certainly, it avoided giving rise to the kind of siege atmosphere that developed early in the Cuban Revolution. Carter policy also indirectly facilitated the activities of other democratic governments, particularly of this hemisphere and of Western Europe. The Carter administration avoided the "worst-case scenario" by influencing the policies of the revolution, but had less impact upon its political structure.

Having tried to do "everything right," the Carter administration did not prevent the ascendancy of the FSLN. The Sandinistas did not abandon their goal of a socialist state, but recognized the need to be practical and make concessions, even to the bourgeoisie. The FSLN was not retributive and avoided the error of the Cuban Revolution of dependence upon the Soviet bloc. It kept open all channels of trade and welcomed assistance from a diversity of sources. The Sandinistas, aware of the risks involved in these tactical decisions, sought to protect themselves by achieving political control.

The Sandinista National Directorate, made up of the nine military commanders representing the three FSLN tendencies, served as the vehicle for the acquisition of political control. It possessed a majority within the five-person Junta of Government of National Reconstruction, effectively subordinating the Junta to its will. The two moderate members, Violeta Chamorro and Alfonso Robelo, resigned in April 1980 in frustration, but moderates Arturo Cruz and Rafael Córdoba were persuaded to replace them. (Cruz has since become the Nicaraguan ambassador to the United States.) Since the Junta appointed the Cabinet and the Council of State, the Sandinista Directorate extended its influence over these organs as well. A number of Sandinista commanders assumed key cabinet posts, including Tomás Borge (interior), Humberto Ortega (defense), Jaime Wheelock (agriculture and agrarian reform), and Henry Ruiz (economic planning). The important position of foreign minister remains in the hands of Father Miguel d'Escoto, a holdover from the Los Doce connection, but his future is uncertain in view of the Vatican's 1979 position forbidding priests to hold political office.

The Sandinistas also enjoyed a majority in the quasi-legislative Council of State. In May 1980 the Directorate secured the expansion of the Council of State from 33 to 47 (a factor in Robelo's decision to resign), in order to add representatives of new Sandinista "popular" organizations. The most significant of these was the Sandinista Defense Committee (CDS), organized in every neighborhood in the same manner as the Cuban Committees in Defense of the Revolution (CDRs). The CDSs are in themselves a powerful instrument of political control, involved in political indoctrination and the dispensing of favors, including jobs, and constitute one of the most disturbing developments of the Nicaraguan Revolution. Bayardo Arce, a member of the

Sandinista Directorate, became president of the Council of State. By establishing an interlocking relationship with the principal organs of the state, the Sandinista Directorate has become the nerve center of the bureaucratic apparatus. Its success in achieving political supremacy was enhanced by its control over the military.

The Sandinista Directorate exercises direct control over the armed elements of the state, including the Sandinista Popular Army (EPS), the police and state security force, and the Sandinista Popular Militia (MPS). Although the army and police are organized as separate units, they are actually closely coordinated by means of the three-member military sub-committee of the Sandinista Directorate, made up of Humberto Ortega, minister of defense and commander-in-chief of the EPS; Tomás Borge, minister of interior, with jurisdiction over the internal security forces; and Luis Carrión, vice-minister of defense and second in command of the EPS. The Directorate has been very vigorous in carrying out political indoc-trination of members of the police and EPS, and has been sensitive to who may make contact with them. Despite the presence of 200 Cuban military advisers in Nicaragua, the Ministry of Defense rejected U.S. offers of military advisers and prohibited contact between the U.S. embassy and EPS personnel without prior approval.[21] The Sandinista Popular Militia, desig-nated to function as army reserves and police auxiliaries, are recruited by the Sandinista Defense Committees. No one is enrolled in the militia, now over 100,000 strong, without political clearance. The only force the Sandinistas did not control was the Popular Anti-Somoza Militias (MILPAS), a far-left armed group of the insurrection, but the FSLN has tried slowly to render it superfluous with the MPS. By treading lightly, the Sandinistas have con-solidated political power; but, early in 1981, Viron Vaky still insisted: "viable non-Marxist elements function in the society. . . . The ball game is still on, whatever the inning."[22]

If Carter policy and Sandinista pragmatism have combined to enable these elements to function, they are viable also because they have a legitimate claim to the revolution. Their position is difficult; there have been incidents of official harassment and repression, as well as episodes of mob violence, but they are intelligent, courageous, and enjoy substantial public sympathy. The church, which opposed Somoza, is not opulent and is dedicated to the poor. Unlike the church in Mexico, it was not a target of the revolution. Archbishop Miguel Obando Bravo is a respected, independent figure. Although the Sandinistas control television and publish their own newspaper, *La Barricada*, the most popular news medium in Nicaragua is still *La Prensa*. The Chamorro family continues the tradition of opposition to injustice. When Borge warned, "I think it is counterrevolutionary to criticize the government," *La Prensa* responded, "We are the revolution. We, *La*

Prensa, have been in the forefront of this. We have a martyr and, indeed, the revolution has to be criticized, otherwise we will find ourselves ending up in tyranny."[23]

This same spirit prevails within organized labor, the private sector, and numerous political parties. At least one-third of the workers have refused to join the Sandinista Workers Confederation and remain organized under independent unions. On March 26-29, 1981, the Union of Nicaraguan Workers (CTN) held its fourth national congress in Managua, with over 200 delegates in attendance, representing 100 affiliated unions. Despite intimidation, the CTN spoke out forcefully in favor of free, democratic unionism and in opposition to "statist and vertical unionism." The private sector, for its part, controls 60 percent of the economy, and the Superior Council of Private Enterprise (COSEP) has vigorously defended its interests in negotiations with the government. The Junta expropriated the vast Somoza holdings early in the revolution, plus banks and insurance companies and a few other properties, which gave it enough to handle, given the small public sector that existed before. Vaky claims that the FSLN "cannot by itself manage the economy."[24] As for political parties, there are several and they are independent. The Sandinistas lack a traditional electoral organization, which may explain their decision to postpone elections until 1985. The Conservative and Independent Liberal parties are still a force, especially among the old families, and the Christian Democratic and Social Democratic parties retain close ties with their counterparts in Costa Rica, Venezuela, and Western Europe. Coming up very fast is a new party, the Nicaraguan Democratic Movement (MDN), and its leader, former Junta member Alfonso Robelo, is emerging as the claimant to Pedro Joaquín's mantle.

Nicaragua's leaders pursued a diversified foreign policy, aware of the support they had received and might hope to receive from many nations. Mexico, Costa Rica, and Venezuela, especially, were supportive of the insurrection and have since provided technicians and aid to help in the task of reconstruction. As noted, Nicaragua has sought economic assistance from a variety of sources, realizing that it was folly to be dependent upon either the United States or the Soviet Union, and that it could not ignore the facilities of international lending institutions dependent upon the wealthy industrial nations. At the same time, it was apparent that the leaders of the FSLN were strongly influenced by those of the Cuban Revolution. As Ambassador Pezzullo observed, "There is a closeness, and there is a great deal of sympathy between the two movements."[25] While Nicaragua rejected U.S. offers of military advisers and even Peace Corps volunteers, it welcomed a sizable number of Cubans (at least 2,000) to work in the areas of education, health, and security. The warm reception given Castro and Yasser Arafat on July 19, 1980, commemorating the first anniversary of the revolution, was disturbing to the Carter administration and placed it on the defensive before its critics. Nicaragua also established diplomatic relations with the Soviet Union, and Junta member Hassan, along with cabinet and directorate members Borge, Humberto Ortega, and Ruiz, went to Moscow in March 1980, where they negotiated a series of agreements dealing with trade and economic, technical, cultural, and scientific cooperation. Soviet aid appears to be modest so far, although there have been reports of an arms shipment, including tanks, to Nicaragua. These actions caused concern, but the most serious development involved the charge that Nicaragua was supporting international terrorist activity and was interfering in events in El Salvador.

The outbreak of violence in El Salvador in mid-1980, and the open sympathy of the Sandinistas toward Salvadoran guerrilla forces, placed the $75 million in assistance to Nicaragua in jeopardy. Under the amendment, Carter could not disperse the funds unless he certified that Nicaragua was not "aiding, abetting, or supporting acts of violence or terrorism in other countries." Even after Carter made the certification, some members of Congress virtually accused him of lying. Representative C.W. Bill Young of Florida, the amendment's sponsor, claimed on September 30, 1980, to have seen intelligence reports that confirmed "in overwhelming detail" that the Sandinistas were engaged in the export of violence and terrorism. "I frankly don't see how he [Carter] could have honestly made that certification if he has seen the same information I have seen,"[26] Young asserted. The Carter administration held firm to its position, even as the issue intensified during the presidential campaign of 1980. Defeated for reelection, and one week before Ronald Reagan took office, Carter suspended disbursement of the remaining $15 million of the economic support fund, because it required a further presidential certification.

The Reagan administration did not lift the suspension and, furthermore, announced in April 1981 that all aid to Nicaragua was being cut off. In the meantime, on February 23, 1981, the Reagan administration issued a "White Paper" on El Salvador, in which it charged that Nicaragua, along with Cuba, had provided a conduit for the flow of arms from communist countries to the guerrillas in El Salvador. Since the maintenance of the government of El Salvador is the principal goal of Reagan policy in Central America, Nicaragua can expect no assistance as long as it is perceived to be aiding the guerrillas. As the same time, the refusal of assistance probably reflected the Reagan administration's fundamental hostility toward the Nicaraguan Revolution. It is difficult to predict the effects of this policy.

This approach asserts U.S. power and prestige, but fails to take into account Nicaraguan nationalism, which the regime can use to rally support. It may achieve its purpose of forcing concessions and even causing the revolution to fail, but it may radicalize the situation further and drive Nicaragua closer to the Cuban model. So far, the latter has not happened, as the Nicaraguans are selling their meat to Canada, and Libya has offered $100 million in aid. The Sandinistas are trying to improve conditions internally, creating the National Forum to promote dialogue between the FSLN and the democratic organizations. However, they closed *La Prensa* for two days in July 1981, on charges that it was printing "lies"; in the same month they suspended the telecasts of Archbishop Obando's Sunday mass, which may portend trouble for the democratic sectors. The Sandinistas have plans to increase the popular militia to a force of 200,000, alleging that the United States is sponsoring counterrevolutionary activity. It may be nonsense, but a hard-line policy converts imagination into belief, fed by the news of the renewal of military assistance to Guatemala and the reports of former Guardsmen training in Florida and Honduras. As Arturo Cruz, Jr., stated, perhaps melodramatically, in a session of the American Historical Association in December 1980, "Not all Nicaraguans are Sandinistas, but all Nicaraguans are nationalists, and they will all fight if the Marines come."

More recently, the Reagan administration has proposed a program of aid for the Caribbean, demonstrating its awareness that overcoming economic misery is the best means of combatting extremism. However, the plan contains certain punitive features: the Reagan administration wants to exclude Cuba and Nicaragua. Mexican President José López Portillo opposes this, even though he endorsed the plan in principle during his meeting with Reagan in June 1981. López Portillo has pledged assistance to Nicaragua, and the Caribbean aid plan, if broadened, may be one way in which the United States can cooperate with other nations in promoting democracy in Nicaragua.

It took over a half-century for U.S.-Nicaraguan relations to reach their present state, so improved conditions are not going to occur overnight. The United States owes it to Nicaragua to exercise patience and goodwill. In striving to preserve the original democratic and mixed economy concepts of the Nicaraguan Revolution, U.S. policy ought to consider that pluralism exists within the FSLN itself. The Tercerista tendency maintains contacts with the social democratic movements of Cost Rica, Venezuela, and elsewhere; its influence may evolve with the help of these allies and an enlightened U.S. policy. The latter means renewed economic assistance and the making of new offers of specialists, technicians, and Peace Corps volunteers. It means, in the words of Representative Gerry E. Studds of Massachusetts, who visited Nicaragua in January 1981,

> not deluging Nicaragua with aid, or becoming blind to the mistakes Nicaraguan leaders will continue to make; but instead dealing maturely, from the sense of security which national wealth and power ought to bestow, with a struggling, courageous, and not really that threatening, potential friend.[27]

United States policy toward Nicaragua, and Central America in general, has been inconsistent. The remarkable American political system has contained more checks than balances in the matter of Nicaragua. This is a subject for serious study. One solution might be an enhanced policymaking role for career foreign service officers, avoiding, in any event, the forced retirement of those who rise too high during a particular presidency. The events in Nicaragua were predictable, but no one wanted to rock the boat. The record of U.S. relations with the Somozas evoked the lament, "the United States does not really care about Central America."[28] Central American democratic leaders express concern that the United States only pays attention to the region when there is a crisis affecting its security and that, when the crisis passes, it loses interest, even if a new Somoza has emerged. More than U.S. intervention, Central American democrats fear U.S. neglect. The United States needs to develop long-range goals, in a spirit of bipartisanship and in dialogue with leaders of the region. Otherwise, it will continue only to react to events in Nicaragua and Central America, not to influence them.

NOTES

1. U.S., Congress, House, Subcommittee on Inter-American Affairs of the Committee on Foreign Affairs, *Central America at the Crossroads,* 96th Cong., 1st Sess., 1979, p. 52.

2. Anastasio Somoza and Jack Cox, *Nicaragua Betrayed* (Boston: Western Islands, 1980), p. 58.

3. Somoza and Cox, *Nicaragua Betrayed*, p. 312.

4. U.S., Department of State, *Bulletin* 78, No. 2020 (November 1978): 52–53.

5. Somoza and Cox, *Nicaragua Betrayed*, p. 28.

6. U.S., Department of State, *Bulletin* 79, No. 2029 (August 1979): 59.

7. Somoza and Cox, *Nicaragua Betrayed*, p. 144.

8. U.S., Congress, House, Subcommittee on Inter-American Affairs of the Committee on Foreign Affairs, *United States Policy toward Nicaragua,* 96th Cong., 1st Sess., 1979, p. 6.

9. House, Subcommittee on Inter-American Affairs, *Policy toward Nicaragua*, p. 48.

10. Alfred Stepan, "The U.S. and Latin America: Vital Interests and the Instruments of Power," *Foreign Affairs* 58, No. 3 (1980): 681.

11. House Subcommittee on Inter-American Affairs, *Policy toward Nicaragua,* p. 74.

12. Thomas W. Walker, "The Sandinista Victory in Nicaragua," *Current History* 78, No. 454 (February 1980): 59.

13. House, Subcommittee on Inter-American Affairs, *Policy toward Nicaragua*, p. 76.

14. House, Subcommittee on Inter-American Affairs, *Central America at the Crossroads*, p. 28.

15. Ibid., p. 34.

16. U.S., Congress, House, Subcommittee on Inter-American Affairs of the Committee on Foreign Affairs, *Assessment of Conditions in Central America,* 96th Cong., 2d Sess., 1980, pp. 53, 75.

17. House, Subcommittee on Inter-American Affairs, *Conditions in Central America*, p. 70.

18. U.S., Congress, Senate, Committee on Foreign Relations, *FY 1981 Foreign Assistance Legislation,* 96th Cong., 1st Sess., 1980, p. 387.

19. Senate, Committee on Foreign Relations, *FY 1981 Foreign Assistance Legislation*, p. 416.

20. U.S., Congress, House, Subcommittee on Inter-American Affairs of the Committee on Foreign Affairs, *Review of the Presidential Certification of Nicaragua's Connection to Terrorism*, 96th Cong., 2nd Sess., 1980, p. 25.

21. Stephen M. Gorman, "Sandinista Chess: How the Left Took Control," *Caribbean Review* 10 (Winter 1981): 16–17.

22. Viron Vaky, "Hemisphere Relations: 'Everything is Part of Everything Else,'" *Foreign Affairs* 59, No. 3 (1981): 621–22.

23. House Subcommittee on Inter-American Affairs, *Central America at the Crossroads*, p. 30.

24. Vaky, "Hemisphere Relations," p. 622.

25. House Subcommittee on Inter-American Affairs, *Assessment of Conditions*, p. 77.

26. House Subcommittee on Inter-American Affairs, *Review of Presidential Certification*, p. 18.

27. U.S., Congress, House, Committee on Foreign Affairs, *Central America, 1981*, 97th Cong., 1st Sess., 1981, p. 15.

28. Quoted in Richard Millett, "Central American Paralysis," *Foreign Policy*, No. 39 (Summer 1980): 117.

9

El Salvador:
Influence in Trouble

Thomas P. Anderson

The ability of the United States to influence events in El Salvador appeared to be stronger in the early 1980s than it had ever been before, largely because of the civil war that has rampaged through that country since the coup of 1979.

Until the late 1970s, it is safe to say that El Salvador did not loom large in the consciousness of the North American people. Only the tragic events of the last several years have sparked an interest in this tiny land.

Even for Spanish America, the country was something of a backwater. Until the arrival of commercial air travel early in the 1930s, it took a great deal of time and effort even to travel from the United States to El Salvador, for the country lacks an Atlantic coast and the Pacific steamers were irregular.

The one thing that might have brought close U.S. scrutiny, a substantial economic tie, was lacking. The major export of El Salvador, until the development of cotton and sugar in the 1950s, was coffee. This was raised on relatively small fincas and did not bring in large foreign corporations as did, for instance, the banana trade in neighboring countries. A part of the coffee went to North America, but much of it was shipped to Germany (except during the world wars), where it was highly prized. Raising no fruit for export, El Salvador did not attract the fruit companies, nor did it appear to offer much else for the foreign investor. Only after the rise of cotton did textile mills come into existence, and when they did they were built and operated not by North Americans but by Japanese.

El Salvador first made headlines abroad in 1932, when the country experienced the first major communist uprising in the Western Hemisphere.[1] This revolt was led by a dedicated communist, Agustin Farabundo Marti, and several other members of his Communist Party of El Salvador (Partido Comunista de El Salvador, PCES). However, the bulk of the manpower for the movement came from the Pipil Indian peasants in the western part of the country, who were increasingly unhappy as the Salvadoran oligarchy encroached upon their traditional lands to create coffee fincas. The revolt took place in January, only a month and a half after General Maximiliano Hernández Martínez had overthrown the moderately progressive civilian government of Arturo Araujo. The United States at that time had a policy of nonrecognition of Central American governments that took power by coup, in accordance with a 1923 treaty signed by the Central American states and adhered to by the United States as well. Despite this, several North American warships rushed to the scene. They offered to land a force of marines and sailors to aid the government, but General Hernández Martínez haughtily refused this offer, declaring that he could handle the situation.

Indeed, he crushed the revolt within three days, and then the great massacre began. Some 10,000 to 20,000 peasants were machine-gunned by his troops, while Marti and the ringleaders were formally executed by firing squad. This was a calculated example of frightfulness to cow the peasantry into permanent submission, and for a long time it worked. During the 1950s and 1960s, when social ferment tore through the neighboring countries, El Salvador remained strangely quiet. It is ironic and tragic that this event that first caused the United States to examine El Salvador was a communist uprising, the name of whose leader has been taken by the Farabundo Marti National Liberation Front (Frente Farabundo Marti de Liberacíon Nacional, FMLN), which in the 1980s waged an armed, Marxist struggle that has caused the United States to volunteer aid and advisers.

Between the death of Marti and the rise of the several movements that eventually came to take his name, the country slipped out of the consciousness of all but the coffee importers in the United States and a few investors. But there were occasions when the United States had to take official action. One vexing problem of the 1930s was the recognition of the government of Hernández Martínez, who had overthrown Araujo. The United States might have wanted to recognize the government, if for no other reason than to support it against any lingering communist menace, but its agreement to the 1923 treaty decreed otherwise. Too strongly entrenched to be ousted by the North American nonrecognition policy, the general blithely ignored the United States. Only military intervention or economic sanctions could have driven him out, and these the Roosevelt administration had pledged itself not to undertake unilaterally. When the Central American states themselves abandoned the nonrecognition policy, the United States had little choice but to follow suit and recognized the government on January

24, 1934. Kenneth J. Grieb comments: "The collapse of the treaty and the successful defiance of the United States by Martínez ushered in a new era in Central American politics, making possible the rise of a new series of dictators."[2] He was overthrown in 1944, but through coup and countercoup the rule of the military continued, partly because the traditional landholding aristocracy had been so badly frightened by the 1932 rising that they left everything but their wealth to the military. In 1961, tired of the instability, Colonial Julio Adelberto Rivera established a ruling party, the Party of National Conciliation (Partido de Conciliacion Nacional, PCN), which subsequently won every presidential election until the coup of October 1979.

Colonel Rivera and his successor, General Fidel Sánchez Hernández, presided over a serious international controversy that again led to intervention by the United States. This was the controversy with Honduras over the hundreds of thousands of Salvadorans who had been lured to that country by the high wages of the banana firms and the increasing difficulty of farming conditions at home. At first welcomed next door, they became the target of political agitation in the mid-1960s, when the wily dictator, Gen. Oswaldo López Arellano, ruled Honduras. Further, disputes persisted over the undefined border between the two countries. There were a number of "pockets" (bolsones) claimed by both countries. In 1967 this situation was dramatized by the arrest of a prominent Honduran border bandit by Salvadoran troops in one of these bolsones. Tension grew in June of that year when a Salvadoran patrol of no less than 43 men supposedly strayed across the border and was captured in Honduras. Both sides threatened war and, despite the mediation of the other Central American states, things might have come to that pass had not President Lyndon Johnson used personal diplomacy. In Central America for a regional conference, he met with López Arellano and Sánchez Hernández and convinced the two soldier-presidents that negotiations were better than fighting. The United States was deeply concerned that the controversy might damage the Central American Common Market, an organization backed by the United States as a means of increasing regional prosperity and warding off Marxist radicalism. Eventually the 43 Salvadorans were exchanged for the one Honduran.

That, however, was not the end of the tensions between the neighboring states. Anxious to implement a land reform scheme without hurting the powerful local landlords, López Arellano hit upon the idea of seizing the lands "illegally" held by Salvadoran nationals. This policy was carried into effect in May 1969 with grim results. Thousands of Salvadorans in Honduras were driven from their meager plots with threats and sometimes violence.[3] This coincided with a bitterly contested series of World Cup Soccer matches between the two countries; when El Salvador, feeling it had exhausted diplomatic resources, launched a surprise attack on July 14, the conflict was given the misleading title, "the Soccer War."

The war caught the United States by surprise. Only a week earlier the U.S. military mission in El Salvador appeared convinced that nothing of the sort would happen. The conflict also was a profound embarrassment to the United States, as both sides used North-American-made aircraft and, to a certain extent, weapons. Further, they had been trained in the use of this equipment by the U.S. Military Advisory and Assistance Groups in the respective countries, as part of the scheme for protecting the region against communism. Murat W. Williams, U.S. ambassador of the Kennedy years, recently recollected that he had warned Secretary of State Dean Rusk that our military mission was "excessive," but Pentagon interests had successfully blocked any reduction.[4] Prior to the outbreak of hostilities, mediation efforts had been undertaken by the other members of the Central American Common Market, but after the fighting began, the Organization of American States appointed a seven-nation commission to conduct an investigation and to make recommendations. The United States was one of these seven.[5]

The commission recommended a cease fire on July 18, withdrawal of the Salvadoran forces from Honduras within 72 hours, and a supervision procedure by the OAS. The seven-nation panel was viewed with extreme hostility in El Salvador, which refused to withdraw its troops until the threat of economic sanctions forced it to do so. A popular, though irrational, Salvadoran slogan of the time was, "We will get out of Honduras when the United States and Russia get out of Germany." Although the Salvadorans departed from Honduras, no peace treaty was signed until October 31, 1980, and there were frequent border incidents. For this reason, the OAS maintained a surveillance along the demilitarized zone separating the combatants. In this the United States played a very active part, providing the helicopters and pilots used in the surveillance.

During the war, the small North American community in El Salvador had spared no pains to indicate their approval of the Salvadoran government and their opposition to Honduras. Joseph E. Maleady, president of the United States Residents Association, even wrote a pamphlet that strongly defended El Salvador against the accusations of barbarism toward Hondurans in the country and defended the invasion. All the same, many Salvadorans blamed the United States for taking the lead in the OAS and forcing the withdrawal of the Salvadoran army under threat of sanctions. Although the military group was maintained on a reduced scale during the 1970s, the United States ceased to supply El Salvador with much in the way of military aid. In 1977 Congress blocked $600,000 that the Carter administration had wished to send as a training grant to the army.[6]

This brief sketch of the relationship between the United States and El Salvador prior to the origins of the current crisis suggests a number of points that indicate that this relationship was profoundly different from that of the

United States to many other Latin American countries. First of all, there was little economic interpenetration between the two countries. The giant fruit companies and the mining interests, such as Rosario Mining, had stayed out of El Salvador. The largest U.S.-owned plant in the 1970s was that of Texas Instruments, which employed no more than 200 Salvadorans. While the United States brought substantial amounts of Salvadoran coffee and cotton, it was by no means the sole customer.

Second, the United States seldom tried with any real degree of seriousness to influence events in El Salvador. It tried to aid the government (although it did not officially recognize it) in 1932 against the communist rising, and was rebuffed. It sought to maintain a nonrecognition policy against Hernández Martínez, and was forced into a recognition that destroyed the whole policy of not recognizing illegal regimes. President Johnson successfully fended off armed conflict between El Salvador and Honduras in 1967, but the conflict broke out in 1969 and the United States actively participated in the OAS settlement.

Third, there was no clear-cut policy toward El Salvador. The chief efforts of the United States were directed toward the country in instances when it became a threat to the peace and stability of the region, either as a potential communist base or through an aggressive military policy. Internally, El Salvador mattered very little and so there was no need to work out a permanent, long-term set of U.S. objectives. This tradition would be a great handicap to U.S. planners during the growing crisis of the 1970s.

The troubles that were to convulse the country in recent times sprang from the profound dissatisfaction on the part of the peasant community over the fact that the land (and therefore the wealth) of the country was being concentrated in fewer and fewer hands. The "fourteen families," which was a way of saying the very wealthy, had most of the resources of the country. Of Central American countries, only Honduras (the second poorest country in the Western Hemisphere) had a lower per-capita income. Further, with the population growth running at around 3.5 percent a year, the country was becoming grossly overpopulated in terms of its ability to feed its people.

Since 1932 the political atmosphere of the country had been harshly repressive. The army, and such militarized police units as the Guardia Nacional, insured peace in the countryside by terrorizing the peasant population and preventing them from protesting against the poor wages and miserable conditions under which they worked on the estates of the mighty. Although, under the system established in the early 1960s by Colonel Rivera, opposition parties were allowed to function, their toleration was always precarious and fraud was common. In the presidential elections of 1972, the Christian Democratic party (Partido Demócrata Cristiano, PDC), the socialist Movimiento Nacional Revolucionario (MNR), and the communist front party ran the PDC leader José Napoleón Duarte for president. Although Duarte appeared to have won a plurality in the election, a hastily called congress declared the PCN candidate, Colonel Arturo Armando Molina, to be the winner. Shortly thereafter, Duarte made the mistake of involving himself in an abortive coup of younger officers and was exiled from the country. The same three opposition parties, although disheartened by their previous experience, ran Colonel Ernesto Claramount Rozeville in the 1977 election. This time massive fraud and violence was used by the PCN.

Many persons opposed to military rule had not needed a second fraudulent election to tell them that only an armed struggle could topple the entrenched political system. Salvador Cayetano Carpio, a breakaway former secretary-general of the Communist party, had formed the Popular Liberation Forces (Fuerzas Populares de Liberación, FPL) in 1970. Following the 1972 election, this guerrilla-terrorist band swung into action. There were three major guerrilla movements terrorizing the country by 1975.

Even more alarming from the point of view of the government was the emergence of several broadly based peasant unions. In the mid-1970s, these peasant unions spawned the massive "popular organizations": the Unified Popular Action Front (Frente Acción Popular Unificada, FAPU) and the Popular Revolutionary Block (Bloque Popular Revolucionario, BPR). These combined peasants, labor unions, student and teacher groups, and various other associations under a single banner. Even though the Catholic church had a good deal to do with the formation of these movements, they moved rapidly to the left; by 1979 Facundo Guardado, leader of the BPR, declared his movement to be Marxist-Leninist.[7] By that time, the various guerrilla movements had been "adopted" as the fighting arm of the various popular organizations.

Although the North American public was unaware of peasant discontent in El Salvador until the late 1970s, the State Department had long been aware of potential problems from that sector, as had the American Institute for Free Labor Development (AIFLD), an international branch of the AFL-CIO specifically charged with encouraging "free" labor unions (that is, non-Marxist ones) among the peasants of Third World countries. Although AIFLD was and is a nongovernmental body, some 90 percent of its activities have been funded by the United States Agency for International Development (AID), an arm of the federal government. It was frequently charged in the 1960s that AIFLD had close connections with the Central Intelligence Agency as well as AID.

In 1961 the United States and El Salvador had signed a General Agreement for Economic and Technical Assistance as part of President Kennedy's Alliance for Progress. Under this it was envisioned that the United States would help to train peasant leaders in order to pave the way for land reform. The following year, AID, the Salvadoran ministry of labor, and

AIFLD signed an agreement to begin the training of these leaders, and the process actually began in 1965. Out of AIFLD's experience in this work grew the Unión Comunal Salvadoreña (UCS), founded in 1968. This was not judged to be a peasant union of the sort considered illegal and was granted legal status (personería jurídica) by the government, which seemed to regard this as a safe alternative to less controllable peasant movements. The organization remained under the tutelage of its founder, AIFLD, and through that organization received large amounts of money from AID, beginning with a grant for $136,600 in 1970. Grants for 1971–72 totaled half a million dollars.[8] UCS established peasant cooperatives and communal farms on a small scale, often with the direct support of the Salvadoran government, which became increasingly cooperative as the menace of more radical peasant organizations grew. Thus the UCS became a powerful link in the early 1970s betwen the government of El Salvador, the United States government, and the AFL-CIO. One of the chief AIFLD men involved in the program was Michael Hammer, who would be assassinated in El Salvador in January 1981.

Then, in a dramatic move, AIFLD was expelled from El Salvador in August 1973. There were a number of reasons behind this expulsion. For one thing, certain members of the military government felt that some Institute officials were interfering in the internal affairs of the country. Further, there was controversy within the UCS over AIFLD allegations of corruption and mismanagement. This did not mean the end of U.S. involvement with the UCS, for funding continued to come through the Inter-American Foundation, a semiautonomous government agency established by the U.S. Congress in 1969. This foundation expended almost $1 million in aid between the expulsion of AIFLD and the coup of October 1979. Meanwhile Michael Hammer, based in Venezuela, continued to keep an eye on the situation. After much negotiation, AIFLD was readmitted to El Salvador in summer 1979.[9]

The involvement with the UCS indicates once again the concern, both of the U.S. government and the labor movement, to ward off the threat of Marxism in El Salvador, not because of the importance of the country itself, but out of regional strategic concerns. Again the fear was that El Salvador would become a disturber of the peace, as it had been in 1932 and, for quite different reasons, in 1969. Involvement with the UCS proved to be a powerful means of influencing the government of El Salvador, which was closely identified with the movement.

That government, however, found its base of support rapidly deteriorating during the 1970s; only the guns of the security forces prevented total collapse. Faced with an increasingly vociferous and sometimes violent opposition, the governments of presidents Molina and Romero resorted to a heavy-handed repression, carried out through the security forces and through the paramilitary group known as ORDEN. Simple peasants were killed when they protested their condition, but lay workers of the Catholic church, known as catechistas, were also eliminated on the grounds that they aided the illegal peasant unions. Then, starting in March 1977, there was a string of murders of priests, blamed on the security forces and a rightist-terrorist movement, which was said to work with the government.

The murder of priests led to a direct confrontation between the government and the new archbishop of San Salvador, Oscar Arnulfo Romero y Galdámez. Humberto Romero assumed the presidency. The new archbishop was radicalized by the death of priests and began to denounce the government's campaign of repression. His weekly sermons from the cathedral of San Salvador became famous throughout the region.[10] The publicity that this "war of the two Romeros" received in the United States had its effect upon the North American clergy and the Catholic laity as well. Such influential journals as *America* and *Commonweal* began to run pieces highly critical of the Salvadoran government.

In one case at least, a North American citizen was the victim of the repression of the PCN government. This was a ne'er-do-well drifter and self-proclaimed soldier of fortune by the name of James Ronald Richardson, who was arrested by the Policía Nacional in the fall 1976 on drug-smuggling charges. Richardson was even brought to the U.S. embassy and interrogated, but the next day he was "disappeared," as the Salvadorans say. The government claimed to have put him on a flight to Guatemala, but he never arrived there. An investigation conducted by the embassy itself showed that he had been the victim of a Colonel René Chacón. The United States ambassador at the time was Ignacio Lozano, Jr., a California newpaper publisher and a political appointee of the Nixon administration. Lozano sought to push the investigation into the disappearance of Richardson, but received scant cooperation from the State Department. Shortly after, Lozano was turned out by the Carter administration and the Richardson matter was allowed to drop. Although the case seemed trivial in light of the massive human rights violations going on daily in El Salvador, it contained a symbolic value. To the military it sent a signal that the United States was not really concerned enough about human rights to investigate the disappearance of one of its own citizens.

Nevertheless, the new administration of Jimmy Carter had an announced policy of championing human rights. The career officer who replaced the able Lozano, Frank Devine, was charged with pursuing this policy. But Ambassador Devine received mixed signals from Washington, and was himself unclear how much emphasis should be placed on this matter in the light of the growing menace of Marxism. "I am an unreconstructed cold warrior," he once declared.[11] What was evidently intended by Washington was a carrot-and-stick approach, in which gradual rewards would be given for an improvement of the human rights situation, while rewards would be withheld should the government fail to cooperate.

One particular carrot desired by the government of El Salvador in 1977 was $90 million in loans from the Inter-American Development Bank (IDB) for the massive San Lorenzo hydroelectric project. The United States had a virtual veto over the actions of the IDB. When General Romero replaced Molina on July 1, 1977, he seemed to hold out the promise of a better human rights policy. He declared that he started with a "clean slate," and that "people would be surprised" at the changes we would make. In view of his promises, the State Department had urged Congress to approve U.S. participation in making this loan. Interestingly enough, the State Department lobbyist in this matter was the ambassador-designate, Frank Devine.[12] The loan was approved in November 1977. Three weeks later the government of El Salvador promulgated the infamous Law of Public Order, which imposed a perpetual state of siege in the country. Further, disappearances and massacres began to occur at an increased tempo, and the only active opposition newspaper in the country was suppressed.

Ambassador Devine believed in a low-key, cooperative approach to the question of human rights. One approach he tried was to invite prominent members of the government to his residence and to leave scattered about various clippings from the world press that condemned the actions of the Salvadoran government. By such methods he hoped to shame the government into a better human rights policy. One critic of this policy commented at the time that this was "rather like shaming a fox into not killing chickens."

The left in turn began to dramatize their own actions, knowing that world opinion was against the government. Such tactics as the seizures of churches and foreign embassies became common, with hostages being taken in the latter case. Only the fortress-like U.S. embassy, which loomed over one of the city's principle squares, was immune to seizure, though not to occasional gunfire. These tactics resulted in two appalling massacres in May 1979, which sealed the fate of the Romero government.

Following the arrest of its leader, Facundo Guardado, the BPR seized the cathedral of San Salvador, with the acquiescence of the clergy. Taunting BPR demonstrators would stand on the steps of the building, waving banners and shouting slogans. On May 3, this became too much for the Policía Nacional which opened fire, killing 24 persons and wounding many more. A major U.S. television network was present and caught the entire action, which was broadcast to a horrified North American audience. The Venezuelan embassy and a number of hostages were then seized in reprisal. Three weeks after the cathedral steps incident, a march of women and children, bringing food into the besieged embassy, was machine-gunned and 20 persons were killed.

A plot to topple Romero was launched about this time by a number of junior officers, led by Captain Francisco Mena Sandoval. Colonel Jaime Abdul Gutiérrez, known as a middle-of-the-road officer between the hardline advocates of repression and the leftist sympathizers, was soon brought into the plot. Much later, another powerful colonel, Adolfo Arnoldo Majano, considered more leftist, was also brought into the plot. The Jesuit University, Universidad Centroamericana, which had become the focus of antigovernment activity since the government's seizure of the National University in 1972, was consulted as to the program to be presented by the pronouncement of the coup. It seems quite certain that feelers were also made to the U.S. embassy, which is said to have given the movement its blessing.[13] In any event, a bloodless military rising toppled the 18-year-old regime of the PCN and sent General Romero packing into exile on October 15, 1979. The United States, greatly relieved, quickly recognized the new regime and hailed its makers as reformers.

In the Latin American tradition, a governing junta was then set up, composed of Colonels Gutiérrez and Majano, Guillermo Manuel Ungo, the socialist leader, Román Mayorga, rector of the Jesuit University, and a San Salvador businessman. Archbishop Romero gave the new regime cautious approval and counseled a wait-and-see attitude to the mass organizations. Indeed, a truce of sorts was established between the security forces and the leftist opposition that ran from November 7 to December 7. After that it broke down. The BPR assaulted a march of middle-class women in the capital, and shortly thereafter the security forces raided two villages and massacred the inhabitants.

The key to the problem was the junta's control over its own military. Unless they could prevent further outbreaks of violence by the security forces, they could neither pacify the leftist forces nor effect the necessary social reforms. On December 27 Ungo, Mayorga, and most of the civilian members of the cabinet presented a list of demands to the Superior Military Council, the governing body of the security forces. These amounted to an assertion of civilian control. But the military had been out of control for 50 years, setting its own budget, running its own prisons, and dispensing its own brand of justice. Compromise proved to be impossible; the junta and cabinet resigned on January 3, 1980.

This development created a momentary crisis in the capital, with rioting crowds burning busses and shops. However, behind the backs of the civilian members of the government, the military, led by Minister of Defense Colonel José Guillermo Garciá and Colonel Gutiérrez, had been negotiating with the leaders of the Christian Democratic party, and the PDC had agreed to help form a new government in which it would be the dominant civilian voice. Such a government was announced only two days after the fall of the first junta. Antonio Morales Erlich, the secretary-general of the party, and Héctor

Dada, a prominent PDC intellectual from the Jesuit University, were named to the new junta; a majority of cabinet members were also party members. Colonel García retained his post as defense minister, and the same two colonels also sat on the junta.

The United States breathed a sigh of relief at this turn of events. But all was not well with the new government. Violence between the military and the left continued, as did atrocities by the security forces and the White Warrior Union (UGB). Archbishop Romero began both to criticize the PDC members of the junta as ineffective and to justify the right of insurrection when all peaceful means of change had failed. On the other side, Major Roberto D'Aubuisson, one of the 60 officers removed from the military in the October coup and the deputy chief of military intelligence under President Romero, was advocating a coup by the right in order to save the country from communism. Finally, the murder of PDC leader and Attorney-General Mario Zamora by the UGB sparked a series of defections to the opposition by prominent Christian Democrats, including his brother Rubén and Hector Dada, who charged the government with being unwilling to put down right-wing terrorism. Dada's place on the junta was taken by José Napoleón Duarte, the leading figure in the PDC, who had been waiting in the wings.

The crisis with D'Aubuisson and the right reached a critical point in late February, when a coup seemed imminent. At this time Ambassador Devine was slated for retirement and departed the country. Until the new ambassador, Robert White, could arrive, the post was taken by Deputy Assistant Secretary of State for Central American Affairs James Cheek. Sending Cheek was an indication of how seriously the United States regarded the situation. Cheek immediately began to make contact with leading landholders, businessmen, and members of the armed forces, "spelling out in cold terms U.S. policy and the consequences of defying it."[14] Cheek's strategy worked, and although D'Aubuisson hatched several more plots, none of them ever flew. He was also rumored to have been behind the assassination of Archbishop Romero, which took place on March 24.

It was not enough simply to forestall a coup from the right. The government of El Salvador was in desperate need of financial aid, and this began to be provided in a $49 million package. Of this, $5.7 million was earmarked for the military, the first military assistance since the start of the Carter era. The "nonlethal" military aid, trucks, radios, and other such equipment, was designed not only to strengthen the hand of the military against the Marxist guerrillas, but also to buy the loyalty of the military to the junta. This initial aid package was the beginning of a very substantial North American investment in the junta and its success.

The Christian Democrats on the junta, and Colonel Majano, believed that only major reforms could possibly create a constituency for the junta, but they hesitated, knowing that the powerful business lobby, known as

ANEP, was against any sweeping social changes. However, at the urging of the United States, they decided to launch a land reform. The U.S. State Department saw land reform as a means of undercutting the radical left by giving the peasantry a stake in society. The scheme was largely conceived by AIFLD, which had been back in the country since the preceding summer. Technical advice came from the institute's consultant, Roy Prosterman, who had been in charge of setting up the land reforms of the ill-fated South Vietnamese government. AID provided a grant to enable Dr. Prosterman to do this work. The on-the-spot advice came from Michael Hammer.[15] The first phase of the reform, along with the nationalization of all Salvadoran banks, got underway on March 6, 1980. It was designed to transfer 263 estates of 500 hectares (1,250 acres) or more to the permanent and temporary workers on them. The plan was to be administered through the Instituto Salvadoreño de Transformación Agraria (ISTA), working through the UCS and other peasant groups loyal to the government. The head of the UCS, Rodolfo Viera, himself a peasant, was made director of the land reform, his deputy and the real organizer of the process being Leonel Gómez Vides, a maverick member of the upper classes and long-time advisor to UCS. This immediately made for tension because Gómez Vides had an intense dislike for AIFLD and had played a role in its expulsion from the country in 1973.

The first phase was hastily conceived and hastily carried out, ignoring a perfectly sensible land reform plan that had been drawn up under the Molina government. The military inevitably played a role in the expropriations, and, just as inevitably, tried to use the reform to reward peasants loyal to them, which generally meant members of the now-outlawed ORDEN. This was discouraged by Viera and Gómez. Phase two was to confiscate a portion of estates between 100 and 500 hectares, but this was not carried out in the first year of the reform.

A third, more controversial aspect of the land reform program was Decree 207, the Land-to-the-Tiller program, which came out shortly after the initial seizure of the great estates. AIFLD largely wrote the decree and gave it to the junta, ignoring the minister of agriculture and the officials of ISTA. Behind the move as well were the U.S. embassy and the State Department, which desired a dramatic reform for political purposes.[16] Indeed, Prosterman himself hailed the Land-to-the-Tiller program as "the most dramatic aspect of the reform, and the one most likely to have the most immediate impact on both the political and agricultural spheres."[17] The idea of Decree 207 was to transfer all rented land from the current owners to the renters. This would be automatic and self-enforcing. It was a beautifully simple idea, and one totally out of touch with Salvadoran realities. For one thing, many of those who rented land were not great hacendados, but were as poor as the people they rented to. Second, the majority of rentals were of marginal land given over to food crops and land upon which slash-and-burn agriculture was practiced, necessitating moving from one strip of land to another every couple of years. The last thing renters wanted was to be saddled with such property. Further, while it was imagined to be self-implementing, in reality most peasants feared reprisals from the current owners should they attempt to take advantage of the law; even if they should be so bold as to do so, no machinery was set up to process the new titles. ISTA, which regarded the plan as a Yankee imposition, largely ignored it. While one might not fully agree with James Stephens's assessment that the land reform was "flawed to the core,"[18] it was apparent after more than a year of operation that it had many drawbacks, and these stemmed at least in part from the fact that it was largely an outside creation.

The most damaging blow to the land reform program came on January 3, 1981, when Rodolfo Viera, Michael Hammer, and another AIFLD official, Mark Pearlman, were shot to death at the Sheraton Hotel in San Salvador. In May, two young members of the Salvadoran oligarchy were arrested by federal authorities in Miami and turned over to the Salvadoran government to be charged with the crime. Following the death of Viera, Leonel Gómez took over at ISTA; but only ten days after the Viera killing he was arrested by the military on charges of being a leftist. He was released, but that same evening was visited by a right-wing death squad. Barely escaping with his life, he fled to the United States, reportedly with the aid of Ambassador Robert White.

Ambassador White had relieved James Cheek in March 1980. He had been ambassador to Paraguay and was known for his vigor there in carrying out the human rights policy of the Carter administration. In El Salvador he found himself in a much more ambiguous situation. While the government of of El Salvador could certainly be charged with human rights violations, it was at the same time a government to which the United States was deeply committed, and one that had made strenuous efforts at reform. White took the line that the junta was basically reformist, but was caught between right-wing extremists and the Marxist rebels. While there were undeniable excesses by certain military units (indeed, on occasion wholesale massacres of villagers), these White saw as aberrations that the more moderate elements of the military, represented by Defense Minister García, were trying to bring under control. The left was also committing excesses, and, in White's view, represented a group of extremists who wished to created in El Salvador another version of Pol Pot's maniacal government in Cambodia. These leftists did not represent the majority of the Salvadoran people; in proof of this the ambassador cited the repeated failure of their general strikes and demonstrations. The task of the United States, as he saw it, was to continue to encourage reforms, especially land reform, to champion human rights, and to buttress the government against pressures from both the right and the left.[19]

This view of the situation received several shocks in late 1980. On November 27 the leaders of the leftist umbrella movement, the Frente Democrático Revolucionario (FDR), were meeting in Sal Salvador. How it happened that the leaders of this outlawed opposition body presumed that they could meet in broad daylight at the Jesuit academy in the capital city of the enemy has never been satisfactorily explained. Armed government troops sealed off the street and nonuniformed persons arrested FDR president Enrique Alvarez, a minister under the first junta, Juan Chacón, the chief of the BPR, and four other FDR leaders. Their tortured bodies were found the next day. Although the government denied any role in the seizure and murder of these men, it could hardly have been done without governmental complicity. On December 5 there were even more shocking murders. Four North American Catholic missionary women, three of them nuns, and two members of the Maryknoll order, which had a reputation of backing the FDR were killed on their return journey from the new national airport. Their bodies were exhumed from a shallow grave the next day, with Ambassador White in attendence. It was clear that they had been murdered by the security forces. United States aid was temporarily suspended and demands were made that the Salvadoran government track down the guilty parties. A U.S. commission was sent to investigate, composed of Assistant Secretary of State William Bowdler, former Assistant Secretary of State William Rogers, and Luigi Einaudi. No immediate progress was made in the investigation, and Ambassador White soon charged the Salvadoran government with dragging its feet. "We have expressed our concern about the violence to this government for months and months," he declared, "now it is time to act."[20] Months later, six soldiers of the Guardia Nacional, none ranked higher than corporal, were charged with the crime. However, it seemed evident that the two Maryknoll sisters, who had been returning from Managua, had been targeted for death from the time their names appeared on the passenger list of their flight. This meant that someone considerably higher up in the military had been responsible.

The Bowdler Commission's arrival coincided with a crisis within the junta, in which that group was restructured with Duarte becoming president. Colonel Gutiérrez was named vice-president and commander-in-chief of the army, a clear indication that the military balked at civilian control. Colonel Majano was dropped. Bowdler persuaded the junta to restore Majano, but he was dropped later in December, went into hiding, and was arrested in January. Majano was subsequently exiled from the country, another blow to the moderate image projected by the government.

Indeed, after November 4, 1980, the government seemed to trouble less about its image, confident that the new Reagan administration in Washington would back it in any event as a bastion against communism. A report was prepared in early December by Pedro A. San Juan of the Reagan transition team and Frank Carbaugh, an aid to Senator Jesse Helms, which was sharply critical of Ambassador White for having backed the land reform and banking schemes of the Salvadoran government. Ambassadors, said the report, "are not supposed to function in the capacity of social reformers and advocates of new theories of social change with latitude to experiment within the country to which they are accredited." In regard to human rights, the report stated, "Internal policy-making procedures should be structured to insure that the human rights area is not in a position to paralyze or unduly delay decisions on issues where human rights concerns conflict with other vital U.S. interests."[21] The new administration promptly renewed aid to El Salvador.

Seeing that his dismissal was imminent, Ambassador White began to publicly air his differences with the Reagan administration, charging the transition team with undermining his position and renewing charges of a cover-up in the murder of the women missionaries. At the end of January 1981, he was recalled for consultation and promptly dismissed by Secretary of State Alexander Haig. As a measure of the government's displeasure, he was not even permitted to return to El Salvador for the customary round of diplomatic farewells.[22] He was temporarily replaced by Frederic Chapin, a career diplomat, until Dean Hinton, formerly assistant secretary of state for economic affairs, was named to the post in April.

The policies of the new administration did not meet with universal acceptance within the ranks of the foreign policy professionals. A "dissent paper" was prepared, probably by a number of officials in the State Department, Defense Department, and CIA who preferred to remain anonymous, and was circulated throughout the government in January. It warned that the United States had "identified our strategic interests in Central America with a relatively weak, unpopular and isolated regime." It went on to state that "current policy consistently underestimates the domestic legitimacy and international approval enjoyed by the opposition FDR/DRU coalition." It recommended the recognition of the FDR as the government of El Salvador and a lower profile for the United States in the region. Despite this assessment, there was no evidence that the rebels could win on the field of battle. A major offense in January 1981 was beaten back by the security forces, although a number of towns were temporarily lost.

The Reagan administration moved quickly to give massive aid to El Salvador. Military assistance had been resumed in October by President Carter, and by March it had reached $41 million. Starting in September 1981, the military was to receive an additional $66 million. Fifty-four military advisers arrived at the beginning of March, with Pentagon sources suggesting that the "optimum figure" would be 270.[23] Commented ex-

Ambassador White, "The Reagan administration has found the only way to revive the left in El Salvador, that is, by sending military assistance and advisers."[24]

To counter such caustic criticisms, the State Department released a White Paper on El Salvador in late February and simultaneously released a number of papers purportedly seized by the Salvadoran security forces from the rebels, indicating Nicaraguan, Cuban, and Soviet involvement in the struggle. According to the White Paper, "the insurgency in El Salvador has been progressively transformed into a textbook case of indirect armed aggression by Communist powers."[25] Plainly, the United States could be expected to have considerable involvement with El Salvador for some time to come.

It is the thesis of Marxists that North American involvement in Third World countries is based upon the economic needs of American captalism. But, in the case of El Salvador, there was very little economic penetration. The United States had little investment in the country, and those products the United States bought from El Salvador, such as coffee and cotton, could easily be procured elsewhere. El Salvador had other customers such as West Germany and Japan. Direct economic considerations therefore played a very small role. Because of this, it was very difficult for the United States to bring much influence to bear upon the Salvadoran government, nor were there frequent motives for so doing. Only occasionally, as in the San Lorenzo dam project, was there much economic leverage to be asserted.

The United States has become so heavily involved with El Salvador due to fears that events within that country might have serious regional consequences. The idea that El Salvador might follow Cuba and Nicaragua into the socialist camp greatly alarmed Washington officials, who feared a chain reaction, leading perhaps to revolution in always volatile Guatemala or even Mexico, two oil-producing countries strategically close to the United States. Another geopolitical concern was for the Panama Canal, should the wave of revolutions spread southward. Even in the days of the Carter administration, the growing turmoil in El Salvador was seen less in Salvadoran terms than as part of a regional consideration. However, concern for human rights did force the Carter government to address directly problems within the country. The Reagan administration, backing off from the human rights approach, wishes to bring about a military victory by noncommunist forces of whatever stamp.

El Salvador, even without civil war claiming 15,000 lives a year at its current tempo, would be in pitiful shape. Desperately overcrowded and overfarmed and with a surging population, El Salvador would need massive aid to survive without the dislocations of the war. But the war has greatly intensified all the problems. Much of the agriculture has been ruined by the fighting, and the land reform, while eventually beneficial, has had the temporary effect of furthering agricultural disruption.

All this greatly increased the United States potential for influencing events in the country. The government of President Duarte had to be responsive to North American policy because only the United States would supply the military hardware to win the war. Indications of the importance of U.S. influence could be shown in the land reform program and in the ability of the United States to persuade the military not to go along with the projected coup of Major D'Aubuisson, although many of them doubtlessly wanted such a coup to succeed. The government of El Salvador under Duarte had a relatively narrow power base, being tolerated rather than supported by the military, and having alienated the landed oligarchy through its reforms. The United States represented a powerful constituency for the government of El Salvador. But if the Duarte government was tied to the United States, the United States was likewise tied to the Duarte government, which it could not allow to fail. While, as a gesture, the United States might temporarily suspend aid after the murder of the missionary women, it could not realistically maintain that suspension for very long without bringing down a government it was committed to support. Even if the guerrillas were defeated, terrorism would probably be a problem for the foreseeable future, and the economic situation of the country would probably not show any dramatic improvement. Therefore, the United States and El Salvador appear to be linked in their fortunes for some time to come.

NOTES

1. For an account of the uprising, see Thomas P. Anderson, *Matanza: El Salvador's Communist Revolt of 1932* (Lincoln: University of Nebraska Press, 1971).

2. Kenneth J. Grieb, "The United States and the Rise of General Maximiliano Hernández Martínez," *Journal of Latin American Studies* 3 (1971): 72.

3. For the background of the war, see William H. Durham, *Scarcity and Survival in Central America: Ecological Origins of the Soccer War* (Stanford: Stanford University Press, 1979). The war itself is covered in Thomas P. Anderson, *The War of the Dispossessed: Honduras and El Salvador, 1969* (Lincoln: University of Nebraska Press, 1981).

4. *New York Times*, April 17, 1980.

5. Mary Jane Reid Martz, *The Central American Soccer War: Historical Patterns and Internal Dynamics of OAS Settlement Procedures* (Athens, Ohio: Ohio University Center for International Studies, 1978), p. 76.

6. Robert Drinan, John McAward, and Thomas P. Anderson, *Human Rights in El Salvador—1978: Report of Findings of an Investigatory Mission* (Boston: Unitarian Universalist Service Committee, 1978), p. 15.

7. Thomas P. Anderson, "El Salvador," *Yearbook on International Communist Affairs—1979* (Stanford: Hoover Institution Press, 1980), p. 355.

8. Carolyn Forché and Philip Weaton, *History and Motivations of U.S. Involvement in*

the Control of the Peasant Movement in El Salvador: The Role of AIFLD in the Agrarian Reform Process, 1970–1980 (Washington EPICA, 1980), pp. 3–6.

9. Forché and Weaton, History and Motivations, pp. 6–8.

10. Washington Post, 22 May, 1977.

11. At an embassy briefing with the writer being present, January 9, 1978.

12. Drinan, McAward, and Anderson, Human Rights in El Salvador, pp. 12, 30.

13. Robert White stated to the writer on May 28, 1981, "It is reasonable to think that we knew about it [the coup] in advance."

14. This Week Central America and Panama, February 11, 1980.

15. Forché and Weaton, History and Motivations, p. 27.

16. Mac Chapin, A Few Comments on Land Tenure and the Course of Agrarian Reform in El Salvador (privately circulated document of June 1980), p. 20.

17. Roy Prosterman and Mary Temple, "Land Reform in El Salvador," Free Trade Union News 3 (June 1980): 4.

18. James C. Stephens, Jr., "Land Reform's Faded Promise," Democratic Left 9 (April 1981): 13.

19. Interview of the writer with Robert White in San Salvador, August 1980.

20. Boston Globe, December 9, 1980.

21. New York Times, December 4, 1980.

22. This Week Central America and Panama, February 9, 1981.

23. Central America Update, March 1981.

24. Washington Report on the Hemisphere, April 21, 1981.

25. Central America Update, March 1981.

10

Mexico: Wary Neighbor

Martin C. Needler

The United States relations with Mexico are twofold. Mexico, like other states of Latin America, lies in the economic and strategic zone dominated by the United States, and thus is subject to the same kind of overwhelming presence with respect to investment and trade as other countries of the region. At the same time it is an immediate neighbor of the United States, which gives rise to a series of problems deriving from the fact of a common border. Difficulties deriving from each aspect of this relationship interact with each other and become compounded; issues become particularly sensitive, but at the same time the interdependence of the two countries is so complex and so intense that powerful forces make for accommodation whatever the magnitude of the difficulties.

The relations between the two countries rest, of course, on an asymmetry of power, as is the case of U.S. relations with other countries of Latin America. But the relation is less asymmetrical between the United States and Mexico than it is between the United States and many of the countries of the region, for Mexico is a substantial power in its own right. Perhaps also the scope for problems to arise out of pure misunderstanding is rather less, from the Mexican side, than in the case of other countries, since Mexicans know the United States well. In some respects Mexico may know the United States better than the United States knows itself.

Today the dominant image the two governments try to present to their peoples is that of partners and allies. The ritual abrazos when the two presidents meet at the border or in either capital, and the rhetoric each engages in about the special relations of neighbors, may cause one to forget that for much of their history as independent countries the United States and Mexico have been hostile. When in 1941 the government of President Manuel Avila Camacho pledged Mexico's support to the United States in its struggle against Germany and Japan, the Mexican public experienced a shock of surprise. World War II was the first foreign war in which Mexico had been an ally of the United States.

The westward expansion of the United States thwarted what seemed at independence the "manifest destiny" of Mexico to be the largest state in the western hemisphere, and certainly the leader of Hispanic America. At that time Mexican territory reached from a frontier with Russian settlements in the north to Panama in the south. Central America seceded, and a series of secessions, purchases, and conquests gave the United States what is today the western half the country, which would otherwise have been the northern half of Mexico. During the nineteenth century, the governments of the two countries were mutually sympathetic and cooperative only when they were facing other threats: that of southern secession in the United States and of French intervention in Mexico. The two great national heroes, Abraham Lincoln and Benito Juárez, corresponded with each other and their cooperation contributed to the defeat by Juárez of the French forces that had attempted to establish an empire in Mexico under Maximilian. The recollection of other heroes contains a different message: the "Niños Héroes" or Boy Heroes of the War of 1848 jumped to their deaths, wrapped in the Mexican flag, rather than surrender their military academy in Chapultepec Castle to the invading U.S. forces under Winfield Scott.

Over the last 100 years, relations between the two governments have been friendly, despite the underlying tensions and occasional flare-ups of antagonism. Under the long rule of Porfirio Diaz (1876 to 1910), relations between the two governments were good in that Díaz guaranteed stability and favorable treatment for foreign investment during a time when U.S. investors were looking for opportunities, and when investor interests were influential on U.S. government policies. Nevertheless, it should be noted that there was popular resentment in Mexico over the favor shown to foreign investors, and Mexico was sometimes called "the mother of foreigners, the stepmothers of Mexicans." At the same time, Díaz was open to all foreign investment, not to U.S. investment specifically; as a matter of fact, British investment was larger than American until after the Mexican Revolution. There is even some evidence that U.S. oil interests favored the revolution against Díaz in the expectation, which seems to have been correct, that as a result of the revolution they would replace the British interests more favored by Díaz.[1]

During the fighting that followed the revolution, the United States intervened on several occasions. Woodrow Wilson sent in an expeditionary force under General Pershing in an attempt to capture Pancho Villa, who had raided the town of Columbus, New Mexico, in retaliation for the favor shown by the Wilson administration to his rival Venustiano Carranza. Wilson also landed troops in Veracruz, ostensibly to retaliate for an insult to the American flag growing out of a confused incident involving a U.S. sailor, but in reality to protect the oil-producing installations there. Substantial pressure was also brought on the U.S. government to intervene by force of arms over two policies of the Mexican government that aroused resentment in some sectors in the United States. One was the anticlerical policy followed during the 1920s that led to extensive persecution of the Catholic church in Mexico. The pro-Catholic guerrilla movement, the Cristeros, was supplied with weapons and funds by U.S. sympathizers, but Washington resisted pressure to intervene. In 1938 when President Lázaro Cárdenas expropriated the foreign oil companies, there was again pressure to intervene, which was also resisted by the administration of Franklin D. Roosevelt.

As already mentioned, Mexico declared war against the Axis powers on the side of the United States in 1941; it sent an air squadron to fight in the Pacific. World War II, with the Roosevelt administration in office in the United States and that of Avila Camacho in Mexico, represented the high point of cooperation and good feeling between the countries. As the postwar policies of the United States became dominated by the cold war and anticommunist ideology, however, Mexico held back. As a semisocialist government still proud of its revolutionary antecedents, Mexico could not identify wholeheartedly with the cause of capitalism against communism. To view that particular conflict as the overriding one in the international arena seems to most Mexican officials to ignore more important realities of the international scene: regional rivalries, the desire of newly independent countries for genuine autonomy, and the struggle of have-not nations and disadvantaged social classes for a greater share of the world's wealth.

Moreover, the policies adopted by the United States in pursuit of its cold war objectives frequently entailed intervention, overt or covert, by political, economic, and even military means, in the internal affairs of other states. This violated long-standing Mexican commitments to nonintervention, the sovereign equality of states, and resistance to the use of trade and investment as tools of strategy. These were principles matured by Mexico out of a long history of subjection to such policies at British, French, and American hands. Accordingly, Mexico held aloof from the military cooperation programs extended by the United States to the countries of Latin America, designed to upgrade the capabilities of Latin American armies and coordinate their organization and attitudes in an anticommunist direction. Mexico also opposed U.S. policies toward the revolutionary governments of Guatemala and Cuba, which included political isolation, economic blockade, and the organizing of exile invasions.

ECONOMIC RELATIONS

The United States is by far Mexico's largest trading partner for both exports and imports, while Mexico is third in rank among the countries with which the United States trades. Although the relation will remain asymmetrical, Mexico has become a more important trading partner with the expansion of its petroleum production, somewhat under half of which is sold to the United States.

The importance of the United States to the Mexican economy has several dimensions. Revenues from tourism and U.S. investments are critical in balancing Mexico's foreign payments, since the country consistently runs a negative balance on trade alone. This situation has not improved with the expansion of oil exports (although it could be expected to improve eventually) since the requirements for importation of equipment for the oil industry are substantial, and since the growth fueled by expansion of petroleum production has led to import-requiring expansion in transportation and infrastructure projects. This dependence on U.S. capital and tourism has, in effect, created political hostages for U.S. policy. Thus, for example, there was a drastic capital outflow after President López Mateos gave a speech in which he identified the position of his government as on "the far left within the constitution."[2] When President Echeverría instructed his delegate at the United Nations to vote for a resolution in which Zionism was identified as a form of racism, so many hotel bookings were canceled that substantial damage to the nation's balance of payments could be expected, and the president backtracked on his position, issuing "clarifications." It should be noted that the capital and tourism "strikes" were not directed by the government of the United States. They were partly spontaneous and partly unofficially organized acts of private U.S. citizens that, in effect, set limits to how far Mexican policy could go contrary to U.S. preferences. Of course, U.S. government actions with similar effect take place. For example, when the Mexican government seemed reluctant to collaborate in U.S. antidrug efforts, President Nixon ordered border authorities to adopt a "go-slow" strict enforcement policy with respect to customs and immigration formalities, whereupon the lines of people waiting to cross the border were backed up for several hours. The Mexican government capitulated on that issue.[3]

Although foreign investment plays a significant role, the bulk of Mexico's capital is domestically generated. Airlines, railroads, utilities, and petroleum, along with some other sectors of the economy, are publicly owned; foreign direct investment is allowed into other areas only on certain conditions. Increasingly, a firm operating in Mexico should have majority Mexican ownership, although administrative authorities have a great deal of latitude in interpreting and enforcing the law. Other regulations limit the fields of activity foreign firms may engage in, restrict the fees that can be paid for licensing of patents and the like, and forbid ownership of land by foreigners close to the national borders. The general feeling among foreign businessmen is that it is possible to do business in Mexico despite these regulations, although bribes may have to be paid or Mexican partners taken on whose contribution is not economic but political, smoothing the way for government contracts or favorable interpretations of regulations. Although the foundations of the Mexican system are nationalist and thus anti-Yankee, U.S. businesses have learned to work within the system with no more than minor inconvenience or loss. In addition, Mexico's basic nationalism is tempered with the realistic appreciation that it is necessary to get along with the United States. For example, Mexico decided not to join OPEC despite domestic pressures to do so; the United States would have interpreted this as an unfriendly act.

United States economic relations with Mexico have to be understood within the context of the objectives of Mexican development policy. Mexico was one of the first Latin American countries to try to industrialize on the basis of substitution for imports; that is, to develop industries to supply the domestic market while competitive foreign products were kept out by import restrictions. As economic theory teaches, this leads to higher prices to the consumer, and possibly to inferior quality of goods. However, it creates urban employment, whereas the international division of labor might other-wise confine Mexicans to work in mining and agriculture, an option that is no longer viable at a time when there is a tendency for migration to urban areas. At the same time, the desire to have control of the direction of the growth of the Mexican economy in Mexican hands has led to the reservation of some areas of economic activity for state control and to require majority Mexican ownership of firms doing business in Mexico. The large area left to administrative discretion insures that the policy is applied flexibly, and American businesses have found ways to live with (or in some cases to circumvent) the law.

At least since the late 1960s or early 1970s, it has become clear that import substitution alone is not an adequate policy for economic development in Mexico. Mexican governments regard as unacceptable the other grand alternative that presents itself to developing countries: operating an open economy in which there is free movement across international borders of goods and capital. This is seen as involving excessive foreign influences, which tend to force down wages and benefits and lead to an outflow of capital. Accordingly, the direction taken by Mexican policy is, in the words of José López Portillo, to "increase the depth and scope of the process of import substitution and to penetrate foreign markets."[4]

In keeping with this objective, and with an eye on the experience of Japan and (to some extent) Brazil, Mexican governments have been concentrating investments on infrastructure and producers' goods production, and keeping domestic energy costs low, in the expectation that Mexican industry will grow and become internationally competitive. In line with this policy, legislation was passed in 1973 designed to elminate restrictions placed on production in Mexico by foreign companies involved in providing technology under license to Mexican firms.

Thus Mexico's policy with respect to foreign investment remains a balanced one in which foreign investment is welcomed, but at the same time is controlled, supervised, and directed as far as possible to purposes consonant with the government's development program. In view of the country's unfortunate history, beginning with independent Mexico's first trade treaty with Britain, of economic relations detrimental to the nation's sovereignty and resulting in unfair treatment of Mexican interests, Mexico insists that disputes over interpretation of contracts and other economic agreements between Mexicans and foreigners relative to business in Mexico be dealt with in Mexican courts. It resents attempts by U.S. government officials to bring influence to bear.

Doubtless there will continue to be problems in the economic relations between the two countries. At different times, different issues flare up. For example, Florida tomato growers charged that Mexico was shipping tomatoes to the United States at prices below the cost of production, a practice prohibited by U.S. law. The charge was found to be groundless by U.S. courts. When the United States sells minerals, such as lead and zinc, from its emergency stockpiles when these are found to be in surplus, Mexico complains that such sales depress the prices of those products, which it exports. To the great disappointment of the United States, Mexico has held out against joining the General Agreement on Tariffs and Trade (GATT), which requires its members to reduce their tariffs to each other reciprocally, agree not to subsidize exports, and so on. Mexico is not yet prepared to take such a large step away from protecting its domestic industry, despite heavy U.S. pressure. Accordingly, the position of Mexican exports to the United States with respect to tariff liabilities is still unsettled.

Another sensitive fact from a nationalist perspective is that Mexico is no longer self-sufficient in basic foodstuffs; it must import corn, wheat and other commodities. The López Portillo administration has engaged in various policies to augment domestic production of basic food crops through technical assistance, marketing organization, the bringing of new land into cultivation, irrigation, and so on. But the president has made clear that he will not follow the urging of nationalists that land now devoted to cash crops for export should be diverted to the production of foodstuffs for domestic consumption. Such a course of action would only entail the substitution of lower value crops for those of higher value and would in any case worsen the balance of payments, thus forcing further foreign indebtedness.

PRIOR CONSULTATION AND BORDER ISSUES

It is difficult for the United States, as a powerful country used to getting its own way, to treat Mexico on a genuine footing of equality and to be conscious at all times of Mexican interests and sensitivity to slights. To be sure, U.S. presidents use the language of partnership and equality, but in the abstract; when specific issues arise, they forget the general pledges of equality and consultation. A striking case occurred during the Nixon administration, when the president promised to consult in advance with Mexico before taking action that might adversely affect Mexican interests. Subsequently, as the U.S. balance of payments deteriorated, Nixon imposed a surcharge on imported goods with no pretense of consultation, although the act affected Mexico quite drastically. If they had indeed been consulted in advance on that occasion, the Mexicans would no doubt have pointed out that U.S. trade was not in balance primarily because of a large excess of U.S. imports from Japan over exports to Japan; the United States balance of trade with Mexico was positive. It hardly seemed to make sense to penalize Mexican exports to the United States because Americans were buying Datsuns and Toyotas.

With respect to the bilateral and border issues that continually plague relations between the two countries, the record on consultation is mixed. For many years the demarcation of the border of the two countries was unclear after the Rio Grande shifted its channel. The United States refused to abide by the procedures for settling the dispute it had itself agreed to in advance; it was finally resolved in a statesmanlike manner by Presidents Lyndon B. Johnson and Gustavo Díaz Ordaz with a settlement on balance advantageous to Mexico. Similarly, a long-running dispute about the United States creating an excessively saline condition in the waters of the Colorado River that subsequently irrigated Mexican agriculture, on which the United States was for some years uncooperative, was finally resolved by modifications in the hydraulic engineering on the U.S. side of the border. Other successes of consultation and joint negotiation have been the conclusion of a civil aviation agreement that responded to Mexican charges that the allocation of air routes between the two countries was unfair, and agreements on reduction of pollution in the border area. Major continuing issues that still await satisfactory resolution are those concerning Mexican migration to the United States, fishing rights within territorial waters, control of narcotics traffic, and reduction of tariffs.

One of the difficulties involved in dealing with the migration issue is the lack of symmetry in the nature of the problem on the two sides of the border. Thus the United States regards the migration of undocumented Mexican workers as a problem. Those most opposed to such migration charge that illegal Mexican workers take jobs away from American workers, depress the general level of wages in the Southwest, and constitute a burden on the provision of public services in the areas of education and welfare. From the Mexican point of view, there is no particular desire to do anything about illegal migration to the United States since it is not a problem but rather a solution to a problem, that of unemployment and underemployment in Mexico. At the same time, returning migrants are a source of funds and skills for the Mexican economy. Mexican authorities also argue that most un-documented migrants are seasonal agricultural workers, unskilled con-struction laborers, and the like. Therefore it is unlikely that they displace many American workers, who would generally receive more in unem-ployment insurance or welfare payments than they would working at the wages given illegal migrants. Moreover, undocumented aliens do not con-stitute an appreciable burden on local public services of health, welfare, and education—in fact, they avoid such services, as they are afraid of giving away their illegal status if they come into contact with public officials. On the contrary, it is argued, U.S. public revenues benefit from the work of illegal migrants, since taxes and social security are often withheld from their wages, but they do not usually receive social security or claim tax refunds.

Attitudes toward undocumented workers cut across normal political lines of division in the United States. Favoring a more open policy to the migrants, or at least laxity in the enforcement of immigration rules, are both liberals and U.S. Hispanics sympathetic to the needs of the migrants, and Southwestern ranchers and growers eager to employ them; against such a policy can be found both union officials and right-wing chauvinists and racists. The thrust of U.S. policy will probably be to continue the present state of affairs, in which it is difficult to migrate legally but easy to do so illegally; or alternatively, to make it possible to receive legal temporary entry and work permits. The latter solution was favored by over 80 percent of a sample of opinion in Mexico City in 1979.[5]

After initial reluctance, Mexico has cooperated fully in U.S. anti-narcotics programs. The United States provides some financing and tech-nical assistance for the enforcement efforts, and the two governments cooperate in exchange of intelligence, investigation, and prosecution. This collaboration has apparently resulted in a decrease in the traffic and production of heroin in Mexico. There has also been cooperation with respect to other criminal activities, such as the transportation of stolen vehicles and the repatriation of convicts to serve their sentences in their country of nationality.

Another binational program that seems to have met with success is the arrangement for "in bond" assembly plants, called by the Mexicans "maquiladoras." These are factories established on the Mexican side of the border that can import components from the United States, and reexport the finished product to the United States, without paying tariffs to either country.

In effect, Mexican labor works in U.S. factories without having to migrate across the border; the factory is brought to the work force and not the work force to the factory. These factories have created some employment in the border area and have contributed to economic development through "backward linkages."

PETROLEUM

The biggest reason for the current emphasis in U.S. policy on good relations with Mexico is that Mexico holds vast supplies of oil in an era in which some Arab producers have shown their willingness to interrupt supplies for political reasons, and in which collusion among producing states and major companies has led to exorbitant increases in price that place substantial strain on the balance of payments of consuming countries. Under these circumstances, Mexican oil is an attractive way of meeting U.S. consumption needs. The extremely rapid growth in Mexican production since the mid-1970s placed the country in fourth place among world oil producers in 1981. Production reached 2.7 million barrels a day, of which about half was exported. On the order of three-fourths of Mexico's oil exports have been going to the United States, an amount Mexicans consider excessive. If Mexico becomes dependent on oil exports, and if most of them go to the United States, then it is conceivable that in a time of excess supply on the world market the United States would be in a position to bring pressure on Mexico to modify its foreign policy, or its rules governing the operation of foreign corporations, as a price for continued oil purchases. In more extreme versions, some Mexicans fear that the United States might choose at some future time of oil shortage to occupy Mexican oilfields so as to assure itself of supplies. In order to reduce dependence on the U.S. market, Mexico has been trying to diversify oil sales to countries other than the United States.

In addition, the government has been attempting to insure that oil revenue is used productively. With the example of Venezuela in mind—not to say Iran—Mexico wishes to avoid a situation in which revenue from oil is used only for luxury imports, leaving no productive capacity against the day when oil is no longer a reliable basis of the economy, either because supplies have become exhausted or because cheaper substitutes have been developed. Accordingly, Mexico has been attempting to negotiate deals for oil sales in which the country receives not only payments in money form, but also investments and technical assistance that create new productive capacity. The energy-poor Japanese have been particularly willing to engage in deals of this type, involving the supply of Japanese capital and know-how. It is thus no coincidence that in an opinion survey taken by the United States

International Communications Agency (ICA) in August 1979, Japan led the United States among a Mexico City sample as a preferred source of future foreign investment.[6] Japan also led the United States in general feelings of favorable opinion toward various countries.[7] As President López Portillo has put it:

> Petroleum paves the way for authentic balanced development with financial autonomy, but we should be aware that this opportunity will not last forever. Today we are in a propitious stage that we must use to the best advantage.[8]

There are dissenting voices on the question of oil policy in Mexico. Among more nationalist currents of opinion, the view is expressed that Mexico should cut back on its oil exports and instead reserve the fuel for Mexico's own use, especially in building the petrochemical industry. These views are hardly likely to be embodied in government policy, however. There is enough oil for the development of a petrochemical industry and for export also. Moreover, the country's economic needs are substantial enough that the export of oil is absolutely necessary to secure foreign exchange. Prior to the era of massive oil exports, in fact, the country was in a serious deficit position in its balance of payments and was becoming heavily in debt, a situation that could hardly be endorsed by nationalist opinion.

DIFFERENCES OF FOREIGN POLICY

A source of tension between the United States and Mexico has been their differing perceptions of the world, and thus their divergent policies with respect to problems and areas of the world in which the bilateral relationship between the two countries is not directly involved. Regardless of what policies they might be pursuing at home, recent Mexican governments have taken seriously Mexico's vocation as a revolutionary power, as part of the Third World resentful of the assumption by the developed countries that the world's affairs are theirs to arrange. The United States, by contrast, conceives of its military and economic power as carrying with it the responsibility for assuring world peace and civilized behavior on the part of other states, and of assuring that world trade and economic development can go forward on a free enterprise basis for the benefit of all concerned. On some issues, the two countries can disagree amicably. Other questions, such as the vote that equated Zionism with racism, touch sensitive issues—differences that lead to tension and recrimination.

One such policy area concerns Central America. Mexico has become especially concerned with Central American affairs in the second half of the twentieth century. The Central American countries were, in the first few years after independence, federated with Mexico. But in the ensuing century

Mexico was too preoccupied with its own affairs to bother much with those of the republics to the immediate south. There have been exceptions to this general rule. Sandino, the Nicaraguan patriot who fought against both domestic tyrants and the U.S. marines in Nicaragua, was influenced by the ideology of the Mexican Revolution, having worked for some time in Mexico; he looked to Mexico for both moral and material support. But Mexican interests in Central America grew with the expansion of Mexican industry following World War II, and especially with the development of the Central American common market. This afforded an opportunity for Mexican industry to expand into Central America. The establishment of joint Mexican-Central American companies made it possible to operate inside the common market, an attractive possibility, as the common market provided a total of 15 million potential customers and Mexican industry had in some respects exhausted the possibilities of the domestic market. Beginning with President Gustavo Díaz Ordaz (1964 to 1970), it became customary for each Mexican president to pay a visit to Central America.

As Mexico became an oil-exporting power, other opportunities presented themselves, since Central America (except for Guatemala) is an oil-importing region. In 1980 Mexico and Venezuela jointly offered to sell oil to the countries of Central America and the Caribbean at prices below those generally prevailing, with the difference between the two price levels to be used for an investment fund. The hope was clearly that this fund would provide credit for purchases of equipment, technology, and so forth in Mexico.

Meanwhile, in Central America the old political order has been breaking down. The rule of long-entrenched oligarchies has been challenged by a rising middle class, a small urban working class, and a peasantry long downtrodden but given new hope by the socially more progressive teachings of a Catholic church trying to come to terms with the conditions of twentieth-century life. For the Mexicans, upheavals of this kind seem to echo their own revolution, and they extend to them strong moral support.

For the United States, things appear somewhat different. While the U.S. government does not particularly sympathize with the social and political order represented by landed oligarchies or military dictators, it prefers quiet and predictability in the area it regards as its own backyard. Moreover, the idea of revolution no longer invokes in Washington memories of 1776, but instead echoes of 1917, the year of the Russian Revolution. Accustomed to over 30 years of thinking in terms of a world in which the status quo represents peace and order and drastic change implies increasing Soviet power, U.S. administrations generally react in opposition to social change. They may, however, attempt to promote "third force" solutions in times of social upheaval: governments that represent neither oligarchic landlords and military tyrants on the one hand, nor revolutionary socialists on the other, but plausibly democratic, middle-class advocates of the free market plus social welfare programs. Attempts toward a solution of this type at the collapse of the Somoza regime in Nicaragua in 1979 foundered on the fact that the situation was already polarized to the extent that no constituency for such a third force existed. Similar attempts in El Salvador came not quite so late in the evolution of the revolutionary process, but ten years after they might have been readily successful.

While some Mexican officials would not be quite so happy with revolutionary socialist governments in Central America as official rhetoric implies, Mexico on the whole supports the revolutionary forces in the struggles of Central America. It sees U.S. attempts at devising third force solutions as unviable maneuvers to preserve U.S. hegemony and to protect private U.S. economic interests against the popular will and forces of history. Mexicans are not impressed with U.S. fears of Soviet or Cuban influence in Central America. They know that oil company representatives and right-wing forces in the United States, using alarmist talk of Bolshevism and threats to U.S. interests, attempted in the 1920s and 1930s to get Washington to intervene militarily against revolutionary governments in Mexico.

QUESTIONS OF STYLE AND SUBSTANCE

To a great extent, however, the problems between Mexico and the United States concern matters of style, rather than of substance. It is true that genuine areas of conflict exist between the two countries. But it is equally true that substantial areas of common interest and mutual benefit also exist, so that it is not clear, simply on the basis of the substance of the issues that arise between the two countries, whether their relations will be based on harmony or on conflict. That is up to the leadership on each side.

Because the United States holds the best cards, or most of the cards, in the relationship, it has not been difficult for Washington to assume an attitude of friendliness and cooperation, secure in the knowledge that in quiet negotiations or discussions it will have the best arguments, those with dollar signs on them. Popular opinion in the United States toward Mexico is friendly though vague, thus constituting no constraint on the freedom of action of U.S. governments. Opinion in Mexico toward the United States is bimodal: the ICA poll of opinions in Mexico City referred to above found that 56 percent of the respondents felt that the interests of Mexico were "more or less" in agreement with those of the United States, while 31 percent felt that the interests of the two countries were "somewhat different" or "very different."[9] Those more skeptical of the commonality of interests between the United States and Mexico are the more educated and more influential. This means, in effect, that a president of Mexico has a constituency for friendly relations with the United States, and a smaller but more influential one for circumspection or restraint. The initiative in setting the tone of relations between the two countries thus lies largely with the United States.

While at the rhetorical level U.S. presidents talk of friendship and harmony with Mexico, the reality at the working level is sometimes quite different. For example, Jimmy Carter prepared a program to deal with the problem of undocumented migrants without taking Mexican views into account. Carter's designations first of Patrick Lucey and then of Julian Nava as ambassadors, rather than appointing senior professional diplomats or major political figures, appeared to the Mexicans transparently political gestures that showed that Mexico was not a country taken seriously by the United States, an idea that President Reagan's designation of John Gavin did nothing to dispel.

What is clearly in order now for the United States is not to take Mexico for granted, not to assume that Mexico has no choice but to fall in with policies about which it was not consulted. Nor should consultation be merely pro forma. Mexican interests must genuinely be taken into account in solutions of common problems. Moreover, Mexico's views must be seriously consulted with respect to problems involving third countries. Here Mexico's distinctive point of view and experience can be a valuable resource for U.S. policymakers, who are sometimes recruited from private industry or elsewhere and expected to become instant experts, and who rely all too often on superficial or simplistic conceptions of international relations and foreign politics. Mexico, allied with the United States on a firm basis of common interests, can give valuable support to U.S. policies in the world. A Mexico given reason to suspect and mistrust U.S. intentions, on the other hand, can be a leader and rallying point for anti-imperialist sentiment.

NOTES

1. Richard B. Mancke, *Mexican Oil and Natural Gas* (New York: Praeger, 1979), p. 26.

2. Carlos Astiz, "Mexico's Foreign Policy: Disguised Dependency," *Current History* 40, May 1974, p. 223.

3. Astiz, p. 223.

4. *State of the Nation Report*, September 1, 1980 (Mimeographed English version distributed by Mexican Embassy, Washington, D.C.), p. 11.

5. *Mexico, Reluctant Friend of U.S.: Mexico City Opinion on Bilateral and International Issues*, USICA Research Memorandum, September 12, 1979, p. 22.

6. *Mexico, Reluctant Friend*, p. 47.

7. *Mexico, Reluctant Friend*, p. 41.

8. *State of the Nation Report*, p. 14.

9. *Mexico, Reluctant Friend*, p. 34.

11

Cuba: The Impasse

Edward Gonzalez

Cuba was a vexing issue for U.S. foreign policy in the mid-1970s. It remained a pariah state within the Caribbean basin, closely aligned with the USSR, while challenging U.S. interests both in the region and as far away as Angola. In the meantime, it had become evident that the U.S. policy of denial toward Cuba was no longer effective—if it ever was—because the regime of Fidel Castro was well entrenched, and its survival seemed reasonably certain. In fact, by the mid-1970s U.S. policy appeared more counterproductive to U.S. interests than it was harmful to Castro's regime. Having broken diplomatic relations with Havana in January 1961, and having thereafter maintained a trade, economic, and travel embargo against Cuba, the United States gave Cuba no option but to increase its dependence on the USSR, while denying itself the political and economic presence with which to gain influence over Cuban domestic and foreign politics.

The Carter administration moved to break this impasse with Cuba in the hopes that a more normal relationship between the two countries would serve to moderate Castro's policies and lead to some measure of U.S. leverage over his regime. This chapter examines the reasons why such leverage ultimately eluded the United States, and why U.S.-Cuban relations again deteriorated after 1977 despite innovations in U.S. policy.

THE FAILED THAW IN U.S.-CUBAN RELATIONS

Relations between the United States and Cuba soon entered an era of mutual hostility following the overthrow of Fulgencio Batista and the rise to power of Fidel Castro in January 1959. Beginning in the fall of that year, the rapid radicalization of the Cuban Revolution not only affected domestic Cuban interests, but also U.S. investments on the island and U.S. security interests throughout the Caribbean and Latin America. By October the two countries had become locked into a pattern of mutual recriminations, hostility, and conflict. This intensified the following year as Castro success-fully realigned Cuba with the Soviet bloc and transformed his revolution along Marxist-Leninist lines.[1] Thereafter, four successive U.S. administra-tions—starting with Eisenhower's and ending with Nixon's—sought to resolve the Cuban problem through a variety of pressures that aimed at ending or destabilizing the Castro regime, or at forcing it to yield to U.S. conditions for normalization.[2]

The Ford administration did initiate changes in U.S. policy with the aim of moving toward a more normal relationship with Cuba. Thus, a round of secret, high-level talks were held between U.S. and Cuban officials in Washington and New York on four different occasions between November 1974 and November 1975.[3] Although exploratory, the talks did lead to an initial reduction in tensions between the two countries. On March 1, 1975, for example, Secretary of State Henry Kissinger declared that the U.S. government saw "no virtue in perpetual antagonism" with Cuba. For his part, Castro responded by describing Kissinger's statement as "positive," while noting that there had been a decline in tension between the two countries. Later, the U.S. government yielded to changing sentiment within the hemisphere and voted with the majority of the members of the Organiza-tion of American States in July 1975 to free them from enforcing the 1964 OAS sanctions against Cuba. Then, on September 23, 1975, Assistant Secretary of State William Rogers announced that the United States was "prepared to improve our relations" with Cuba and "to enter into a dialogue with Cuba."

At the time of Rogers's statement, however, Cuba was already on its way to becoming deeply involved in the Angolan civil war on the side of the Marxist-oriented Popular Movement for the Liberation of Angola (MPLA).[4] Thus, Rogers registered strong U.S. opposition to Cuba's Angolan inter-vention at the final round of secret talks held in November 1975. Nonethe-less, he urged that the talks continue, and that Cubans be allowed to travel between the two countries for purposes of family visits. According to Rogers, the Cubans never responded and the talks lapsed.[5]

In the meantime, Cuba's growing "internationalist" activities—in Puerto Rico as well as Angola—became a major matter of public dispute between Washington and Havana. On December 23, 1975, President Ford ruled out any further possibility for improvement in U.S.-Cuban relations because of the Castro regime's policies toward Angola and the Puerto Rican independence movement.[6] For his part, Castro responded two days later by declaring that "there never will be relations with the United States" if the "price" had to be Cuba's abandonment of its "solidarity" with anti-imperialist movements in the Third World.[7] Thereafter, Cuba increased its military buildup in Angola to 36,000 troops during 1976, enabling it to score a major battlefield victory and to install the MPLA in power.[8] Worse still for U.S. interests, Havana aligned itself ever more closely with the Soviet Union and continued to increase its political and military presence in other parts of Africa during 1976 and 1977.

The new administration of President Jimmy Carter set out both to break the new deadlock between the two countries and to moderate Cuba's international behavior along lines less damaging to U.S. foreign policy interests. In this regard, both the White House and State Department recognized that the United States would continue to possess little leverage over the Castro regime as long as there were no political and economic linkages with Cuba that Washington could use to exert influence on Havana. Short of military threats and coercion, in other words, continued U.S. isolation from Cuba virtually denied the United States the possibility of exercising effective influence over Cuban behavior. As a first step, therefore, it was necessary to establish a diplomatic presence in Havana, however limited, and to move along several fronts toward a more normal set of political and economic relationships between the two countries.

Toward this end, the Carter administration played down Cuba's continuing military involvement in Africa, to the extent that U.N. Ambassador Andrew Young even called Cuba's presence a stabilizing force in the region.[9] Meanwhile, the administration moved quickly to open the way for more normal relations. In April 1977 the U.S. government signed a fisheries agreement with Cuba to regulate and demarcate access to each other's fishing grounds. The following June, the two governments reached agreement on the establishment of mutual Interests Sections in each other's capitals starting in September 1977, thereby establishing subdiplomatic relations and ending 16 years of mutual isolation. In the meantime, there were prospects for the normalization of commercial relations between the two countries, as Cuba's minister of foreign trade and other economic officials visited the United States. In turn, groups of U.S. businessmen were given the red carpet treatment in Havana in an apparent bid to gain the support of the American business community for the opening up of the U.S. market to Cuban exports and the extension of U.S. credits to Cuba for the purchase of needed U.S. goods.

Despite the headway made toward normalizing diplomatic relations and the promise of restoring commercial intercourse between the two countries, U.S-Cuban relations once again became stalemated. Notwithstanding the Carter administration's conciliatory stance, Cuba intervened militarily for the second time in Africa. Starting in late 1977, and at the request of the beleaguered Marxist regime of Lt. Col. Mengistu Haile Mariam, Cuba dispatched some 12,000 combat troops to Ethiopia to help that country defend its Ogaden region following Somalia's declaration of war and invasion of that contested area.[10] Whereas Cuba's Ethiopian operation did not precipitate a new rupture with the United States, it did bring a halt to the normalization process that had been gathering momentum since spring 1977.[11] Thereafter, U.S.-Cuban relations steadily deteriorated as a result of three additional incidents. These involved U.S. allegations regarding Cuban complicity in the Shaba II affair between Angola and Zaire in May 1978; U.S. allegations concerning the existence of a Soviet combat brigade in Cuba in August 1979; and U.S.-Cuban tensions over the unregulated exodus of 125,000 Cuban refugees that came across the Florida straits in the "Freedom Flotilla" between May and September 1980.

THE PERSISTENCE OF THE CUBAN PROBLEM

This brief review of recent U.S.-Cuban relations suggests that there is no simple solution to the perennial Cuban problem. Whereas the U.S. policy of reprisals and denial in the 1960s failed in overthrowing or destabilizing the Castro regime, so did the more conciliatory Ford and Carter initiatives of the mid-1970s fail to moderate the regime's international behavior. The policy failure of the Carter administration is particularly perplexing not only because it was the most innovative, but also because it appeared to be on the verge of breaking the long-standing deadlock. The remainder of this chapter will explore the following central questions concerning the period from 1977 to 1980:

● Given what was newly at stake with the United States in 1977, why did Havana launch a new overseas military operation in Ethiopia? In other words, why did the new administration's conciliatory posture fail to deter Castro from embarking upon a second major African intervention?

● More fundamentally, why did the Carter administration's innovative posture fail to achieve its stated purpose—to compete effectively with the Soviets over Cuba with the aim of lessening the latter's dependence on the USSR in order to gain Castro's moderation in international affairs?

● Finally, why did U.S.-Cuban relations in fact worsen by the late 1970s after having made a promising start toward reconciliation at the beginning of the Carter administration?

One possible explanation for both the failure in U.S.-Cuban policy and the eventual deterioration in the relations between the two countries would involve the idiosyncratic character of the Carter administration's foreign policy behavior. As with its erratic policy toward the Soviet Union, Carter's policy toward Cuba also zigged and zagged from an initial softline to growing bellicosity. The latter culminated with the administration's charges over the alleged presence of a Soviet combat brigade on the island in August 1979, and with U.S. steps to increase its military presence in the Caribbean, which critics in and outside of the United States suspected were prompted as much by the president's domestic political concerns as by Cuban developments.

However, such an interpretation does not explain why the Castro regime ignored U.S. policy concessions and the possibility of even greater break-throughs in the future, when it embarked upon its Ethiopian operation in late 1977. Indeed, as will be shown below, Cuba not only resumed its military adventurism, but also aligned itself militarily more closely with the Soviet Union precisely at a moment when the Carter administration was in its most conciliatory phase. In short, the Carter administration can be criticized for its inconsistent policies, but such inconsistencies were not yet present at the time of Cuba's renewed thrust into Africa; thus, they cannot adequately explain the Castro regime's return to a highly militant and activist foreign policy beginning in late 1977.

The argument to be advanced below is that U.S. policy failed and relations worsened from 1977 to 1980 because of the following related factors:

- The interests at issue between the United States and Cuba are not only conflictive, but also contradictory;
- The Castro regime's dominant leadership elements pursue maximum foreign policy goals that invariably make for contradictory interests with the United States, and that thus cannot be satisfied by conciliatory U.S. postures;
- The Castro regime found that it could in fact pursue its maximalist strategy abroad, and simultaneously obtain even higher levels of Soviet economic and military support, by serving as an international paladin allied with the Soviet Union; and
- As a result of the above three factors, the United States possessed insufficient leverage to constrain and moderate Cuba's international behavior.

CONTRADICTORY INTERESTS

Three types of interests characterized relations between the United States and Cuba during the 1970s and continue to govern those relations today. First of all, there are *congruent* interests involving those issues in which both the United States and Cuba are able to derive mutual advantage through joint cooperation. For example, both countries have long cooperated on weather and hurricane forecasting; they reached agreement in the early 1970s on controlling the hijacking of commercial aircraft; they later signed additional agreements demarcating the respective fishing rights and territorial boundaries of the two countries; they also agreed to establish Interests Sections in each other's capitals and thereby reopen direct channels for diplomatic communication and negotiation; and they both could potentially gain economically from the normalization of commercial relations.

Second, as is customary in most bilateral relationships, there also exist *conflictive* interests whereby each country has staked out an opposing stand, but which could be resolved through eventual compromise by one or both parties. Examples of conflictive issues include U.S. insistence on Cuban compensation for the $1.8 billion in certified claims against the Castro government as a result of the latter's nationalization and expropriation of U.S. property; and Cuban demands for the return of the territory occupied by the U.S. naval base at Guantanamo Bay. Both of these conflictive issues are potentially resolvable within a larger political settlement between Washington and Havana. Were such a settlement to occur, then a compromise solution of the U.S. claims question might thus be attained by scaling down the amount and specifying the method of Cuban compensation. Similarly, Guantanamo Bay might ultimately be ceded to Cuba were the latter to alter its close military ties with the Soviet Union, as well as its confrontation posture toward the United States.

However, there remains a still more critical third category of issues that pertain to the *contradictory* interests standing in the way of the United States and Cuba. These form the basis of the profound antagonism between the two countries, which in turn make it virtually impossible for either to expand the area of congruent interests or to compromise on conflictive interests. Contradictory interests involve not only mutually antagonistic stances as in conflictive interests, but also firm adherence to fundamental principles and issues that are essential to the international role of each country. These cannot be sacrificed by either actor without irreparable harm to its power, influence, and status in world affairs.

For example, contradictory interests were clearly at stake over the issue of Cuba's dispatch of combat troops to Ethiopia beginning in late 1977, which in turn halted the normalization trend. As a superpower with global responsibilities and commitments, the United States could not reward Cuba for embarking on yet another military operation in Africa, nor for its role in advancing Soviet interests on the Horn of Africa, by continuing the normalization process. To encourage normalization under such adverse circumstances, moreover, would most likely have had domestic political repercussions that no U.S. administration could afford. For its part, the Castro regime was unwilling to forego its internationalist role in the Third World, and its heightened leverage with Moscow as the latter's most effective ally in Africa, in order to minimize conflict with the United States or to improve the chances of eventual trade normalization.

In this regard, for Havana to have acceded to U.S. wishes would have entailed abandoning Cuban efforts to assert leadership over the Third World countries, including its efforts to radicalize the nonaligned movement. More critically, it would have required that Cuba give up its new role as a global paladin that effectively promoted Soviet interests in the Third World and Africa. Indeed, as will be seen later, Soviet economic and military assistance to Cuba rose dramatically in the post-1975 period; clearly, such a rise was not simply coincidental with Cuba's combat role in Angola and Ethiopia, but was instead an outcome of that role.

As the Ethiopian case illustrates, contradictory interests lock Washington and Havana into virtually irreconcilable positions. Part of the reason for the persistence of such a situation lies in the mentality, objectives, and interests of the Cuban leadership, particularly those of the two Castro brothers and their veteran guerrilla followers.

CUBAN OBJECTIVES AND INTERESTS

In spite of the commanding presence of Fidel Castro, his regime is not a monolithic entity. Instead, it comprises a coalition of different elites that represent the old political parties and movements of the revolutionary period and the new organizations and forces that have developed in the post-1959 period. During the 1970s three elite groupings and respective foreign policy tendencies were discernible within the regime.[12]

The first and least influential of the three can be called the pragmatic economic tendency. This was led by Carlos Rafael Rodríguez, who was appointed to the Political Bureau of the Communist Party of Cuba (PCC) in December 1975, and who also became a vice-president in both the Council of State and Council of Ministries the following year. This pragmatic economic tendency represented the economic technocrats and managers who had gained increased importance following the economic debacle associated with the attempted $10 million sugar harvest in 1970.[13] Buttressed by close ties with Soviet economic technicians and planners, this elite grouping stood for greater rationalization of the Cuban economy at home and for improved trade and technology ties with both the socialist and industrialized Western world. Hence, it pushed for the normalization of relations with the United States.

The second and most influential of the elites comprised the revolutionary political tendency. This was headed by Fidel Castro, and backed by his personal fidelista guerrilla followers in the upper echelons of the party and government. This revolutionary political tendency remained concerned with problems of Cuba's underdevelopment, but it attached far greater importance to the fulfillment of ideological, political, and security imperatives than did the economic pragmatists. While initially willing to work toward more normal relations with the United States, this tendency nevertheless impelled the Cuban regime toward adopting maximum foreign policy postures that aimed at promoting "liberationist," "anti-imperialist," and "socialist" causes in the Third World, securing new Third World allies, projecting Cuba's regional and global influence, and gaining greater international autonomy and leverage for the regime. The fidelista tendency stood ready to sacrifice more pragmatic economic goals if necessary in order to attain higher revolutionary objectives.

The third and organizationally most critical elite grouping consisted of the military mission tendency. This was headed by Army General Raúl Castro in his capacity as minister of the Revolutionary Armed Forces (FAR). This military mission tendency was made up of the top professional soldiers within the FAR, including both ranking raulista officers who had long been associated with Raul, and ranking fidelista officers who had remained in the military.[14] During the 1960s the FAR became the most powerful institution within the regime, serving in a developmental and national defense capacity. As the U.S. security threat to Cuba eased under détente, and as party and governmental organs were strengthened in the post-1970 period to assume the developmental role previously performed by the army, the FAR strengthened its military capabilities to encompass overseas operations beginning in the early 1970s.[15] Thus, prior to Angola, a 600- to 700-man advisory force was stationed in South Yemen in late 1973, while 600 to 750 tank troops were also dispatched to Syria in the latter stages of the October 1973 War.[16] The successful outcome of Cuba's intervention in Angola, which led to the commitment of 36,000 combat troops during the course of 1976, thus confirmed the FAR's new military mission: it would serve as a principal instrument for advancing the Castro regime's maximalist foreign policy objectives. The FAR's new role also served the military's own professional interests, at first Angola and then Ethiopia; improved the combat proficiency of the Cuban armed forces; enhanced the FAR's international prestige; and led to the acquisition by the FAR of new Soviet military equipment in the post-1976 period. Thus, the FAR developed a vast organizational interest in supporting Castro's activist foreign policy inclinations.

They were already on the ascendancy when Angola reinforced the revolutionary tendency of Fidel Castro and the military mission tendency of Raúl Castro and the FAR. Even in the very midst of the Angolan operation, the First Party Congress in December 1975 confirmed the renewed dominance of the Castro brothers and their civilian and military followers: they continued their tight control over the party's principal policymaking and supervisory organs—the Political Bureau and Secretariat—whereas the FAR alone accounted for over 32 percent of the newly expanded Central Committee's regular membership.[17] Moreover, the total percentage of fidelista and raulista guerrilla veterans—including long-time civilian leaders, former FAR officers occupying civilian posts, and active duty FAR officers—actually showed an increase from 55 percent in the 1965 Central Committee (n=100) to 63 percent in the new 1975 body (n=124).

With the reorganization of the state and governmental structures under Cuba's new socialist constitution in 1976, there occurred a still further concentration of power by the two Castro brothers and their followers. By December 1976 Fidel and Raul Castro not only remained as first and second secretary of the PCC, respectively, but also they became president and first vice-president of the Council of State and Council of Ministers. In turn, their followers occupied four out of five vice-presidencies in the Council of State, and the major share of that organ's membership, while also securing five of the eight vice-presidencies in the Council of Ministers—a more administrative and managerial body in which greater representation by the economic pragmatists would normally have been expected. Indeed, the pragmatic economic tendency was underrepresented in all four of the principal party, state, and governmental bodies. Only Carlos Rafael Rodríguez held membership in the PCC Political Bureau and Secretariat, and was named as a vice-president in both the Councils of State and Ministers.

The distribution of power within the Cuban regime after 1975 had important consequences for Cuban-U.S. relations, as well as for overall Cuban foreign policy. First, it meant that the technocrats and managers led by Rodríguez, which was the one elite grouping with the most interest in normalizing relations with the United States, and which was the least committed to a highly activist and militant foreign policy, remained less influential in the formulation of high policy. Second, it signified that the two predominant leadership elite groupings—the fidelista guerrilla veterans that identified themselves with Fidel, and the military headed by Raúl—shared a basic commitment to the pursuit of maximum foreign policy objectives that could be achieved only through a highly activist and expansionist foreign policy.

Consequently, headway toward more normal relations with the Carter administration could initially be realized as long as it did not impede the realization of the value preferences of the dominant elites. From the latter's perspective, therefore, Cuba's new military thrust into Ethiopia would in fact jeopardize the prospects for trade normalization with the United States, but these were problematical in any event owing to the need for congressional as well as White House action. In the meantime, the new Ethiopian venture offered immediate and far higher economic, military, and political returns to Cuba in its paladin role.

THE CUBAN-SOVIET RELATIONSHIP

Cuba's Ethiopian operation needs to be viewed in the context of its earlier triumph in Angola—specifically, the way in which that operation advanced the Castro regime's economic, military, and diplomatic interests after 1975 with both the USSR and on other fronts as well. Because of its singular success in promoting Soviet interests and ambitions in southern Africa, Cuba in effect became a privileged ally of the USSR, enjoying a new favorable relationship with its patron superpower in the aftermath of Angola. Cuba became the beneficiary of massive increases in Soviet economic assistance in the post-1975 period. Additionally, the Cuban armed forces received new arms and equipment following Angola, thereby upgrading and modernizing their weapon systems.[18] Fidel Castro himself evidently enjoyed new standing in Moscow as an effective champion of the USSR and the socialist camp in Africa and the Third World.[19]

Within Africa, too, Cuba acquired new prestige in large part because its military presence in Angola was seen as having been directed against the South Africans, who had invaded the Portuguese colony in late October 1975 just prior to the latter's independence. Owing to the South African incursion, Cuba's own military intervention acquired a legitimacy in much of Africa that it might otherwise not have obtained. In any event, Angola gave Cuba's Africa policy renewed impetus: Castro made a triumphal extended tour through part of the continent in spring 1977; Cuban-African diplomatic exchanges, and African visitations to Cuba, increased markedly after 1975; and Cuba gained a greater political, technical, and military presence in Africa in the post-1975 period.[20] Cuba also gained new status in the Third World in general as a result of its apparent willingness to commit combat forces on behalf of a national liberation movement and against South African racism. As a result, the Castro regime was in a better position to try to assert leadership over the nonaligned movement as the 1970s drew to a close.

Cuba's growing African involvement in the latter half of the 1970s, however, prompted debate as to whether Cuba was: an autonomous, selfless, and ideologically motivated revolutionary actor committed to promoting liberationist and socialist movements in Africa; a Soviet-directed surrogate that served as the cutting edge for Moscow's policies in Africa; or a self-directed international paladin that pursued its own interests and objective, but that also necessarily had to operate within the parameters of Soviet global interests.[21] Angola appeared to support the third interpretation because the surrogate thesis neglected Cuba's long-standing involvement and interests in Africa dating back to the early 1960s, and the revolutionary thesis overlooked Cuba's Soviet connection and the nonideological gains that Cuba secured from its Angolan action.

The dispatch of Cuban combat troops to Ethiopia was another matter, however. Indeed, Ethiopia seemingly lent greater credence to the surrogate interpretation regarding Cuba's overseas activities:

• Unlike in Angola, Cuba had not had a long history of ties to the Ethiopian revolutionary movement;

• Unlike in Angola, there existed a high degree of Soviet-Cuban military coordination from the very outset of the operation: the Soviets supplied the logistical support to transport and equip the 12,000 Cuban combat forces deployed in Ethiopia, whereas Soviet pilots subsequently flew Cuban MiGs in Cuba, which enabled Cuban pilots to fly combat missions over Ethiopia; and

• Unlike in Angola, the Cuban expeditionary force in Ethiopia, serving under Division General Arnaldo Ochoa, was placed under the overall strategic command of Lt. General Vasiliy Ivanovich Petrov and his Soviet general staff.[22]

Nevertheless, Cuba's Ethiopian action still appeared to correspond more closely to the paladin model. To be sure, Cuba's combat role was indispensable to the preservation of power by the new Marxist-Leninist regime in Ethiopia and to the consolidation of the Soviet presence in that country. But while promotive of Soviet ambitions on the Horn, Cuba also had its own concrete interests to advance, which were congruent with those of the USSR. As a paladin, Cuba thus moved to capitalize on Soviet objectives and interests as a means of securing new gains for itself.

To begin with, the professional and organizational interests of Cuban armed forces were directly advanced as a result of the Ethiopian operation. The Cuban army acquired valuable combat experience in the execution of the successful counteroffensive in the Ogaden; Cuban officers also were able to collaborate professionally with and to learn from the Soviet officer staff; and the FAR as a whole gained additional international standing because of the proficiency displayed in the Ethiopian campaign. As had occurred following Angola, Cuba also became the recipient of new Soviet arms shipments with the Ethiopian operation, thereby furthering the modernization of the FAR's weapons inventories. Thus, after Cuban pilots had been flying MiG 23s over Ethiopia, Cuba received the first 12 of these advanced fighter-bombers in spring 1978. Some 15 months later, the USSR delivered 20 An-26 medium-range military transport planes capable of ferrying 40 combat troops over a range of 900 miles. In early 1980, the Cuban navy received three Foxtrot class, diesel-powered Soviet submarines.

In the meantime, Cuba's services as a military-political paladin enabled Castro to command not only new weapons systems from the USSR, but also greater levels of Soviet economic support. As seen in Table 11.1, data

Table 11.1 Total Soviet Economic Assistance to Cuba: Cumulative Yearly Totals, Annual Grants, and Per Annum Totals

(in million U.S. $)

	1961–1970	1975	1976	1977	1978	1979
Cumulative Yearly Total	3,568[a]	7,099	8,606	10,588	13,556	16,664
Annual Grant Total[b]	1,018[a]	901	1,357	1,672	2,638	2,667
Per Annum Total Assistance		1,051	1,507	1,982	2,968	3,107

[a]Figures represent cumulative totals for entire 1961–70 period.
[b]Includes sugar, petroleum, and nickel subsidies, as well as nonrepayable aid.

Source: Adapted from the National Foreign Assessment Center, Central Intelligence Agency, *The Cuban Economy: A Statistical Review – A Reference Aid,* ER 81-10052 & PA 81-10074, March 1981, p. 39.

compiled by the Central Intelligence Agency from official Cuban and Soviet sources show that the USSR had supplied Cuba with nearly $7.1 billion in total cumulative economic assistance—consisting of repayable aid, trade subsidies, and grants—from 1961 through 1975. From 1976 through 1979, however, total cumulative economic assistance reached $9.6 billion, representing a 135 percent increase over the 1961-75 figure in only a four-year time frame. Of that $9.6 billion in total assistance, nonrepayable trade subsidies and grants alone accounted for $8.4 billion. When further broken down on a yearly basis, the per annum aid levels showed a dramatic increase beginning in the 1976-79 period, with 1978 and 1979 in particular being banner years for Cuba (see Table 11.1).

One could argue that developments in the world economy accounted for the sudden growth in Soviet assistance. Thus, increased Soviet trade subsidies were needed to compensate for the drop in world sugar prices and for the rise in world oil prices during the last half of the 1970s, since the USSR was both Cuba's principal sugar purchaser and sole petroleum supplier. Still, as a dependent client state, and faced with adverse conditions on the world market, Cuba demonstrated a remarkable ability to extract ever-higher levels of Soviet assistance and on better terms than before. Surely, the key to Havana's success lay in its paladin role which, beginning with Angola and extending through Ethiopia, enabled it to gain leverage on the USSR after 1975.

Cuba's political gains from its Ethiopian action were less clear-cut in Angola, however. Many states in and outside the Third World were critical of the Ethiopian venture. Yet other states saw Cuba's actions as legitimate: Havana, after all, had dispatched combat troops only after the Mengistu regime had requested assistance, and only after Somalia had invaded the contested Ogaden region. Most African states sided with Ethiopia in retaining the Ogaden, owing to their overriding concern with maintaining their own territorial integrity. Thus, the initial deployment of Cuban forces to Ethiopia probably did little damage to Cuba's overall standing in the Third World, although the Cuban role in supporting Ethiopia in the struggle against Eritrea drew greater criticism from African and Middle Eastern governments.[23] In any event, on balance, neither Ethiopia nor the Eritrean issue prevented Havana from hosting the sixth summit meeting of the nonaligned movement in September 1979, nor from assuming official leadership of NAM in its capacity as the host government.[24]

Whereas Cuba's standing in the Third World was neither greatly damaged nor enhanced by Ethiopia, the latter did strengthen the Castro regime's relationship with the USSR. By dispatching combat forces to Ethiopia, and by again proving to be the decisive force on the field of battle, Cuba had demonstrated for the second time within two years that it possessed a singular capacity and willingness to insure the survival of a new

Marxist regime in Africa, and thereby to advance Moscow's strategic, political, and ideological interests as no other member of the Soviet bloc could. The Ethiopian action conferred new leverage on Cuba in its dealings with the USSR.

THE DENIAL OF U.S. LEVERAGE: A SUMMARY ANALYSIS

In the context of U.S.-Cuban relations, international leverage can be conceived as involving a situation whereby the United States could influence Cuba's behavior to the U.S. advantage through the Castro regime's own recognition that it could best minimize its vulnerabilities and maximize its interests by satisfying Washington. Because of the contradictory interests of the two countries, the value preferences of the dominant Cuban elites, and the rewards offered by Cuba's relationship with Moscow, however, the United States was prevented from acquiring such leverage over Cuba in the late 1970s because:

- The contradictory interests between the two actors could be overcome only if the Castro regime were to abandon its maximalist foreign policy postures as a political-military paladin and as a close ally of the USSR, in exchange for the continuance of the normalization process after 1977;
- While there might be economic and technological advantages to further normalization, the value preferences and organizational interests of the dominant elites within the Cuban leadership—the fidelistas under Fidel and the military under Raúl—were ultimately committed to pursuing a maximalist strategy that could yield far higher and far more certain returns for the regime on the military, economic, and political fronts; and
- Cuba's relationship with the USSR, and its role as a global paladin that advanced Soviet as well Cuban interests in Africa, the Third World, and the nonaligned movement, not only permitted the Castro regime to fulfill its preferred foreign policy inclinations, but also to generate new leverage with Moscow and ever-higher levels of Soviet economic, military, and political support.

In short, the United States could not satisfy the major interests of the dominant elites within the Castro regime. Conversely, it was unable to exploit the regime's potential vulnerabilities in both the security and economic fields as these were largely offset by Cuba's ties with the USSR. The end result was that the Carter administration was precluded from exercising effective leverage over Castro following the initial modus vivendi in 1977.

There were also additional related factors that further worked against the United States acquiring leverage, even had the Cuban leadership been willing to concede its maximalist foreign policy postures in exchange for trade or the necessary credits to purchase U.S. agricultural commodities, manufactured goods, and high technology. Trade normalization and the extension of credits remained highly problematical as they were contingent upon congressional as well as executive action, upon support by U.S. interest groups and public opinion, and upon the general U.S. perception of Havana's good behavior. In the meantime, Cuba's foreign policy would be held hostage by Washington.

Furthermore, even had the prospects for trade normalization been certain, there was simply no way that the United States could displace the USSR as Cubas's economic patron and supporter. Soviet economic assistance to Cuba's after 1975 grew at a rate the United States could not hope to match. Cuba's economy had become closely integrated with that of the Soviet Union as the latter absorbed 73 percent of Cuban exports and supplied the island with 65 percent of its imports as of 1979.[25] Cuba's trade dependency was further intensified by the fact that it received preferential prices from the USSR for its sugar exports (upwards of $.40 per pound), and for its petroleum imports (roughly one-half the world price), neither of which the United States could provide.

Finally, apart from the above political and economic obstacles, the United States could not satisfy the organizational interests of the Cuban armed forces. As noted earlier, the FAR remained the most important institutional force within the Castro regime. Staffed at its highest levels by former guerrilla veterans who had served under Fidel and Raúl Castro, it had performed both civilian and military roles, and its position within the regime had been further strengthened with the victory in Angola. Moreover, the FAR was the governmental institution in Cuba with the longest and most professionalized ties to a counterpart organization in the Soviet Union, as it predated the formation of the party by six years. These bonds between the Cuban and Soviet military, along with the FAR's organizational interest in modernizing its arms and equipment and in improving its level of combat proficiency and professionalization, impelled the Cuban armed forces to support a maximalist foreign policy that promoted both Cuban and Soviet interests.

Without effective sources of leverage, therefore, the Carter administration was unable to deter Cuba from embarking upon its Ethiopian venture. However, U.S. policy toward Cuba in the post-1977 period was not entirely ineffective. Washington regained a window on Havana through the presence of its Interests Section, which had been missing for more than 15 years. In turn, the initial thaw in U.S.-Cuban relations opened the way for the eventual return of over 120,000 Cuban exiles from the United States, who were allowed brief visits to the island begining in late 1978.

The return of the exiles had a profoundly disturbing impact upon Cuban society. Having long been depicted as *gusanos* (worms) who were exploited by U.S. capitalism, the returning exiles demonstrated how much better off they were in the United States than the relatives, friends, and neighbors they had left behind in Cuba, who in turn had suffered severe and recurrent privations in the intervening years. This revelation, together with the renewed austerity that Cuban society was again experiencing, served as the principal catalyst for rising popular discontent within Cuba in 1979 and 1980.[26] As a result, the Castro regime was confronted with increased lawlessness, delinquency, and declining labor productivity. Two examples of this were the April 1980 occupation of the Peruvian embassy by 10,000 Cubans seeking asylum, and the exodus of some 125,000 Cubans to the United States, principally through the hastily improvised boatlift across the Florida straits, from May to September 1980.

These developments had major political repercussions for the regime. To regain control over the deteriorating economic and political situations, Castro carried out sweeping personnel changes and governmental reorganizations in late 1979 and early 1980, while embarking upon a new hardline against domestic dissent. Confronted with unrest at home and with rising tensions with the United States during 1980, the regime came to resemble a garrison that saw itself besieged from within as well as without—a perception that was intensified with the election of Ronald Reagan in November 1980.[27] Thus confronted with a hostile domestic and international environment, the Second Party Congress that was held in December 1980 saw the further strengthening of the hold by the fidelista and raulista elites, and by the military as an institution, over the highest government and party organs to an extent unmatched since the 1960s.[28]

As his newly reconstituted regime enters the 1980s, Castro continues to be faced with a lagging economy and public restiveness at home. Abroad, new strains are being placed on his regime because of Cuba's overextended foreign policy in Africa and elsewhere, and because of growing anxiety over the Reagan administration's confrontational stance on Cuba. In the meantime, his earlier successful Third World strategy has been dealt a body blow owing to the December 1979 Soviet invasion of Afghanistan, which his regime was compelled to support before the U.N. General Assembly the following month, and which he publicly defended at the Second Party Congress.

While thus beset with new vulnerabilities, the Castro regime now has an even greater interest in insuring its survival and distancing itself from the Soviet Union, which are interests that only the United States can ultimately satisfy. Consequently, the 1980s may well present the United States with the opportunities needed for finally gaining leverage to constrain Cuban behavior along lines less inimical to U.S. security interests in the Caribbean basin and elsewhere in the world.

NOTES

1. Although not initially a communist, Castro began a preemptive alignment with the USSR starting in February 1960, which entailed his formal conversion to Marxism-Leninism the following year in order to insure his regime against anticipated U.S. aggression. See Jacques Levesque, *The USSR and the Cuban Revolution* (New York: Praeger, 1978), pp. 48–68; Edward Gonzalez, "Castro's Revolution, Cuban Communist Appeals, and the Soviet Response," *World Politics* (October 1968): 39–68.

2. On U.S. policy see Lynn Darrell Bender, *The Politics of Hostility* (Hato Rey, Puerto Rico: Inter American University Press, 1975); Cole Blasier, *The Hovering Giant* (Pittsburgh: University of Pittsburgh Press, 1976), pp. 177–210 and 211–78. See also U.S. Senate, Intelligence Committee, *Alleged Assassination Plots Involving Foreign Leaders, An Interim Report*, 94th Cong., 1st sess., November 20, 1975.

3. See David Binder's account in the *New York Times*, March 29, 1977, pp. 1, 8.

4. Some 230 Cuban civilian and military advisers had already been sent to Angola the previous June. The first large-scale contingents of Cuban combat troops probably left Cuba by ship no later than early September. For the background and details to the Cuban involvement, see Nelson P. Valdes, "Revolutionary Solidarity in Angola," in *Cuba in the World*, eds. Cole Blasier and Carmelo Mesa-Lago (Pittsburgh: University of Pittsburgh Press, 1979), p. 87–118.

5. Binder, loc. cit.

6. *New York Times,* December 21, 1975, p. 1.

7. Radio Havana, December 22, 1975.

8. The 36,000 troop figure was given by Fidel Castro in his then "secret speech" to the National Assembly of People's Power in Havana, on December 27, 1979, which has since been published in the West. Castro's figure for the Cuban expeditionary force in Angola was 50 percent higher than the highest Western intelligence estimate, whereas his figure for Cuba's Ethiopian expedition force, 12,000, was about 25 percent lower than had been estimated.

9. On January 27, 1977, just prior to assuming his post as U. N. ambassador, Young declared in a television interview that in a sense Cuban troops had brought "stability and order" to Angola. Although both Young and the State Department later denied that he had condoned the Cuban troop presence, his statement certainly signaled a less militant U.S. stance against Cuba's military operations in Africa.

10. Some 40,000 Somalian troops invaded the contested Ogaden region in July 1977, leading to increased Cuban and Soviet aid to Ethiopia, and to Somalia's break in diplomatic relations with Cuba in November. Cuban and Soviet aid to Ethiopia thereupon intensified, with Cuban Defense Minister Raúl Castro visiting Moscow and reportedly Addis Ababa in January 1978 to coordinate Cuban-Soviet operations in the Ogaden. The 12,000 Cuban troop figure is taken from Castro's December 27, 1979 address.

11. At the request of Castro, according to CBS news, a secret negotiating channel was opened between Cuban and U.S. emissaries in March 1978, but talks over normalization finally collapsed in 1979 over the issue of Cuba's international behavior. *San Diego Evening Tribune,* July 7, 1981, p. B-6.

12. For a more extensive discussion of these tendencies, see Edward Gonzalez, "Institutionalization, Political Elites, and Foreign Policies," *Cuba in the World,* pp. 3–36.

13. The 1970 harvest attempt was a watershed in Cuba's revolutionary development as it opened the way for the so-called institutionalization of the revolution. See Edward Gonzalez, *Cuba Under Castro: The Limits of Charisma* (Boston: Houghton Mifflin, 1974), pp. 190-236.

14. The distinction between the fidelistas and raulistas derives initially from their primary associations with the Castro brothers during the anti-Batista struggle: the former grouping started with Fidel in the 1953 attack on the Moncada barracks, and remained with him on the First Front during the later guerrilla war (1956 to 1958); the latter grouping followed Raúl when he established the Second Front in 1958. The fidelistas assumed the bulk of the civilian posts in the government and party in the post-1959 period, but were augumented by raulistas from the military beginning in the late 1960s. Today, the FAR contains nearly as many fidelista senior officers as raulistas.

15. On the professionalization and changing military missions of the FAR, see Jorge I. Dominguez, *Cuba: Order and Revolution* (Cambridge, Mass.: Belknap Press of Harvard University Press, 1978), pp. 341–78.

16. On Cuba's military involvements prior to and including Angola, see William J. Durch, *The Cuban Military in Africa and the Middle East: From Algeria to Angola,* Professional Paper No. 201, Center for Naval Analysis, September 1977. For a later assessment that includes Ethiopia, see William M. LeoGrande, *Cuba's Policy in Africa, 1959–1980,* Policy Papers in International Affairs (Berkeley: Institute of International Studies, University of California, Berkeley, 1980).

17. For further details, see Gonzalez, "Institutionalization, Political Elites, and Foreign Policies," pp. 7–17.

18. It was estimated that most of the Cuban military equipment used in Angola was replaced within two years by new and more modern weapon inventories, including T–62 tanks, ZSU–4 self-propelled anti-aircraft guns, Saggers, and SA-3 missiles. See the testimony of Lt. Col. John A. Fesmire, Defense Intelligence Agency, in *Hearings before the Subcommittee on Inter-American Affairs of the Committee on International Relations,* House of Representatives, 95th Cong., 2d sess., March 14 and 15; and April 5 and 12, 1978, pp. 4–9, 14.

19. For a further analysis of Cuba's new privileged relationship with the USSR, see Edward Gonzalez, "Cuba, the Soviet Union, and Africa," *Communism in Africa,* ed. David E. Albright (Bloomington: Indiana University Press, 1980), pp. 145–67.

20. Approximately 13,000 civilian technicians, teachers, and medical personnel were in Africa by 1979, whereas 10,000 African school children were studying in Cuba by the end of that year. In the meantime, the number of African high-level delegations visiting Cuba increased as follows: 23 (1976), 29 (1977), 44 (1978), and 26 (Jan.–June 1979). In additional to PCC Politburo members, the number of high-level Cuban delegations visiting Africa also increased over the same period: 7, 24, 20, and 5, with the decline in the last figure due to preparations for Havana's hosting of the nonaligned movement's meeting in September 1979.

21. On these three interpretations, see Gonzalez, "Cuba, the Soviet Union, and Africa," pp. 145–57.

22. For a detailed analysis of Cuba's Ethiopian involvement, see LeoGrande, *Cuba's Policy,* pp. 35–51.

23. Thus, at the Organization of African Unity meeting in July 1978, Nigeria warned that the USSR and Cuba should not overstay their presence in Africa "lest they run the risk of being dubbed a new imperialist presence." *New York Times,* July 20, 1978, p. 1.

24. On the summit conference, see William M. LeoGrande, "Evolution of the Nonaligned Movement," *Problems of Communism* (Jan.-Feb. 1980): 35–52.

25. National Foreign Assessment Center, Central Intelligence Agency, *The Cuban Economy: A Statistical Review—A Reference Aid,* ER 81-10052 & PA 81-10074, March 1981, p. 23.

26. In his report to the Second Party Congress, Castro complained that "a number of bad habits were spreading in our country," adding that:

there were increasing signs that the spirit of austerity was flagging, that a softening up process was going in which some people tended to let things slide, pursue privileges, make accommodations and take other attitudes, while work discipline dropped . . . . Was our Revolution beginning to degenerate on our imperialist enemy's doorstep? Was that an inexorable law for any revolution in power? Under no circumstances could such a thing be permitted (*Granma Weekly Review*, December 18, 1980, p. 13).

27. For an analysis of these developments, see Jorge I. Dominguez, "Cuba in the 1980s," *Problems of Communism* (March-April 1981): 48–59.

28. In the new and expanded 16–member PCC Political Bureau, the fidelistas accounted for ten, the raulistas for three, and the "old communists" from the defunct PSP for three members. In the newly created eleven-member alternate membership of the Political Bureau, three division generals headed the list; and in the new nine-member Secretariat, the fidelistas accounted for three, the raulistas for five, and the ex-PSP for only one member.

12

Conclusion

Robert Wesson

It is clear that the ability of the United States to sway the course of events in Latin America is complex and variable. Despite memorable shortfalls and failures, it is still impressive. There is, indeed, some inclination in both the United States and Latin America to regard the latter as what it has historically been: a sphere of influence and responsibility of the former.

Leftists in nonleftist Latin American countries are especially disposed to view their governments as dependent and subject to the political and economic sway of the leading hemispheric and world capitalist power. This view has great political appeal as it gives an acceptable interpretation of many unpleasant situations and events; it has, moreover, an obvious basis in reality. The Latins are aware of history and the direct and indirect interventions of the United States in many countries of the hemisphere, and they are not easily convinced that conditions and policies have genuinely changed. They know about the activities of the CIA and do not know the limits of its mysterious powers. They see their economies under the shadow of the still prominent multinational corporations, many or most owned by or affiliated with U.S. interests. They have a perhaps overblown image of the powers of international finance, in which the United States plays the largest role and its capitalist allies usually second its purposes. They see the disproportionate contribution of the United States to their entertainment by television, movies, and the press. They may be aware of the numbers of U.S. personnel in their countries, in missions of many kinds, from scientific studies of the local flora to exchange students. It is typical that U.S. embassies have large professional staffs, whereas most Latin American countries are rather casual about the conduct of foreign affairs. They see the United States as overwhelmingly rich, strong, expansive, technologically advanced, and perhaps dangerous.

The various aspects of domination add together to form a single conglomerate, an overall feeling of the overweening presence of the leading hemispheric power. From the point of view of most Latin American critics, the domination of the United States is not so much a matter of specific decisions taken according to the desires of the hegemon, as the broad support of an economic and political system many find oppressive. The essential matter, in this view, is not the specific outcome of the many contentions that inevitably arise in economic and political questions between Latin American nations and the United States, but the support of the latter for more or less undemocratic governments, highly unequal societies, and the capitalistic, allegedly exploitative, economic order.

The overshadowing presence of the United States certainly makes it less likely that countries will break away from the broad patterns of society favored and promoted by it. The United States may be fairly considered a basic cause of frustration of the parties of the radical left (and perhaps also of radical rightist parties so far as they exist). One of the enduring objectives of U.S. policy in the hemisphere has been stability, and stability has meant avoiding radical change and favoring private property and pluralistic societies. United States policy has usually been successful in defending these and related values.

It has not been entirely so, however. The United States came somewhat unwillingly to live with a Marxist-Leninist, Soviet-allied Cuba. It has also not known how to prevent weak, poor Nicaragua from coming under a political movement whose rhetoric and policies are sharply hostile to the United States. It tells something of the limitations of U.S. influence that the radical Left has triumphed in three countries in the area most closely under the sway of the United States: what would seem to be strong potential influence obviously may turn counterproductive.

In South America, where U.S. influence is considerably attenuated, radical movements have been uniformly defeated—with some help or encouragement from the United States, but primarily by native forces. The prime examples are Brazil and Chile. The United States also assisted the forces of order in Venezuela, Colombia, Peru, Argentina, Uruguay, and elsewhere; but its role has apparently been rather distant and secondary.

The successful efforts of the United States to turn South American countries in a desired direction also belong to a receding past. It is apparent, as detailed in preceding chapters, that not much is left of habits of deference to the supposedly hegemonic power anywhere in the hemisphere. Whatever might have remained was much and permanently diminished by the experience of Vietnam, which seemed to show the United States as a ruthless but unsuccessful imperialist that could be defied with impunity. Nowadays the various republics overtly, even ostentatiously, look out for their own interests, drive stiff bargains, and assert the primacy of their national sovereignty. The United States seems to have to make repeated concessions, such as acknowledging Colombian sovereignty over reefs that might logically be claimed for the United States for strategic purposes, as pointed out in Chapter 6. The goodwill of Colombia also had to be bought by surrender of the Panama Canal Zone. Despite such concessions, Colombia failed to react effectively to U.S. concern over the narcotics trafffic until it became evident that Colombian society was being poisoned.

The self-will of Brazil is understandable. That huge, rapidly industrializing nation has much confidence in its destiny and sees little reason to accommodate U.S. desires. It seems to take satisfaction in acting in ways not approved by the United States, and Brazilian presidents made a point of not visiting Washington.

The growing independence of small, once pliable countries is more striking. Panama has overcome the weaknesses that made it more fully subject to U.S. influence than any other Latin American country. It has built up an army of its own, has done away with the division of the country and the economy by the Canal Zone, and, as shown in Chapter 7, has substantially reduced the cultural influence of the United States. In their effort to assert the national personality, Panamanians increasingly look to Latin America for education. In Nicaragua, U.S. influence seemed to be very strong before 1979; but it was concentrated on a small oligarchy, so not much remained when Somoza fell. As made clear in Chapter 8, Somoza did not actually do much for the United States, although he persuaded some members of Congress and other high officials that he was the best anticommunist and loyal supporter of the United States. He gave economic privileges to Somoza-held enterprises, not, generally speaking, to U.S. corporations; and he stiffly resisted efforts to impel him toward more observance of human rights.

In El Salvador, rather exceptionally, the U.S. influence has risen markedly, as pointed out in Chapter 9. The reason, however, is strictly internal: the government, under assault by the radical Left, became dependent on aid from the United States for its survival; need is the chief maker of dependency. This kind of power is not, however, beneficial to the United States. It represents a large material cost and some political loss elsewhere; it is not a matter of American choice, but is imposed by fears of a strongly negative outcome. It is the exercise of influence not in order to secure an advantage, but to avoid a feared major loss of standing in Central America. But even El Salvador, totally dependent as it is on American largess, is not wholly amenable to American wishes. The United States was unable to persuade the regnant powers and recipients of U.S. weaponry to halt the numerous murders that embarrassed the effort to defeat the guerrillas and bring stability to their country. The Salvadorans have not even been willing to go through the motions of punishing the murderers of American nuns.

Most U.S. relations with Latin American countries, at least in terms of diplomat-hours, have to do with practical, especially economic, issues. Dealings with Mexico, for example, revolve around questions of trade, oil, tourism, legal and illegal immigration, and investments in Mexico. Although Mexican freedom of action is considerably narrowed, as Chapter 10 makes clear, by economic dependence on the United States, it hardly seems that the United States enjoys special advantages in negotiations on such matters. In many cases the Latins may have a stronger bargaining position because of the idea, accepted on both sides, that the richer power should assist in the development of the poorer. The Latin Americans want more than formal equality. They insist not only that the United States owes it to them to admit their products duty-free, but also that prices of various commodities be supported. While Mexico, Colombia, Brazil, and other nations demand unhampered access to the U.S. market, they do not consider permitting free entry of U.S. goods to their sheltered markets. The United States has not even been able to persuade Mexico to open its economy to the extent of adhering to GATT. It sometimes seems that the weaker country may use the United States more than the reverse. For example, long-term influence with the Somoza government was never gratuitous, but was paid for in economic and military assistance and political deference; Somoza's return concessions were mostly symbolic.

It is true that the stronger economy has inherent advantages, but the political tendency is often to compensate for the inequality (presumably inadequately) than to reinforce it. The United States at the height of hemispheric dominion hardly ever claimed special commercial advantages for itself or its business interests, but worked, openly at least, only for general reduction of barriers. Recently it has felt inhibited in doing much for U.S. corporations beyond the normal services of information and advice governments provide for their citizens abroad, because political costs outweigh commercial benefits. United States interests, however strong statistically, have not staked out a preserve for themselves or been able to influence governments to exclude competition. To the contrary, most Latin American countries have gone counter to the United States by taking active measures to broaden their economic relations, that is, to favor trade with Europe, Japan, other Latin American countries, the Soviet Union, and other countries completely alien to U.S. influence. They have been successful, of course, in reducing their dependence on trade with the United States and the actual or potential economic influence of the latter. There is no longer much that Latin America cannot procure elsewhere than in the United States.

Competitive markets also reduce economic alignment with the United States. Argentina's ability to sell large amounts of grain to the Soviet Union (its largest single customer) adds to its freedom of action.

In political questions, as economic, the weaker countries commonly fare well. In nonsecurity issues, the United States is ordinarily quite respectful of the rights and equality of the Latin Americans. For many years the United States vainly opposed the 200-mile territorial waters claimed by first a few, then more and more Latin American states. It continues to react very mildly to the frequent seizures of American tuna vessels by Ecuador, desisting from trying to impose its view that the tuna, as migratory fish, do not become Ecuadorean by entering Ecaudorean waters. United States persuasion helped to bring elections in Honduras and Bolivia from 1978 to 1980, but the concession was not deep, as in both countries the military retained or reasserted much or all of its power.

The undoing of the Somoza dictatorship in 1979 showed some of the ability of the United States to influence events, together with the limitations of that ability. It was impossible to assure a moderate outcome. Whatever influence the United States had with Somoza was vitiated by his loss of contact with reality—the exercise of influence presupposes a certain degree of rationality of the party to be influenced. The outcome was a situtation of negative influence, that is, one in which the Nicaraguan government was predisposed to oppose U.S. purposes and made its defiance of this country a major article of faith.

The ability of the superpower to get its way in negotiations with weaker powers and to impose its views in areas subject to its power is curtailed by public opinion and concern for image in Latin America in general, in the allied and nonaligned countries, and in the United States itself. It would obviously be very difficult for any administration to send forces into Central America, short of invasion by a hostile army. The negative reaction in Latin America, Europe, and the United States to the Reagan administration's initial focusing on the military dimensions of the Salvadoran problem led to a rapid broadening toward political and economic factors. Panama secured revision of the Canal treaties partly by the threat of an unfriendly population in case of emergency, and partly by appealing to Latin American and world sympathies for a nation subjected to an arrangement considered proper in 1904 but no longer acceptable. Even economic reprisals, legitimate enough under international law, are difficult. An embargo against Grenada, however abusive its leaders may be of the United States, would be hard to justify in the contemporary temper of international affairs. Such a nonviolent act as cutting off aid is widely denounced as imperialism, as though the aid were an entitlement—which it is often held to be. The Nicaraguan Sandinistas have many precedents in their condemnation of the halting of free grain shipments as imperialist coercion.

Where considerations of public opinion are ineffective at the time of action, they may operate post factum. For example, the sending of marines to the Dominican Republic in 1965 was widely condemned as an overreaction. It doubtless made any subsequent similar intervention more problematic, just as the experience of Vietnam made Americans allergic to other ventures. So far as the CIA was responsible to the overthrow of Allende, it was successful at low material cost. But the subsequent investigations, revelations, and innumerable denunciations have certainly served to inhibit repetition of such actions. Not only does it not appear that there has been any subsequent effort to destabilize a legal government, but there seem to have been no further efforts to influence democratic elections, like those in Chile in 1964 and 1970.

Increased concern for world opinion, the growing self-assertiveness of the Third World, the Latin American tendency to identify with the Third World rather than to view itself as part of the New World, and the expanded expectations of peoples everywhere have been important factors in the shrinkage of U.S. influence in Latin America since the early 1960s. More concrete factors include the relative success of economic development—growth of GNP—in at least some Latin American nations, and the rise of alternative powers to which they may turn.

The former is well illustrated by the Brazilian case. At the beginning of the 1960s, the freedom of action of the Brazilian government seemed to be hedged by the necessity of securing loans of a few hundred million dollars from Washington. The amounts that seemed vital then would seem trivial now, even indexed for inflation, as Brazil's needs are measured in billions and are far beyond the available resources of the U.S. government. The giving or withholding of aid is no longer a potent means of pressure on major Latin American countries, in present conditions of parsimony; whether it proves usable in regard to one of the smallest, Nicaragua, remains to be seen.

The diminution of U.S. influence because of the progress of rivals is most obvious in the increased share of Western Europe and Japan in the foreign trade of the republics and the investments made in them. Their technological prestige, especially that of Japan, is also rising; and the image of technological virtuosity has been a major element in the Latin American esteem for the United States. So far as oil-rich powers—whether Mexico or Venezuela or Arab states—enter the field of international loans, probably helping states differing politically with the United States, the ability of the latter to veto international loans loses effect. There is also increased political competition, as detailed in Chapter 5 in regard to Venezuela; Latin Americans are free to look in various directions for encouragement and guidance. In fact, Christian Democratic and Social Democratic parties of Europe have been much more active in promoting their ideas in Latin America than any similar groups in the United States.

Much of the decline of U.S. influence, however, may be laid to the flagging of will and attention—the means of influence are effective only when put to use. From the beginning of serious engagement in Vietnam and after the assassination of John Kennedy, Washington allowed the Alliance for Progress to wither and backed away from the kind of commitment it represented. The low profile of the Nixon-Ford years encouraged Latin Americans (perhaps salutarily) to go their own way with their own resources. However one may judge the Carter approach and its centerpiece, the emphasis on human rights, its style did not incline Latin Americans to pay more attention to the desires of the United States. It is clear that, especially in critical conditions, skill of diplomacy and wise leadership may be the most critical single factor in the exercise of influence; but these qualities have not been conspicuous in the foreign policies of recent administrations.

The decline of the capacities of Washington in hemispheric affairs is related to the rise of military rule, especially in the Southern Cone and Brazil. It would seem prima facie that the installation of nontemporary military governments replacing the unfriendly regimes of Goulart and Allende represented major victories for the United States. Leftist governments were overturned and succeeded by firmly anticommunist regimes favorable to private (including foreign) enterprise. This is, however, a somewhat superficial view. The fact that anti-U.S. movements came to power in countries previously exceptionally friendly to the United States was very negative, and the fact that popular democracy led to such an outcome showed a basic weakness of the U.S. position. In reaction against the socialistic-collectivist politics that seemed to threaten their hierarchy and standing, the generals instituted military regimes cooperative with the United States in many ways. They also seek foreign capital and technology for the development that is one of their main concerns, and these are to be had from the economic system led by the United States. Moreover, they lack an acceptable alternative on the world stage. If there were a strong, rightist-authoritarian power, like Nazi Germany in the 1930s, such governments as those of Chile, Argentina, and perhaps Brazil might be tempted to align themselves with it. But when the world economy is dominated by the liberal-capitalist powers, and the great antagonist to the United States is nominally dedicated to proletarian revolution, the military governments have no real choice.

An authoritarian regime can be more faithful to market economy theory than the United States, as shown in Chapter 2 in the case of Chile. The administration of General Pinochet has lent both ears to theorists of free enterprise and has conducted a remarkable (and decidely successful) experiment in liberal capitalism. But this is decidedly contra naturam for a state in which there are no constitutional or institutional barriers to political domination of economic activity. It is rather to be expected that a military government will keep much of the economy in its own hands, as in Argentina and Brazil, and probably regulate the remainder rather closely. It is significant that both of these countries, especially Argentina, have been apparently pleased to undertake large-scale dealings with the Soviet Union, despite the total antithesis of political theory. There is an inherent contradiction between the political system of the United States and that of Latin American military dictatorship, and it would be relatively easy for this to turn to truculent nationalism—inevitably anti-United States—whenever this seemed to be in its interests.

Relations are likely to be more cordial with governments that share much of the political outlook of the United States, such as Costa Rica, Venezuela, Colombia, the Dominican Republic, and recently Peru and Ecuador. It is true that populist politics may result, in the future as in the past, in opposition to foreign corporations and to the United States. The likelihood of this, however, may be reduced by the relative dissociation of the United States from the multinationals, by the increased disposition on the part of the corporations to accommodate the needs of the host country, by the growing competition of non-American interests, and by the heightened sensitivity of the United States to the rights and feelings of the Latin republics.

The open, pluralistic society permits multiple links of independent organizations (commercial, cultural, and political), the action not only of private corporations but also of political parties, labor unions, and universities, as well shown in the Venezuelan case in Chapter 5. The United States is especially strong in such unofficial penetration. It goes both ways, however. Latin Americans can lobby with the American Congress, address themselves to U.S. media, and work with sympathetic organizations in this country. Unless the democracy goes to a populist-nationalistic ferment, it is the form of government most favorable to the broad interests of the United States—and indeed of international peace. Democracies never go to war against democracies.

It is clear that the United States has a major interest in promoting democratization, or regularized, constitutional, responsible political systems in Latin America. It is notable, however, that American public opinion and the media have long been more inclined to emphasize democracy in Latin America than the government, and Congress, as a democratic body, more than the executive branch. It is characteristic that Congress made an issue of human rights long before the Carter presidency raised the banner, and Congress has recently seemed more inclined to keep the issue to the forefront than the presidency. This is understandable because the most effective promotion of democracy is by means with which the administration in Washington has little immediately to do, that is, by the health and attractiveness of the open, democratic society of the United States, which is inevitably the preeminent model for Latin America. The preparation for democracy, moreover, is slow and protracted, while decision makers aim for results that are politically rewarding, that is, quick.

Despite these several negatives, the influence of the United States on its southern neighbors, especially its diffuse influence, economic and cultural more than political, remains very great. Correspondingly, the United States is much more influential in the big issues than the smaller ones. Latin American states are unanimously desirous of asserting their national personality, even taking satisfaction in crossing the United States, as in scorning the boycott of the 1980 Moscow Olympics. Yet the basic orientation of the overwhelming majority remains rather favorable to the United States and its values.

Almost any Latin American country might serve as an example of this generality. Brazil, for example, asserts its aspiration to great power status primarily by demonstrating autonomy vis-à-vis the big brother of earlier times, with whom it prized a "special relation." Yet there is no important clash of interests between the two powers; the United States generally views Brazilian purposes sympathetically, especially so far as the "abertura," or opening to democracy, is serious. The fact that the United States is the prime buyer of Brazilian products and the ultimate source of most Brazilian borrowings certainly makes it difficult for Brazil to strike out in ways basically hostile to the United States. Panama has gone contrary to U.S. wishes in many minor ways, for example, in its votes in the United Nations. But Panama is bound to remain basically cooperative because much of its prosperity depends upon its attractiveness as an international financial center.

If the United States perceived a real strategic threat in Latin America, it would doubtlessly assert its vital interests forcefully and would probably do so successfully, to the general applause of the American public. Although it must be concluded that the political position of the United States and its ability to work its will in Latin America have declined, Latin America remains an area of great concern for the United States. Its economic importance, especially as a source of petroleum, is on the rise. It is the part of the Third World where the United States has most influence and is most admired, although much resented. It is the sector of the Third World for which the United States inevitably has responsibility; happily, it is also the sector that is most promising and may conceivably show the way for the less well-situated countries of Africa and Asia. If the United States cannot make itself felt in Latin America, its position in the world will have sunk low indeed.

In this situation, the United States is likely to continue to be mostly reactive and is not likely to do much to promote long-term goals except peace and stability in the region—the biggest concern ever since American presidents began, close to a century ago, to take a serious interest in hemispheric affairs. But now, more than ever, wise and sophisticated statesmanship is essential to make the best use of the shrunken but still vast assets of potential influence for the welfare of the United States, the hemisphere, and the world.

Index

About the Authors

CHARLES D. AMERINGER received his doctorate from the Fletcher School of Law and Diplomacy, and is professor of Latin American history at Pennsylvania State University. He is the author of *The Democratic Left in Exile: The Antidictatorial Stuggle in the Caribbean, 1945-1959* (1974) and *Don Pepe: A Political Biography of José Figueres of Costa Rica* (1979), along with numerous articles in scholarly journals on the subject of Caribbean and Central American affairs.

THOMAS P. ANDERSON is professor of history at Eastern Connecticut State College. His books include: *Politics in Central America: Guatemala, El Salvador, Honduras and Nicaragua; The War of the Dispossessed: Honduras and El Salvador, 1969;* and *Matanza: El Salvador's Communist Revolt of 1932.* Dr. Anderson holds a B.A. from Saint Louis University and an M.A. and Ph.D. from Loyola University, Chicago.

DAVID E. BLANK is professor of political science at the University of Louisville. He is the author of several monographs and articles on politics and urban and regional planning in Venezuela, Mexico, and the Caribbean, including *Politics in Venezuela.* He worked as an urban planner in Puerto Rico from 1961 to 1963 and was a Fulbright lecturer in Argentina in 1971. Field research for his chapter was funded by a 1980 grant from the American Philosophical Society.

EDWARD GONZALEZ is a specialist on Cuban domestic and international affairs, a professor of political science at UCLA, and a consultant to the Rand Corporation. He is the author of *Cuba Under Castro: The Limits of Charisma* (1974) and *Post-Revolutionary Cuba in a Changing World* (1975), coauthored with David Ronfeldt. Dr. Gonzalez has published many other articles and monographs on Cuban developments.

KENNETH F. JOHNSON is professor of political science at the University of Missouri-St. Louis and Great Plains Fellow at Emporia State University of Kansas. Since receiving his Ph.D. from UCLA in 1963, Dr. Johnson has done extensive field work in a number of countries. He is perhaps best known for *Mexican Democracy: A Critical View* (1978) and for *Illegal Aliens in the Western Hemisphere* (1981), with Miles W.

Williams. His current work focuses on the political psychology of Peronism and on inter-American migration.

MARTIN C. NEEDLER is professor of political science and sociology at the University of New Mexico. He has held research appointments at Harvard, Oxford, and elsewhere, and is the author or editor of ten books and 70 articles on European politics, Latin American politics, and U.S. foreign policy. Dr. Needler received his Ph.D. from Harvard.

DANIEL L. PREMO is associate professor of political science at Washington College. He earned his Ph.D. in Latin American studies at the University of Texas at Austin. Before joining academe, he served with the U.S. Information Agency in Guatemala and Colombia. His publications have appeared in numerous journals, and he has contributed to the Hoover Institution's *Yearbook on International Communist Affairs* since 1972. A Wye Institute Fellow in 1980-81, Dr. Premo is currently writing a book on contemporary Colombian politics.

STEVE C. ROPP is associate professor of government at New Mexico State University in Las Cruces, New Mexico. He has published a number of articles and book chapters on various aspects of Central American politics. His book, entitled *Panamanian Politics: From Guarded Nation to National Guard,* is now in press. Dr. Ropp holds a B.A. from Allegheny College, an M.A. from the University of Washington, and a Ph.D. from the University of California, Riverside.

PAUL E. SIGMUND is professor of politics and chairman of the Latin American Studies Committee at Princeton University. He has written nine books and many articles on political theory and Latin American politics, including *The Overthrow of Allende and the Politics of Chile, 1964–1976* (1977) and *Multinationals in Latin America: The Politics of Nationalization* (1980).

ROBERT WESSON is a senior research fellow at the Hoover Institution and a professor at the University of California–Santa Barbara. After earning an A.M. in International Relations from the Fletcher School of Law, he lived in Latin America for 14 years, spending part of that time as a businessman and dairy farmer, part as an English teacher, and part in the U.S. Foreign Service. He returned to the United States in 1958 to earn a Ph.D. in political science at Columbia University. Dr. Wesson specializes in Latin American politics.